Corporate Responsibility and Sustainable Development

Corporate responsibility and sustainable development are two concepts that may be able to reconcile many of the big challenges facing the world; challenges such as tensions between respect for the natural environment, social justice, and economic development; the long view versus short-term imperatives and the competing priorities between developed and developing economies.

This book explores the gaps and overlaps between corporate responsibility and sustainable development. These concerns overlap because they implicate corporate practices, state development policy challenges, the concerns and priorities of non-governmental organisations, and the potential for innovative forms of organisation to address these challenges. This collection examines these questions in terms of tensions and interdependencies, between competing claims to resources, rights and responsibilities, strategy and governance, between public and private interest, and the implications for equity and the common good over the long term.

This is a valuable resource for researchers, lecturers, practitioners, postgraduate and final year undergraduates in business strategy, international business and international management, public sector policy and management, international development, political economy. It is also suitable for more specialist courses on sustainability, corporate responsibility, governance and international development.

Lez Rayman-Bacchus is Visiting Research Fellow at University of Winchester Business School, UK.

Philip R. Walsh is Associate Professor at Ryerson University, Canada.

Routledge Research in Sustainability and Business

Corporate Responsibility and Sustainable Development

Exploring the nexus of private and
public interests

**Edited by
Lez Rayman-Bacchus and
Philip R. Walsh**

Routledge
Taylor & Francis Group

LONDON AND NEW YORK

from Routledge

First published 2016
by Routledge
2 Park Square, Milton Park, Abingdon, Oxon OX14 4RN

and by Routledge
711 Third Avenue, New York, NY 10017

First issued in paperback 2017

Routledge is an imprint of the Taylor & Francis Group, an informa business

British Library Cataloguing-in-Publication Data
A catalogue record for this book is available from the British Library

Library of Congress Cataloging-in-Publication Data
Corporate responsibility and sustainable development: exploring the
    nexus of private and public interests / edited by Lez Rayman-Bacchus
    and Philip R. Walsh.
    pages cm. – (Routledge research in sustainability and business)
    1. Social responsibility of business. 2. Sustainable development.
    3. Corporate governance. I. Rayman-Bacchus, Lez, editor.
    II. Walsh, Philip R., editor.
    HD60.C6396 2016
    338.9'27 – dc23
    2015023557

ISBN 13: 978-1-138-30420-8 (pbk)
ISBN 13: 978-1-138-84595-4 (hbk)

Typeset in Goudy
by Florence Production Ltd, Stoodleigh, Devon, UK

Contents

Figures and tables

Figures

Tables

Notes on contributors

Lez M Rayman-Bacchus, PhD, is a visiting Research Fellow at Winchester University, UK, and Founding Director of the Centre for Corporate Responsibility and Sustainable Development and an international bi-annual symposium. Previously a business practitioner his focus is consulting, teaching and researching strategy, corporate responsibility, ethics, sustainability and related subjects.

Philip R Walsh, PhD, P.Geo., is the Chair of Entrepreneurship and Strategy department at the Ted Rogers School of Management, Ryerson University, Toronto, Canada. A former energy industry executive, he teaches, researches and publishes in the fields of innovation management and commercialization, sustainability and business strategy and is cross-appointed to the Environmental Applied Science and Management graduate program at Ryerson's Yeates School of Graduate Studies. He continues to practice as a registered professional geoscientist.

Nadia B Ahmad, JD, is an assistant law professor at Barry University. Previously a visiting assistant professor at Pace Law School, and legal fellow for the Sustainable Development Strategies Group. She is a graduate of the University of California at Berkeley, J.D. from the University of Florida, and LL.M. from the University of Denver.

Magdalena Paszkiewicz is an Australian lawyer specialized in environmental law and policy reform. Magdalena analyzed the path towards a global framework on corporate sustainability reporting at the Central European University, and has worked with the United Nations Environment Programme on the accountability of financial actors for climate impacts.

Ciprian N Radavoi, PhD, is a former human rights lawyer and diplomat, currently lecturer in International Investment Law at the University of International Business and Economics, Beijing. His research focuses on community – business interaction and more generally, on ethical investment-related matters.

Duane Windsor, PhD (Harvard University), is Lynette S. Autrey Professor of Management in the Jesse H. Jones Graduate School of Business, Rice

University. His work focuses on corporate social responsibility and stakeholder theory. He has published a number of books and in various academic journals.

Michele Filippo Fontefrancesco, PhD, is a trained anthropologist specialized in economic anthropology. He works at University of Gastronomic Sciences and collaborates with Durham University and the University of Turin. His most recent works deal with the cultural impact of the global economic crisis on SMEs and society at large.

Audrey Mocle holds a Bachelor of Laws and Bachelor of Civil Law from McGill University in addition to a Bachelor of Commerce from the Desautels Faculty of Management at McGill and a Masters in Human Rights from the London School of Economics and Political Science.

Stephen Stec, JD, a lawyer, teaches at Central European University and is an Associate Scholar at the Institute of East European Law and Russian Studies of Leiden University. He has written extensively on environmental governance and with Alexios Antypas developed the 'Governance Principles for Foreign Direct Investment in Hazardous Activities' in the early 2000s.

Louise Manning, PhD, has worked in the food supply chain for thirty years addressing food safety, quality assurance, financial and business performance, and environmental management. Her research is published in peer reviewed journals, trade journals and press and she has published several books in the area of food integrity.

Orr Karassin, PhD, Lecturer at the Open University of Israel (OPENU), Department of Sociology, Political Science and Communications; Research Fellow at the OPENU Research Institute for Policy Analysis; Head of the OPENU Program for Public Law. Research interests include environmental regulation, corporate sustainability, climate change adaptation and environmental politics.

Aviad Bar-Haim, PhD, retired Professor at the Open University of Israel (OPENU), Department of Management and Economics; Research Fellow at the OPENU Research Institute for Policy Analysis; Interests include teaching and researching organizational behaviour, human resource management (HRM) and labour relations.

Alex Antypas, PhD, is an Associate Professor at Central European University in Budapest, Hungary. His areas of research include corporate social responsibility, climate change politics, environmental justice, and environmental governance in the Arctic region. He has served as a consultant for the European Commission, the European Parliament, UNEP, UNDP and other international organizations.

Preface

There is no doubt that the world is changing rapidly and that organisations are going to need to re-think they way they interact with their stakeholders if they are to survive and thrive in the 21st century. This book introduces new ideas and ways of looking at organisations in a context of sustainable development and complex interactions between business, investors and civil society. The timing could not be better for we need new ideas and ways of thinking offered by this book.

Between 2006 and 2013 I had the honour to chair the Commission for a Sustainable London 2012. This was a unique body to oversee the promise to deliver the "most sustainable Games ever" by providing independent assurance, and advice as a "critical friend" to delivery bodies and the political leaders responsible for the Games. A global event such as an Olympic Games galvanises stakeholders like nothing else. I had politicians of all colours and government institutions at a local, citywide and national level to deal with along with the myriad of global corporations investing multiple millions to bask in the glory of global brand recognition and many, many special interest groups who wish to use the global focus of the Games to further their own causes. There were also a wide range of organisations responsible for delivering the Games, from building the infrastructure to staging the event to providing transport and security services; the list goes on. Finally, lest we forget, some sport happened too. Over 200 nations coming together to celebrate a shared love of their chosen sport is what the games were all about. But even sports people are surrounded by their own corporate sponsors and national and international governing bodies, with their own political agendas. In many ways, my experience in helping manage sustainability at the games provided me with a clear example of how major stakeholders not only compete and cooperate but are also challenged to deliver on promises around sustainability claims they make, in order to get a share of the benefits of being associated with such an international event.

This nexus of responsibility is much like the theme of this book where its authors have contributed to the debate on the interdependence of private and public interests. They have raised many questions about to the sensibility of seeking a merger of private and public interest including whether that leads to conflicts of interest, or if the ambitions of politicians and managers will interfere with public service and corporate stewardship, and perhaps most importantly how do we define the private-public interest boundary.

Making sense of all this was a daily challenge for me for 7 years, but the notion of a nexus starts to put research and practice together in such a way that helps organise the way we think about how to support sustainable development in the future. Delivering an Olympic Games in a way that supported sustainable development required ALL the actors to come together in ways previously unimagined. It was not a perfect nexus (I doubt if one will ever exist), politicians would laud my organisation as "the single source of the truth about sustainability" one day and call for my head the next, some corporate sponsors engaged enthusiastically in developing new and innovative ways of supporting sustainable development, others threatened to sue me. Some NGOs supported the role of the Commission fully; some tried to bring it down by agitating a mass resignation of my commissioners. The important concept in this book, the nexus, provides a means of making sense of sustainable development in terms of a collective responsibility; a responsibility patterned with gaps and overlaps, tensions and contradictions as well as common interests, and varying degrees of accountability, all infused with many positive and negative influences.

The book comes in four sections; The first section deals with the account-ability for delivering sustainable development goals and the idea of collective accountability, and highlighting the distance between promise and practice. I see this as relating to the differing values of the organisations coming together around common purpose, while holding on to their unique and often competing drivers for sustainable development.

The second calls for a greater voice for community, particularly local communities. This is hard to achieve in practice as most corporate models tend to turn to shareholders and customers as the most influential stakeholder groups. The case for change is compelling if we consider that often, mega projects like the London Olympics leave behind a legacy of various physical structures that local communities may see but not feel connected with.

I recall the sometimes endless negotiating of rights and responsibilities among stakeholders involved in preparing for the Games. The third section looks at ways of thinking about, and possibly reconciling, the diverse interests of groups of stakeholders; the context of "stakeholder" becomes much wider and more diverse than those considered in traditional models of business and government.

The forth section addresses prescriptions for partnership, regulation and state building. I am reminded of the challenges of holding together what was a huge partnership of interests around the London Olympic Games, including myriad firms, central and local government, and NGOs.

I am grateful to the editors for offering me the opportunity to contribute to this thoughtful and timely work. This book introduces important new concepts to the way we think about business and government. I only wish it had been written in 2006!

Shaun McCarthy OBE

Introduction

Conceptualizing responsibility as a nexus

The focus of this book is to explore the notion of a nexus and how it shapes the character and direction of social and economic development and the related environmental impact (sustainable development). In this chapter, we unpack the idea of a nexus. First, the notion of nexus refers not only to the interaction of government, business and multilateral organizations, but to the interdependence of a wider constellation of formal and informal organizations, and tangible and intangible institutions. Their interactions, collectively and separately, generate competitive markets that enable the development of capital (social, manufactured, financial, human talent, natural). Second, while these interactions spur development, they also generate structures that lock-in particular paths of development, resisting change (technological, organizational, governance, cultural). This is clearly visible in the arguments for and against moving from fossil fuel to renewable energy. Third, the resulting construction of markets and competition for resources raises debate about the division of rights and responsibilities between the government and the business for sustainable development. One manifestation of this division is that between the government as a protector of public interests (environment, human welfare, economic development), and firms' corporate responsibility or corporate sustainability strategies. Such divisions harbour conflicts of interest and the need for a regulated environment, infusing strategic choices and institutions with rules of behaviour and ways of thinking that vary with industry, jurisdictional context, and reining ideological preferences. The result is a spectrum of responsibilities. These dimensions (the pattern of interaction, a developmental agenda, institutional commitments, and the character of the regulatory environment) constitute the nexus.

There is no single framework for examining the nature of interactions alluded to here, between the government, the business and other organizations. There is a plethora of separate tools for analysing the workings of particular stakeholders within the nexus, including how businesses make strategic decisions, and frameworks for analysing policy-making such as the 'advocacy coalition framework' of Weible et al. (2009). There is also help with engaging the public with policy-making, such as provided by Steelman (2001) and Fischer's (1993) 'participative' model. Perhaps the lack of tools is due, at least, in part, to researchers tending to work within, rather than across, disciplines, yet there remains need for studies and theorizing around the interdependence of public and private interests (Mahoney, 2009). One cannot be adequately understood without reference to the other. Just as business partnerships are jointly and severally accountable, so too we need to acknowledge that institutional responsibility is not only individual (in an organizational sense), but also reciprocal and collective. When multi-national firms secure a license to develop and exploit local resources (physical, human and others), this right comes with responsibilities (cultural sensitivity, respect for social justice, environmental stewardship and economic). The host government is at the same time invested with reciprocal responsibilities, not only to uphold the legitimate rights of the multinational, but to do so in ways that enable all stakeholders (firm, customers, local government) to flourish. By way of attempting to understand the nexus, we conceive of it as a site of interactions comprising multiple interwoven faces. We highlight these as being the existence of: a developmental agenda, ingrained institutional commitments, some form of regulated environment, and as a spectrum of responsibility that is both individual and reciprocal. Interactions need not include all stakeholders, but can involve parallel interactions over time.

Nexus as developmental agenda

We explore the notion of nexus as a developmental agenda by drawing on three perspectives: the industrial organization economics view of markets, innovation systems theory and industrial district and clusters. From a neo-liberal perspective, a discussion about development invokes concern for the organization of markets, while sustainability draws attention to inter-temporal effects of development, and the role of innovation and supportive institutions. We take as given that economic growth is central to sustainable development, and that innovation (technological, administrative, market) is critical, shaping the direction of development and character of growth. One strand of the industrial organization (IO) perspective focuses on public policy, in particular the enforcing of contracts, property rights and economic governance. From this view, firms exist to maximise profit while government's role is to correct market imperfections and protect the public welfare, through some combination of direct and indirect regulation. From this view, public policy aims for the optimal distribution of resources in an economy (static allocative efficiency) yet as Mahoney and McGahan (2009: 1042) argue, from a sustainability perspective the focus should be on 'inter-temporal innovative efficiency' and while innovation may not be a central concern of the IO perspective, 'once inter-temporal or dynamic efficiency – and thus economic value creation through innovation – is considered, then a range of oligopolistic and even monopolistic industry structures may be superior to perfect competition and contestable markets for innovation and dynamic efficiency' (Mahoney and McGahan, 2009: 1042).

   The limitations of the IO perspective invite reflection on other approaches that add insight to the notion of nexus as developmental agenda. Mahoney *et al.* (2009: 1042) suggests 'the systems of innovation' approach could be an effective alternative policy-making framework where a broader nexus of organizations and institutions and collaborative arrangements such as industry clusters, public–private partnerships and other forms of social capital can encourage innovation and create economic value. Still, the systems view comes with limitations. It does not account for agency problems associated with divergent (public–private) interests at different levels (firm, national, international network), or how these divergent interests shape the character and direction of innovation. The establishment of industrial districts and clusters is a clear example of a site (in spatial terms) with a developmental agenda: to stimulate economic growth, employment and innovation. Government may (or may not) set out to create the initial conditions for a cluster to emerge (through command and control and incentives), but from the view of complexity theory, government cannot control the evolution of a cluster. From this view, the government's impact on social and economic development would be more effective in the role of a facilitator rather than a regulator (He *et al.* 2011).

Industrial organizational economics, the innovation systems approach, and industrial districts and clusters, all focus on value creation for the nation-state and fail to acknowledge that partial interests can undermine the potential of firms in less developed economies, for example in terms of trade or resource development policies, risking the potential for sustainability. Furthermore, a focus on developing firm-level innovation may not lead to inter-temporal sustainability benefits.

Nexus as institutionalized commitments

Within the national innovation systems literature, historical analysis of industrial development in the United States, Germany, and the United Kingdom reveal much useful insight to the emergence and transformative influence of institutions on development. However, there is little in the literature on how institutions adapt and change themselves. Institutions provide the mechanism through which governance is exercised. These institutions reflect accumulated practices and decisions, bringing efficiencies such that stakeholders do not continually have to re-evaluate choices and decisions. However, at the same time, these institutions become constraints, shaping further development (social, political, economic, and technological) in particular directions resisting change along the other dimensions. This resistance to change is common to developed, developing, and undeveloped countries. Moreover, development failures commonly arise due to the particular institutional arrangements (Easterly, 2002). In a globalised world it is in the self-interest of policy-makers and businesses from the developed world to help developing economies build the capacity to learn and transform their own innovation systems, sensitive to their particular institutional context, and not simply transplant developed world innovation systems models (Arocena and Sutz, 2003).

Since institutional commitments exert a powerful steer on legitimate development, then understanding them as a contextual influence is important.

Parto *et al.* (2006: 17) argue that the analysis of institutional contexts of development

> should go beyond specific institutions such as government agencies, business associations, or cultural values . . . [but also consider formal and informal] networks and associations, to examine their inter-relations; reinforcing or neutralizing mechanisms; their relative significance within the system; and the different degree to which each institution may be influenced through policy or other intervention.

In their review of definitions Parto *et al.* (2006) highlight that institutions: comprise a territorial scale of governance (local, national, international); are manifest at differing levels of aggregation (individual behaviour across society, within organizations, among organizations and among nations); and reflect differing antecedent commitments to social, economic and political well-being. They also identify that institutions exercise varying degrees of influence (formal to informal) on social habits (behavioural), values and culture (cognitive), privileging interactions between particular private and public interests (associative), prescriptions and proscriptions (regulative) and the determination of the limits of social relations (constitutive).

Nexus as regulated environment

Two views underscore much of the argumentation about the need for regulation. One view is that more regulation is needed, direct or indirect, in order to rein in a tendency for human self-interest to override any interest in the common good. The other view is that functioning free markets obviate the need for regulation.

Rationale for regulation

Proponents of the free market theory believe in the efficient market hypothesis (EMH) that regulation is an unhelpful intervention in the efficient operation of markets (Rahman, 1992). From this view the share price mechanism reflects all available information equity buyers and suppliers need, making regulatory intervention unnecessary. Regulatory intervention limits choice and increases the cost for products and services. However, there are criticisms of EMH, notably Grossman and Stiglitz (1980) who argue that market friction, such as the cost of trading and analysis, undermine information efficiency in markets, and Schiller (1981), DeBondt and Thaler (1985) and Summers (1986), have all pointed to the existence of mispricing in the market, which is an indication of informational inefficiency. In addition, Beaver (1981: 187–96) argues that business regulation is necessary because of poor incentives for participants to provide legitimate stakeholders with information, the asymmetry of information held across groups in the market, and the tendency for industry groups in unregulated markets to withhold adverse information.

Regulation emerges out of a political determination that certain markets need to be controlled in order to protect the interests of consumers, competitors, the physical environment and society at large (Mitnick, 1980). In his study of insurance companies, Meier (1991) suggests the regulator has five objectives: (i) monitor corporate solvency, (ii) ensure fair trading, (iii) regulate market entry, (iv) promote price stability and (v) meet social objectives. The regulation of business is a feature of all industrializing economies, addressing business conduct and reporting, though of course the nature of regulation varies with particular economies, industries, and markets. Some economies, such as those from (Western) Europe and North America, have been developing and refining regulatory institutions and instruments alongside the evolution of business since the mid-nineteenth century, though this experience does not explain all differences in the regulatory environments across the globe. Ideological commitments to contrasting models of social and economic organization, and peculiar national historical antecedents also shape attitudes towards regulation.

Theories of regulation

Public interest

Arguments around the need for more or less regulation centre on whether there is need for government to protect the public interest. Public interest theory (PIT) holds that regulation is used by government in order to promote social welfare or in response to market failure, or in a crisis such as corporate failure. For example, it is commonly known that in many countries, employment legislation prevents firms from being able to 'hire and fire' at will, and are required to provide adequate compensation for loss of employment should the firm find it necessary to make staff redundant in order to remain solvent. Similarly, firms are compelled to deliver to consumers products (e.g., food, clothing and household) that meet certain standards, and their performance in this is monitored by regulatory agencies.

In the original formulation of PIT, the regulator is assumed to be independent and neutral, responding to a public demand to correct unfair market practices (Peltzman, 1976). However, it has long been established that this assumed neutrality is grossly overstated, and that PIT does not reflect reality (Postner, 1974). Moreover, as Meier (1991; 708) observes, the regulatory agency is likely to fail 'to protect and to promote the public interest' due to bureaucratic ineptitude, a lack of skills and resources, and being unable to understand the complexity of issues faced. In addition, as a bureaucracy, the regulator's office is inclined to pursue self-serving interests, such as the building of bigger bureaucracies, which could work against the public good (Smith, 1986).

Private interest and public choice

PIT sees individual self-interest as the dominating behaviour of all agents, including public figures. From this view, politically effective groups seek to dominate the regulatory process to their benefit (Adams and Tower, 1994). The privatization of state-owned enterprises of all types, from financial institutions such as New Zealand insurance companies (Adams and Tower, 1994), to natural resource companies, provides a clear illustration that such politically motivated initiatives can, and do, work against the public interest. Merino and Neimark (1982) attribute the rise of U.S. corporate disclosure regulation to the growth of share ownership, and that such regulation has intensified during the last two decades in response to corporate wrongdoing; for example, the collapse of Enron and the Sarbanes–Oxley legislative response to name one well-known case. Feroz (1987: 8, 9) sees industry groups as being able to capture the regulatory process, to the detriment of other groups in society (such as consumers), because they possess a number of factors such as economic resources, an interest in the potential benefits arising from capturing the regulatory process, strong organizational capabilities, and industry-specific knowledge. According to Stigler (1971: 5) industry groups seek to capture the legislative process in order to protect their markets against competition and to obtain state subsidies. This restricts consumer choice and induces price increases. This helps explain why farmers (European Union [EU], United States) have been able to secure government subsidies at the expense of (unorganized) consumers. Further, Peirson and Ramsay (1983: 293) and Rahman (1992) argue that politicians are not neutral agents using regulation to secure social welfare objectives, but use public interest in the pursuit of political self-interest. In the United States, politicians are more likely to respond to small organized groups, particularly those representing the interests of business or the economic elite, thus threatening the broader concept of policy creation that is in the public interest and narrowing it down to that of being in the minority public interest or potentially private interests (Gilens and Page, 2014).

Nexus as a spectrum of reciprocal responsibility

The consensus view on the balance of responsibility within the nexus between societal actors has varied over time and by jurisdiction. Certainly, within a U.S. context, the literature (Kaplan, 2015) suggests that a shift towards greater corporate responsibility (CR) for the well-being of the society in which it operates began in the 1970s, perhaps in response to Friedman's classic position that the 'social responsibility of business is to increase its profits' (Friedman, 1970: 32). That is not to say that CR did not have its beginnings earlier on in the twentieth century but rather the combination of deregulation and the globalization of markets in the late 1970s and 1980s, and the social and environmental impacts this created, spawned the growth of shareholder activism. This activism, encouraged by greater media exposure, influenced management of the larger publicly traded firms to begin considering increased CR.

In 1986, J.W. Anderson Jr. wrote about CR as being comprised of three major areas: complying with the law, operating under a set of moral and ethical standards, and procedures and philanthropy (Anderson, 1986). While his view was simplistic in its approach, Anderson was echoing the observation that at that time there was a greater expectation on the part of the public to increased government supervision of the economy and the actions of industry. Industry leaders recognized that while deregulation and globalization was offering increased growth prospects, this was also an opportunity to show that businesses could regulate themselves and reduce government oversight. Arguably, a mix of business leaders exercising moral leadership, a slew of initiatives around sustainable development starting in the 1980s, an open invitation to self-regulate as part of a U.S.- and UK-led deregulating ideological movement, and a growth in activism (consumer, journalistic, and shareholder), all induced an increasing number of firms to invest in CR strategies. Over the past 30 years, CR has grown to become a significant strategic objective of most large global firms. However, the length and breadth of their CR is influenced by both particular industry imperatives and prevailing political climate of the countries they operate in. For example, extractive industries have more observable social and environmental impacts and firms operating in this area promote a more active self-regulating CR agenda, particularly when operating in countries where government oversight and regulation is limited (Walsh, 2012). Yet extractive firms in China are subject to a more significant statist approach to CR and are, for the most part, subject to a state-determined view of what their role and responsibilities are to the communities in which they are active. Spurred on by the practical limitations of government and industry, voluntary and non-governmental organizations (NGOs) have become significant players in contributing to a broad-based concern for the well-being of society (O'Connell, 1996).

These arguments suggest that the nexus between government, industry, and non-aligned institutions is varied, and that a spectrum of responsibilities exists, determined in part by the nature of the industry and the jurisdiction. Gond *et al.* (2011) put forward a typology of configurations, adapted from work by Fox *et al.* (2002) and McBarnet (2007) related to the extent by which government can influence industry-initiated corporate social responsibility (CSR). They propose five types of relationships: CSR as self-government, CSR as facilitated by government, CSR as a partnership with government, CSR as mandated by government, and CSR as a form of government. Adapting their typology to include the role of voluntary and non-governmental agencies as an absolute potential contributor to sustainable development we can construct a spectrum of responsibility (Figure 0.1).

Corporate responsibility as a form of government

When there is a lack of government commitment to the sustainable development of the society it is governing, whether wilful or not, a foreign firm operating within such an environment finds itself free to initiate its own institutional processes for delivering corporate responsibility. This can result in either a lack of responsibility for the social, economic, and environmental conditions associated with the firm's activities (something that risks a backlash from the firm's shareholders and/or the global public) or the establishment of sustainable practices that improve not only

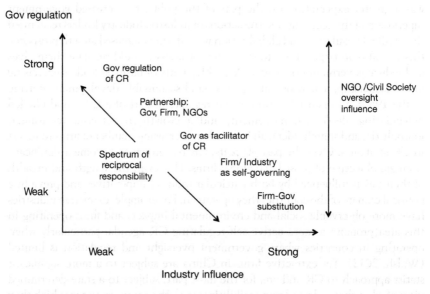

Figure 0.1 Spectrum of responsibility for sustainable development
Adapted from Gond *et al.* (2011)

the lives of those constituents who are directly involved but also the general condition of society itself, therefore supplanting a responsibility that might normally belong to government. Without an effective governance framework being in place, this configuration can result in industry exploitation of the natural and social environment for economic profit. There is also the risk that corporate determination of what counts as responsible behaviour may be inconsistent with what may be in the public interest. Still, government apathy towards sustainable development need not be all bad. The net benefit to the community can still be positive where the firm steps into the void left by government, doing so voluntarily, or quasi-voluntarily, adopting a programmed approach to CR as strategic defence against arbitrary government demands.

Self-governing corporate responsibility

This form of corporate responsibility is also at the sole discretion of the firm but as opposed to corporate responsibility as a form of government, self-governing corporate responsibility does not operate as an alternative to government in providing societal benefits. Rather, government is fully aware and supportive of the corporate contributions but chooses not to interfere in those activities. Generally, firms recognize the strategic importance of their actions as ways to address certain gaps in a jurisdiction's legal and/or institutional frameworks. In undertaking these activities, they establish their social licence to operate not only with the local community but with government as well. Such actions by firms can provide positive benefits for sustainable development, yet the benign involvement of government alongside corporate responsibility activities that are at the discretion of the firm may not entirely be in the public interest.

Corporate responsibility facilitated by government

Governments can have a moderate influence on promoting corporate responsibility by providing firms with incentives, both financial (subsidies or tax exemptions) and political (industry-supporting rhetoric), that encourage them to invest in sustainable practices. Here the government's role in contributing to their society's sustainable development is not absent but there is a greater preference to promote industry investment in social and economic development through more indirect means. This incentive-based approach can help firms rationalize the costs of contributing to responsible development, but it is devoid of any direct influence by government thus increasing the risk that industry could be too selective in terms of its investments that limit benefits to society as a whole. Furthermore, industry supporting rhetoric from government may not always be consistent with the views of affected local communities, raising the risk for firms that their corporate responsibility strategies arising from government facilitation are actually misaligned with the preferences of affected communities. This can limit a firm's ability to work with the community and cause significant disruption of business.

Corporate responsibility as a partnership with government

Corporate responsibility can be influenced through the collaboration of governments, industry, NGOs and civil society bodies such as local community representatives, in order to share strategies and resources. These resources are typically complementary and when combined can provide greater societal benefits than when employed independently. For example, a mining company can contribute capital to the development of government infrastructure such as roads and utilities that serve not only the mining operations but also the surrounding communities who independently could not justify the capital expense for expansion of such services. One of the difficulties with this approach is that the partnership of government and industry requires continual management involving all parties. Recognizing that their interests, while consistent with each other on some dimensions, may be inconsistent on certain other dimensions, can lead to future friction and inaction arising from disagreements. Arguably government is less interested in what specific responsibilities the firm is undertaking and more concerned with the process by which these responsibilities are undertaken. In this scenario, government will have established some legal framework that indirectly influences the corporate responsibility process. The extent to which firms see any such framework as overly onerous can deter the firm from actively participating in a partnership, limiting the potential for investment in social and economic development.

Corporate responsibility as regulated by government

Certain jurisdictions can create a regulatory framework that directly influences the kinds of corporate responsibilities that firms can undertake. This can take the form of compelling firms to comply with certain laws (e.g., employment rights), to requiring firms to invest a predetermined percentage of their profits into CSR initiatives. Examples can be found across all ideological paradigms, including China, India, Nigeria, and EU member states. Such responsibilities are usually monitored though some form of mandatory reporting to ensure that the activities of the firm are in accordance with the regulations. This approach allows for the government to ensure that the public interest is being served. However, under such a configuration industry has little room to manoeuvre, which can have a detrimental impact on social and economic development by discouraging investment from the outset. The challenge for the government is to find ways of encouraging firms to act through a spirit of care rather than through compliance with the letter of the law, and consider a balance of interests.

The role of voluntary and other non-governmental agencies

Underlying all of the potential government–industry configurations for contributing to sustainable development is the role of the voluntary and other non-governmental agencies. As with firms, in the absence of strong government regulation, agencies are largely able to determine the direction and scope of their own missions. It could also be argued that under such circumstances, these agencies have a greater responsibility for providing objective oversight of corporate behaviour and that this responsibility lessens as the influence of government on corporate responsibility strengthens. Gond *et al.* (2011) even suggest that these agencies have been successful in having voluntary corporate responsibilities that were established under the self-governing configuration converted into mandatory actions supported by a legal framework typical of those found under the regulated by government configuration.

Jurisdictional and industry relevance

Gond *et al.* (2011) use typologies, which, they suggest, are of use in theory-building and organizational studies. Through their application of CSR–government configurations found in Western Europe and East Asia, they provide empirical support for the use of their typologies in understanding the dynamic processes at work, in both temporal and spatial terms, under various jurisdictional contexts. We have taken this one step further by arguing that responsibilities form a spectrum where any point along the spectrum can be defined as a nexus of industry, government, and other voluntary and non-governmental agencies, shaped by the peculiarities of particular jurisdictions and/or industries. This nexus is dynamic, so that over time the locus of responsibility moves between self-regulation and government regulated, depending on prevailing attitudes, practices, and accomplishments. This model provides an opportunity for a comparative analysis and we invite readers as they progress through the following chapters to consider where each of the author's arguments or the cases described within their chapters might suggest where the nexus of responsibility is, and should be.

The chapters

This book is organized into sections that reflect a sense of both temporal and spatial terms. We start with a historical review of attempts to encourage business to account for its social and environmental impact, and the extent to which the existing business philosophy is blind to social responsibility. In terms of the here and now there is a strong focus on the place of stakeholders as agents of both change and continuity. We finish with how business and government and multilateral organizations might work together for the common good.

Part 1, 'Challenging corporate accountability', provides two perspectives on where firms stand with regard to their readiness and capacity to be held accountable for their impacts, social and environmental. In Chapter 1, Antypas, Paszkiewicz and Stec argue the need for more regulation requiring corporations to become more accountable for corporate responsibility and sustainable development. The authors argue for a greater focus on measurable 'accountability' because we may not really know what firms are doing despite their claims.

In Chapter 2, Mocle shows that despite the existence of many international treaties and regulations, firms are failing to make substantial progress in meeting human rights obligations. Some of this is due to the nature of business, rather than simply maleficence. In the absence of any international over-arching regulation, an argument is presented for added regulation to make both market behaviour and business organizational models more sensitive in protecting human rights.

The particular and often competing interests of, on the one hand, communities, and on the other hand, business, generates heat that lies at the centre of much debate about where responsibility lies for sustainable development. Indeed this tension can be found in a number of chapters throughout this book. Part 2, 'Community interests and responsibility', explores this through the lens of small and medium enterprise (SMEs) and multinational firms and their relationships with communities. In Chapter 3, Fontefrancesco presents an empirical qualitative study of the impact of the 2007–08 financial crisis on SMEs in northern Italy. In this region of Italy there is an established tradition of small business plus government support for SMEs (principally financial, e.g., tax reduction), which helps create a sense of their belonging to communities. However, the perception among SMEs that government is failing to support them in a time of national economic decline has brought about a feeling among SMEs of isolation from communities and the wider society. Should SMEs be allowed to fail where they form an integral part of communities?

In Chapter 4, Radavoi examines the legal position of local communities, in terms of the control of their own sustainable development compared with the rights of foreign investing firms. Drawing on cases from Romania, Mexico and

Canada, Radavoi shows that in disputes with local communities the law of enforceable contracts requires government to rule on the side of business (except in special circumstances). This raises questions about relative rights and responsibilities of business and community and government as a mediating force.

Part 3, 'Reconciling stakeholder expectations', shifts the focus from being on the contrasting interests of communities and business, to a wider range of stakeholders and which introduces more complex questions about their intersecting rights and responsibilities, power and commitment to securing their interests, all of which cast a long shadow into the future. In Chapter 5, Manning explores the link between the vulnerable (socio-economically disadvantaged) in UK (and U.S.) society, the quality of food they consume, and the consequences for their health. Manning further examines where responsibility lies for the wellbeing of this section of society. Where is the line between consumer sovereignty and state responsibility for consumer welfare? Should food manufacturers take greater care for the nutritional value of their products, regardless of cost, and in light of evidence that meeting the demand for low-cost food carries serious long-term health costs.

In Chapter 6, Karassin and Bar-Haim carried out an empirical quantitative study in Israel of firm behaviour towards corporate social performance (CSP), covering several industry sectors. They examined what promotes self-regulation among corporations by identifying and analysing the factors affecting firm behaviour towards CSP. Looking at the influence of all stakeholders, their findings suggesting the greatest impact on firm behaviour towards CSP is found at the individual level, with the least impact found in the role of outside stakeholders.

Part 4, 'Effecting sustainable partnerships', moves forward from the challenges around competing stakeholder interests and focuses on how stakeholders work together to achieve common purpose. Partnerships between government, multilateral organizations, and firms should represent a coordinated approach to effecting sustainable development. However, the reality can be quite different. In Chapter 7, Windsor proposes a framework for achieving effective partnerships, which he applies to three case studies. The lessons learned include understanding the motivation of stakeholders, principally business; the need for patience while stakeholders work things out; assessing value creation for stakeholders; and the determination of key performance indicators appropriate for each stakeholder.

In Chapter 8, Ahmad explores the combining of government regulation and corporate self-regulation as a policy approach for improving sustainable disclosure and monitoring by operators in the oil and gas industry, primarily environmental, while recognizing the significance of oil and gas reserves to the continued economic and social sustainability of the regions. Using the Colorado oil and gas industry as the principal case, Ahmad argues the need for more 'metaregulation'.

Drawing on the case of a multinational timber company operating in the Congo Basin in Chapter 9, Iff explores the role of corporations in performing social and environmental sustainability initiatives, which in more developed countries would be the responsibility of government and other public institutions. How can companies best work with modern formal government structures as well as traditional tribal hierarchies to effect sustainable development? It is argued that a hybrid model of state-building may be the new direction for firms in developing nations.

References

Adams, M. B. and Tower, G. D. (1994), 'Theories of regulation: some reflections on the statutory supervision of insurance companies in Anglo-American Countries', *The Geneva Papers on Risk and Insurance*, Vol. 19(71): 156–77.

Anderson, J. W. (1986), 'Social responsibility and the corporation', *Business Horizons*, Vol. 29(4): 22–7.

Arocena, R. and Sutz, J. (2003), 'Inequality and innovation as seen from the South', *Technology in Society*, Vol. 25(2): 171–82.

Beaver, W. H. (1981), 'Market efficiency', *The Accounting Review*, Vol. 56(1): 23–37.

DeBondt, W. F. and Thaler, R. (1985), 'Does the stock market overreact?' *The Journal of Finance*, Vol. 40(3): 793–805.

Easterly, W. R. (2002), *The elusive quest for growth: economists' adventures and misadventures in the tropics*, Cambridge, MA: MIT Press.

Feroz, E. H. (1987), 'Financial accounting standards setting: a social science perspective', *Advances in Accounting*, Vol. 5: 3–14.

Fischer, F. (1993), 'Citizen participation and the democratization of policy inquiry to practical cases', *Policy Sciences*, Vol. 26(3): 165–87.

Fox, T., Ward, H. and Howard, B. (2002), *Public sector roles in strengthening corporate social responsibility: a baseline study*. Washington, DC: World Bank.

Friedman, M. (1970), 'The social responsibility of business is to increase its profits', *New York Times Magazine*, 13 September, 32–3.

Gilens, M. and Page, B. I. (2014), 'Testing theories of American politics: elites, interest groups, and average citizens', *Perspectives on Politics*, Vol. 12(3): 564–81.

Gond, J. P., Kang, N. and Moon, J. (2011), 'The government of self-regulation: on the comparative dynamics of corporate social responsibility', *Economy and Society*, Vol. 40(4): 640–71.

Grossman, S. J. and Stiglitz, J. E. (1980), 'On the impossibility of informationally efficient markets', *The American Economic Review*, Vol. 70(3): 393–408.

He, Z., Rayman-Bacchus, L. and Wu, Y. (2011), 'Self-organization of industrial clustering in a transition economy: a proposed framework and case study evidence from China', *Research Policy*, Vol. 40(9): 1280–1294.

Kaplan, R. (2015), 'Who has been regulating whom, business or society? The mid-20th-century institutionalization of "Corporate Responsibility" in the USA', *Socio-Economic Review*, Vol. 13(1): 125–55.

McBarnet, D. (2007), 'Corporate social responsibility beyond law, through law, for law: the new corporate accountability', in D. McBarnet, A. Voiculescu and T. Campbell (eds), *The New Corporate Accountability: Corporate Social Responsibility and the Law*, New York: Cambridge University Press.

Mahoney, J. T. and McGahan A. M. (2009), 'The interdependence of private and public interests', *Organization Science*, Vol. 20(6): 1034–1052.

Meier, K. J. (1991), 'The politics of regulation', *The Journal of Risk and Insurance*, Vol. 58(4): 700–13.

Merino, B. D. and Neimark, M. D. (1982), 'Disclosure regulation and public policy: a sociohistorical reappraisal', *Journal of Accounting and Public Policy*, Vol. 1(1): 33–57.

Mitnick, B. M. (1980), *The political economy of regulation: creating, designing and removing regulatory forms*, New York: Columbia University Press.

O'Connell, B. (1996), 'Guest editorial: a major transfer of government responsibility to voluntary organizations? Proceed with caution', *Public Administration Review*, Vol. 56(3): 222–25.

Parto, S., Ciarli, T. C. and Arora, S. (2006), 'Economic growth, innovation systems, and institutional change: a trilogy in five parts', presented at the Globelics, India 2006 Conference *Innovation Systems for Competitiveness and Shared Prosperity in Developing Countries*, Trivandrum, Kerala, India, 4–7 October 2006.

Peirson, G. and Ramsay, A. L. (1983), 'A review of the regulation of financial reporting in Australia', *Companies and Securities Law Journal*, Vol. 1(6): 286–300.

Peltzman, S. (1976), 'Towards a more general theory of regulation', *Journal of Law and Economics*, Vol. 19(2): 211–40.

Posner, R. A. (1974), 'Theories of economic regulation', *The Bell Journal of Economics and Management Science*, Vol. 5(2): 335–58.

Rahman, A. R. (1992), *The Australian accounting standards review board: the establishment of its participative review process*. New York: Garland Publishing.

Schiller, R. J. (1981), 'Do stock prices move too much to be justified by subsequent changes in dividend?' *The American Economic Review*, Vol. 71(3): 421–36.

Smith, C. W. (1986), 'On the convergence of insurance and finance research', *Journal of Risk and Insurance*, Vol. 53(4): 693–717.

Steelman, T. A. (2001), 'Elite and participatory policymaking: finding balance in a case of national forest planning', *Policy Studies Journal*, Vol. 29(1): 71–89.

Stigler, G. J. (1971), 'The theory of economic regulation', *The Bell Journal of Economics and Management Science*, Vol. 2(3): 3–21.

Summers, L. H. (1986), 'Does the stock market rationally reflect fundamental values?' *The Journal of Science*, Vol. 41(3): 591–601.

Walsh, P. R. (2012), 'Prioritizing sustainability strategies for global extractive sector firms', *Management of Environmental Quality: An International Journal*, Vol. 23(6): 615–29.

Weible, C. M., Sabatier, P. A. and McQueen, K. (2009), 'Themes and variations: taking stock of the advocacy coalition framework', *The Policy Studies Journal*, Vol. 37(1): 121–40.

Part I

Challenging corporate accountability

1 Corporate social responsibility and corporate accountability

A historical overview

Alexios Antypas, Magdalena Paszkiewicz and Stephen Stec

Introduction

From its beginnings in Europe's early colonial ventures of the sixteenth century the multinational corporate form has been both powerful and controversial. Its power in facilitating international trade through the Dutch and British East India Companies was coupled with the excesses of colonialism, and since that time corporations operating outside of their home countries have been subject to debates about the tension between providing economic opportunities in host countries and extracting wealth and resources.

Indeed, the long history of the British East India Company is a prime example of how the limited liability of the owners of a joint stock company can set in motion a dynamic leading to human rights abuses and environmental degradation overseas, leading to movements for regulation at home (Robins, 2006). Even Adam Smith in *The Wealth of Nations* pointed to the East India Company to argue that the separation of ownership and management in joint stock companies invariably leads to reckless risk taking, especially abroad. Edmund Burke eventually led an impeachment proceeding in the British Parliament against the Company's governor-general of Bengal, Warren Hastings, of whom he said:

> Mr. Hastings' government was one whole system of oppression, of robbery of individuals, of spoliation of the public, and of supersession of the whole system of the English government, in order to vest in the worst of the natives all the power that could possibly exist in any government; in order to defeat the ends which all governments ought, in common, to have in view. In the name of the Commons of England, I charge all this villainy upon Warren Hastings, in this last moment of my application to you.
>
> (Burke, 1788)

The East India Company also demonstrates the preferred corporate approach to managing corporate excess – self-regulation. Years before Hastings' impeachment, in 1764, the Company had developed a voluntary internal code of conduct in an attempt to head off more heavy-handed intervention by Parliament.

Yet, the Company's actions caused a famine in Bengal in 1770 that killed up to 10 million people.

To the frustration of Burke and the others who saw in him the symbol of unaccountable corporate power, Hastings was eventually acquitted in 1795. The East India Company continued to operate as a private enterprise, with little to no accountability to the public, until 1858 when it was nationalized. In 1874 its stock was liquidated and it ceased to function (Robins, 2006).

Critics such as Burke and Smith identified three essential flaws in the corporate structure: the impetus to dominate markets and create monopolies, the speculative behaviour of companies in which executives are not owners, and the absence of regulatory mechanisms to check abusive behaviours overseas (Robins, 2006). While many of the particular circumstances under which the East India Company arose and the means by which it operated differ from those of multinationals today – for instance, it employed a private army that directly conquered land and people – the basic structure and drivers of the multinational operating overseas remain similar.

As sustainability issues become more important to stakeholders and many corporations take on sustainability objectives, a growing body of research has examined the business case for corporate sustainability and the motives that corporations have for investing in socially and environmentally beneficial activities (Roca and Searcy, 2012). These studies originally focused on the relationship between a corporation's social, environmental and financial performance, corporate management's appreciation of sustainability and the 'value-relevance' of sustainability disclosures – that is to say, the effect on the bottom line (Othman and Ameer, 2009). Studies have consistently shown that corporate social responsibility (CSR) is fundamentally good for the financial health of business over the long run, providing social legitimacy, competitive advantages and legal security. A seminal study by KPMG, one of the large consulting firms, concluded that 'Corporate responsibility reporting enhances financial value' (KPMG, 2011). The Aviva Report, commissioned by a coalition of institutional investors and insurers to promote sustainability reporting, cited several industry studies establishing a direct relationship between sustainable business practices and longer-term financial success.

As a result, CSR is now a mainstay of business management. Sustainability reporting has substantially increased, from less than 50 non-financial reports produced in 1992, to current global corporate disclosure practices by 95 per cent of the 250 largest companies in the world (KPMG, 2011). Consequently, studies have shifted away from 'debating whether or not corporate sustainability should be implemented to how it can be done in practice' (Roca and Searcy, 2012). Recent decades have seen a proliferation of instruments aimed at setting standards for CSR that take a voluntary, industry-led, self-regulatory approach.

Nevertheless, this has not blunted calls for binding legal frameworks since casual observation suggests that voluntary instruments produce only mild incentives for corporations to moderate their behaviour while unethical practices can bring large short-term gains to shareholders. Moreover, voluntary measures are mainly adopted by high-profile companies worried about their public image, but more easily avoided by the tens of thousands lower profile multinationals that choose to operate unconstrained, including increasingly important corporate players from emerging economies such as China and India.

The 2012 UN Conference on Sustainable Development ('Rio+20') may have marked a turning point in this debate. While industry representatives forcefully brought forward a particular formula for soft reporting obligations ('report or explain'), this approach did not gain traction at Rio. Meanwhile, civil society has renewed its calls for legally binding corporate accountability (CA) that no multinationals can evade. Following Rio+20, some governments, non-governmental organizations (NGOs) and investors are continuing to push for binding CA rules in the post-2015 global development agenda debate.

In this chapter we first distinguish between CSR and CA, arguing that while responsibility is assumed by corporations as a set of voluntary measures, accountability emerges out of the gaps left by CSR and imposes mandatory standards. We show how the voluntary CSR approach evolved over the twentieth and early twenty-first centuries, noting key milestones such as the World Summit on Sustainable Development and the creation of global initiatives such as the Global Compact and the Global Reporting Initiative. We further describe the shift towards an emphasis on reporting, specifically the limited 'report or explain' approach, which has lost the confidence of civil society. We argue that the discourse is shifting towards mandatory approaches, and that a global legal framework is needed.

CSR and CA distinguished

Contemporary approaches to CSR were begun in the 1950s following the post-war examinations of relationships between business, society and governments, and the promotion of obligations on corporations to work for 'social betterment' (Davis, 1960; Frederick, 1994; Othman and Ameer, 2009). These early writings focused on the 'social conscience' of managerial action and business activities (Carroll, 1999), with empirical research notably absent in the development of theories to analyse and explain CSR practices (Carroll, 1999; Moir, 2001).

This early work developed concepts such as 'business ethics' that extended to groups beyond a company's shareholders, and the 'social contract' between business and society that recognized corporate moral obligations to society, in general. This notion found strong support in public opinion surveys in nations whose economies and societies were increasingly dominated by large enterprises (Carroll, 1999). Research studies at this time began to investigate the extent of corporate social engagement and the degree to which they took their greater social responsibilities seriously and how they implemented their social agendas, the type of CSR activities undertaken and the effects of these activities on corporate structures and budgets (Carroll, 1999).

The harnessing of the internet by stakeholder activists to help expose, monitor and challenge corporate wrongdoing (e.g., fraud, environmental harm, human rights abuses), alongside the ongoing expansion of foreign investment and the proliferation of international supply chains (globalization), has not only raised popular awareness but also stimulated the growth of organized movements intent on prodding corporations into demonstrating more socially responsible behaviour. In this chapter we will distinguish between CSR and CA. While CSR by and large is the corporate world's preferred voluntary approach to addressing demands for more socially responsible action, CA uses a mix of instruments, including voluntary and especially regulatory and legal ones. The focus of CSR is on self-regulation, while the focus of CA is on legal accountability.

With the emergence of the discourse around sustainable development following the publication of the World Commission on Environment and Development's report called 'Our Common Future' in 1987, the role of corporations in achieving sustainability became a globally discussed topic, drawing the attention of not only civil society but of corporate leaders themselves, who viewed it as both a threat and an opportunity (Moneva *et al.*, 2006). The interaction between discourses on CSR and sustainable development produced the term 'corporate sustainability', still a variant of the voluntary CSR approach to achieving changes in business practices. CSR is now increasingly rebranded as corporate sustainability as voluntary social and environmental objectives and projects are increasingly integrated into business practices (Hohnen and Potts, 2007). Today, the terms 'corporate social responsibility' and corporate sustainability are often used interchangeably, despite divisions in academia on whether the concepts have the same meaning or remain subtly distinct (Roca and Searcy, 2012), with the concept of CSR often considered more representative of traditional notions of voluntary corporate philanthropy and social engagement (Correa-Ruiz and Moneva-Abadía, 2011).

The CSR movement is cooperative, has industry backing and is soft and persuasive in its ethic and approach. The ISO 26000 set of standards, a voluntary certification scheme, exemplifies this movement. The standards define corporate social responsibility as the

> responsibility of an organization for the impacts of its decisions and activities on society and the environment, through transparent and ethical behaviour that contributes to sustainable development, including health and the welfare of society; takes into account the expectations of stakeholders; is in compliance with applicable law and consistent with international norms of behaviour; and is integrated throughout the organization and practiced in its relationships.
>
> (ISO 26000, 2010)

The ISO standards for CSR define seven core subjects and two funda-mental practices. The core subjects are: organizational governance, human rights, labour practices, the environment, fair operating practices, consumer issues and community involvement and development. The two fundamental practices are stakeholder identification and engagement, and recognizing social responsibility.

Out of concern perhaps that the CSR field was becoming dominated by the voluntary corporate approach, NGOs began to claim new ground through the use of the term 'corporate accountability'. The distinction is made, for example, in the 2005 briefing of *Friends of the Earth*, which defines CA in terms of governance, or the ability of those affected by a corporation to affect or control that corporation's operations, while CSR involves the voluntary actions of companies to improve their social and environmental standards so as to reduce their negative impacts.

The CA movement has arisen to promote a harder, mandatory approach to corporate social and environmental obligations in comparison with the voluntary approach of CSR/corporate sustainability. If CSR was meant to create internal and cooperative mechanisms for 'taming corporate capitalism and minimizing its perverse effects' (Utting, 2008), the CA movement not only takes account of CSR's ambiguous performance history, but begins with the basic axiomatic assumption that only harder approaches will minimize the 'perverse effects' of global corporate capitalism. Utting (2008: 965) delineates the differences between CSR and CA:

> Conceptually and strategically there are several important differences. Whereas CSR is very much about voluntarism, in the dual sense of both individual agents taking action and voluntary initiatives, corporate accountability redirects attention to the question of corporate obligations, the role of public policy and law, the imposition of penalties in cases of non-compliance, the right of victims to seek redress, and imbalances in power relations.

Thus, CA generally has been used with reference to disclosure, transparency and corporate reporting practices, although it is also aligned with corporate governance and ethics principles in some instances. The CA movement embraces a wide array of tactics, including activism and contestation, using consumer and other market mechanisms to influence corporate behaviour, and steadily increasing standards and expectations through multi-stakeholder processes. But it has been the movement to introduce legal standards that has generated the most optimism and attention. The NGO sector has traditionally been the most active in promoting a legally binding instrument to regulate the behaviour of transnational corporations (TNCs) abroad. More recently, investors and insurers began to support CA as a means of predicting returns on investment and avoiding risk and exposure, recognizing that voluntary CSR alone will not get the job done.

Among the limitations of the voluntary approach is the relatively limited engagement of states, particularly the developing countries that are recipients of investment. It is not so much a case of the 'fox guarding the henhouse' in the absence of active exercise of regulatory oversight, although legitimate concerns may be raised on that account as well. More critically, the abdication of responsibility by regulatory authorities makes it impossible to measure the performance of states and also frustrates efforts to improve performance through dialogue and international assistance. Authorities in these countries are essentially given a 'free pass' from the self-regulated business community, meaning that capacities are not built to the extent that would be necessary to assist in implementation and enforcement of a legally binding regime. The lack of involvement by states also inhibits state-to-state exchange of experience and technical assistance.

Listed companies, moreover, which have been the focus of voluntary reporting initiatives, represent only a fraction of companies whose activities should give rise to reporting obligations. While UNCTAD estimates that approximately 4500 corporations are engaged in voluntary sustainability reporting, there are over 80,000 multinational corporations whose activities and performance must actually be reported in order to have a comprehensive picture of the global extent of problems related to corporate accountability in order to enable the development of appropriate policy responses (UNCTAD, 2010). While the response of highly visible, *Fortune* 500 companies to the challenges of corporate accountability has been laudable, other corporations involved in transnational investments with substantial environmental and social risk are less motivated to take on voluntary commitments.

Some of the most intransigent high-risk actors, such as the smaller companies engaged in extractive industries and agricultural commodities, have thus become the target of programmes aimed at increasing transparency and accountability. The UNEP Finance Initiative recognized the problem in certain sectors by focusing for a time on the role of Export Credit Agencies in financing high-risk, 'strategic' industries. Another programme aimed at increasing transparency and accountability is the Extractive Industries Transparency Initiative. Yet such piecemeal actions to extend current achievements into a consistent global regime merely highlight the limitations of the voluntary approach.

Despite the thousands of corporations that actively practice 'good corporate citizenship', the inherent tendencies of multinational corporations to abuse the power that wealth and the low risk of liability gives them continue to pose a threat to communities and the environment today. Moreover, given the absence of an international, universally applicable legal framework that governs the behaviour of multinationals, that number is always subject to fluctuations upwards whenever corporations, new or existing, are tempted to avoid voluntary standards, especially in countries where domestic legal and regulatory frameworks are weak. While the voluntary approach to CSR has certainly raised awareness, and most corporate boards in principle endorse CSR as a matter of course, the race for marginal profits, market share and access to resources often induces companies to cut (UN Human Rights Council, 2011) corners, cooperate with corrupt governments or otherwise undermine their CSR commitments. The countless campaigns against abusive mining, energy and other operations worldwide shows that as the number of transnational corporations has grown, so have the problems they bring.

The evolution of international CSR instruments

While domestic concerns about corporate behaviour have followed the growth of industrialization in nearly every society, on the international level, concerns for the management of corporate behaviour only emerged with the recognition of international human rights to just and favourable work conditions. The United Nations (UN) Declaration of Human Rights in 1948 (UN, 1948) and the International Covenant on Economic, Social and Cultural Rights in 1966 (OHCHR, 2007) recognized the needs to protect worker rights and promote international labour standards and emphasized the importance of protecting social justice in advancing economic policies and business activities (Kolk and Tulder, 2002; ILO, 2012a). However, the need for regulation of multinational corporate behaviour attracted increased international attention in the 1970s amid growing civil and women's rights movements, corporate corruption revelations and the visibility of environmental impacts of industrial activities (Kolk *et al.*, 1999; Kolk and van Tulder, 2002). The success of shareholder activism such as the Dow Chemicals shareholder resolution over napalm production in 1969 gave rise to a major divestment campaign aimed at apartheid South Africa (Guay *et al.*, 2004; Glac, 2010). By the 1980s environmentally and socially responsible investment was well established.

Meanwhile, governments took the first few tentative steps towards voluntary principles and standards for responsible business conduct with the 1976 OECD Declaration on International Investment and Multinational Enterprises, comprising non-binding recommendations on responsible business conduct for governments and companies operating within OECD countries, followed by the adoption of the OECD Guidelines for Multinational Enterprises (OECD Guidelines) (OECD, 2011), which have since been updated several times. Similarly, the ILO Tripartite Declaration of Principles concerning Multinational Enterprises and Social Policy (MNE Declaration) adopted in 1977 offered voluntary recommendations as guidelines for multinational enterprises, governments and employer organizations in employment, work conditions and industrial relations matters (ILO, 2006).

These voluntary initiatives followed the failed mandatory approach taken under the UN Commission on Transnational Corporations, established in 1973 with the goal of formulating a Draft Code of Conduct for transnational corporations. The commission abandoned its efforts to draft the code in 1992 amidst disagreements among states, and ended its work two years later. The initial attempts of international organizations to introduce international codes of conduct in the 1970s demonstrated the 'inability to come to an international agreement on the function, the wording and – especially – the sanctions for non-compliant firms' (Kolk and van Tulder, 2002).

Over the course of the 1980s and 1990s, multinational companies began to voluntarily introduce codes of conduct to placate increasing societal pressures (Kolk and van Tulder, 2002). One of the first was the adoption in 1976 of the Shell General Business Principles (Shell, 2006). These have been revised several times and encompass a commitment to sustainable development and responsible environmental management, employee rights, social responsibility, openness, stakeholder engagement and local community well-being in the context of business integrity and financial responsibility towards shareholders.

In response to a number of environmental disasters in the 1980s, notably the Bhopal gas leak in India in 1984 and the Exxon Valdez oil spill in Alaska in 1989, the environmental movement drove non-governmental campaigns against specific companies and contributed to the larger concern over the risks to the environment and to people that multinational companies could pose. The concern is reflected in Article 36 of the Charter of the Organization of American States, added in 1985, which stated that:

> Transnational enterprises and foreign private investment shall be subject to the legislation of the host countries and to the jurisdiction of their competent courts and to the international treaties and agreements to which said countries are parties, and should conform to the development policies of the recipient countries.

The 1992 UN Conference on Environment and Development in Rio de Janeiro, Brazil (The 'Rio Conference' or 'Earth Summit') was a turning point in the relationship between international organizations, the environmental movement and multinational companies. In the run-up to the Rio Conference, voluntary corporate codes of conduct sponsored by the Coalition for Environmentally Responsible Economies (CERES) promoting environmental awareness and reporting (CERES, 2010) were endorsed by a variety of high-profile companies including The Body Shop, Ben & Jerry's and Aveda (SRI, 2012).

The UN Environment Programme's (UNEP) Finance Initiative was launched around this time as a collaborative effort between UNEP and commercial banks to 'catalyse the banking industry's awareness of the environmental agenda' and integrate environmental considerations into the financial sector (UNEP FI, 2012). The World Business Council for Sustainable Development was formed to represent the business sector in Rio (WBCSD, 2012) and to promote private voluntary efforts by the corporate sector in addressing sustainable development (Clapp, 2005). The Rio Conference recognized the role of voluntary initiatives and self-regulation by business in minimizing impacts on the environment and human health. The conference called on business to recognize environmental management 'as among the highest corporate priorities', in Chapter 30 of the outcome document, Agenda 21 (UNDESA DSD 2009). The rapid globalization of the 1990s (World Bank, 2007) brought even greater influence of corporations on political systems, society and the environment (Deardorff, 2004).

Industry-driven, sector-specific codes of conduct also appeared. For example, the multi-stakeholder Forest Stewardship Council, established in 1993 with the support of the corporate sector, environmental organizations and social groups, promoted improved forest management in the timber industry through global certification and accreditation systems, guidelines and standards (FSC, 2012).

Similarly, the Code of Ethics on the International Trade in Chemicals, which extended earlier London Guidelines for the Exchange of Information on Chemicals in International Trade, encouraged voluntary agreements between industry and government for the disclosure of information and risk management in the use of hazardous substances. Social and environmental responsibility reporting extended into investor responsibility and the foreign investment sector, with the adoption of the Environmental and Social Safeguard Policies of the International Finance Corporation (IFC) in 1998, a set of performance standards for IFC projects in emerging markets, which were later superseded by the Sustainability Framework in 2006 incorporating policy and performance standards on environmental and social sustainability for IFC-supported projects (IFC, 2012).

As national environmental management standards evolved in domestic arenas, the International Standardization Organization developed the ISO 14000 series of environmental management standards in 1996 in response to concerns that the different environmental management requirements that countries imposed on corporations could result in non-tariff trade barriers. The following year, the NGO Social Accountability International created the Social Accountability Standard (SA8000) as a tool for implementing international labour standards and national labour laws (SAI, 2012). This instrument filled a perceived gap in the standards market (as the ISO 14000 series focused on environmental management) and a need from the business sector for a streamlined accreditation process to appease international and national labour law pressures. As of March 2013 there were 3137 SA8000 certified facilities in 69 countries representing 65 industries with over 1.8 million employees (SAI, 2013).

The human rights aspects of CSR continued to develop through the globalization of the Sullivan Principles. The private initiative of the Global Sullivan Principles for Corporate Social Responsibility was jointly re-launched by UN secretary general Kofi Annan and the Reverend Leon Sullivan in 1999 to encourage companies in supporting economic, social and political justice in their business activities (Leon H. Sullivan Foundation, 2012). Similarly, the UN recognized (UN Human Rights Council, 2011) its own agencies face corporate behaviour that is having a negative impact on basic rights, bringing corporate action into clear conflict with UN goals. Many such examples can be found in the work of the UN Special Rapporteur on the Rights of Indigenous Peoples, who has reported on numerous cases of corporate involvement in the violation of indigenous rights, often involving mining or other resource extraction in indigenous areas (UNOHCHR, 2013).

Despite the abandonment of the 20-year-long negotiations on a draft UN Code of Conduct on Transnational Corporations in 1992 (CCC, 1998), initiatives towards a global framework on corporate social responsibility began re-emerging with the OECD-led negotiations on a proposed multilateral agreement on investment that took place from 1995 until 1998. The negotiations sought to produce a 'free-standing international treaty' to 'develop a strong, comprehensive framework for international investment' by providing 'high standards for the liberalisation of investment regimes and investment protection, with effective dispute settlement' (OECD, 1995). The complexity of negotiating an international regime regulating foreign direct investment was demonstrated by the failure of the negotiating group to reach consensus despite consistent efforts over three years to do so (OECD, 1998). Negotiations were discontinued following strong opposition from non-governmental organizations due to the 'pro-investor bias of the proposed agreement and . . . being excluded from the drafting process' (Cohen, 2007). Nonetheless, broad support did emerge for some elements of the proposed agreement relating to labour and environmental issues (OECD, 1998).

The WSSD (Johannesburg 2002)

Despite this failure, expectations were high in 2002 that the World Summit on Sustainable Development (WSSD) in Johannesburg (the 'Johannesburg Summit') would produce an initiative surpassing the results of Rio in 1992, which merely encouraged corporations to 'report annually on their environmental records, as well as on their use of energy and natural resources' (UNDESA, 2009). Leading up to the summit, Friends of the Earth released a detailed blueprint for a global treaty that would regulate transnational corporations, including a provision to extend liability to top executives (Friends of the Earth, 2005). Greenpeace International promoted its voluntary 2002 'Bhopal Principles on Corporate Accountability' as a step towards a legally binding treaty (Greenpeace, 2002).

Corporate accountability was seen as a 'highly contentious' and 'hotly debated' (Khor, 2002) issue at the Johannesburg World Summit as the Business Action for Sustainable Development group, a joint initiative of the International Chamber of Commerce and the WBCSD, called on the corporate sector to assume its obligation for accountability (BASD, 2002) and lobbied for private voluntary measures (Clapp, 2005) by projecting industry as 'sufficiently responsible and capable . . . for implementing sustainable development' (Khor, 2002).

However, strong industry opposition ensured that draft language in the WSSD Plan of Implementation calling for the start of negotiations on a multilateral agreement on corporate accountability was removed from the final text (Clapp, 2005). The Johannesburg Declaration on Sustainable Development agreed on the 'need for private sector corporations to enforce corporate accountability, which should take place within a transparent and stable regulatory environment' (UNDESA DSD, 2004: paragraph 29). The Plan of Implementation also committed states to 'enhance corporate environmental and social responsibility and accountability' through encouraging 'industry to improve social and environmental performance through voluntary initiatives' (UNDESA DSD, 2005: paragraph 18).

Although critics viewed the promotion of voluntary initiatives by the business sector as a means of undermining the development of regulatory measures and 'marginalis[ing] the development of intergovernmental agreements' (*The Guardian*, 2002 quoted in Bendell and Kearins, 2005), others saw the expressed commitment towards corporate accountability as one of the few achievements of the Johannesburg World Summit (Khor, 2002).

The rising tide of voluntary codes of conduct and reporting standards ahead of the Johannesburg Summit further propelled collaboration between industry and international organizations to develop a number of international multi-stakeholder instruments, notably the Global Reporting Initiative and the UN Global Compact. The Global Reporting Initiative was initially developed by CERES and the Tellus Institute to provide sustainable reporting guidelines, and was formally adopted and established by UNEP at the Johannesburg World Summit to provide organizational reporting guidance through its sustainable reporting framework and guidelines (GRI, 2012). The Global Reporting Initiative's guidelines are considered in current literature as the paramount corporate sustainability framework (Ballou *et al.*, 2006; Choudhari and Chakraborty, 2009; Roca and Searcy, 2012). Its sustainability reporting framework is largely recognized as the leading international standard on corporate sustainability reporting, with research identifying that 77 per cent of the top 250 global companies release sustainability reports using the Global Reporting Initiative's framework (KPMG, *et al.*, 2010).

The Global Reporting Initiative is also considered the benchmark for sustainability reporting by other existing international corporate sustainability reporting instruments. For example, the Global Reporting Initiative is explicitly identified by the OECD Guidelines for Multinational Enterprises as a useful reference for reporting standards and as an example of reporting standards developed through cooperation between enterprises, non-governmental organizations and intergovernmental organizations (OECD, 2011). The Global Reporting Initiative, in turn, has formed a strategic alliance with the United Nations Global Compact to provide guidance on transparency and reporting of the United Nations Global Compact principles (UN GC, 2006) and has worked in partnership with the United Nations Environment Programme Finance Initiative (UNEP FI) to develop the revised financial services sector supplement that is recognized by UNEP FI as being 'expected to develop into the standard for reporting on sustainability performance of financial products and services' (UNEP FI, 2012).

Post-Johannesburg

Since the Johannesburg Summit, socially responsible investment was further embedded in the foreign investment sector when the OECD launched its Initiative on Investment for Development in 2003 to complement the existing OECD Guidelines with the development of a policy framework for investment. The IFC and a number of international banking institutions launched the Equator Principles in 2003 to provide a framework for social and environmental policies, procedures and standards in project finance activities (TEPA, 2011). The UNEP Finance Initiative, a merger of its earlier Banking and Insurance Industry Initiatives, and the UN Global Compact launched the Principles for Responsible Investment in 2006, following a multi-stakeholder development process involving the investment industry, intergovernmental and governmental organizations, civil society and academia, to provide a voluntary framework for incorporating environmental, social and corporate governance into investor decision-making (PRI, 2012).

In addition, the development of ancillary accreditation services and standards has assisted the corporate sector in addressing the multitude of initiatives at hand. For example, the Social Accountability Accreditation Services certify compliance with social standards (SAAS, 2012), the AA1000 AccountAbility series of standards provides operational guidance on sustainability assurance and stakeholder engagement (AccountAbility, 2011), and the ISO 26000 guidance on social responsibility, released by the International Standards Organization in 2010, provides guidance to organizations in social responsibility activities (ISO, 2011). Other initiatives in this field include the Climate Disclosure Standards Board climate change reporting framework, and the Sustainable Stock Exchanges initiative.

'Protect, respect and remedy'

After strong opposition from the business sector contributed to the abandonment of draft norms produced by the UN Commission on Human Rights in 2004 to impose binding obligations on transnational corporations and other business enterprises, the Human Rights Council sought to move 'beyond the stalemate' and clarify 'the roles and responsibilities of states, companies and other social actors in the business and human rights sphere' (HRC, 2008). The UN Secretary General appointed a Special Representative on human rights and transnational corporations and other business enterprises to 'identify and clarify standards of corporate responsibility and accountability for transnational corporations and other business enterprises with regard to human rights, including through international cooperation' (OHCHR, 2005). The Special Representative, Professor John Ruggie, developed the UN 'Protect, Respect and Remedy' Framework for Business and Human Rights, more commonly known as 'the Ruggie Framework', which was adopted by the Human Rights Council in 2008 to express the global standard of expected corporate conduct and provide the baseline for corporate responsibility with respect to human rights as 'part of the company's social license to operate' (HRC, 2008; UN, 2010). The framework centres on three 'differentiated but complementary' pillars of responsibility; the State duty to protect against human rights abuses by third parties (including business); the corporate responsibility to respect human rights; and the need for more effective access to remedies (HRC, 2008; UN, 2010).

More recently, the first global standard to prevent and address the risk of adverse human rights impacts from business activities was endorsed by the UN Human Rights Council in 2011 as a set of guiding principles (the Ruggie Principles). These provide a template for business in implementing the 'Protect, Respect and Remedy' Framework and outline the due diligence companies are expected to become aware of, prevent and address adverse human rights impacts (HRC, 2008; UNGA, 2011; UNOG, 2011). The guiding principles were expressly intended to 'elaborat[e] the implications of existing standards and practices for States and businesses; integrating them within a single, logically coherent and comprehensive template; and identifying where the current template falls short and how it should be improved' rather than to create new international law obligations (UNGA, 2011).

Shift towards reporting

Following the Johannesburg Summit and the willingness of the business sector to adopt voluntary initiatives in the absence of universal regulatory requirements, corporations began to proactively embrace corporate social responsibility and voluntarily commit to norms and standards, whether individually or as part of larger coalitions or business-sector organizations (Kolk and van Tulder, 2005). Fuelled by the global financial crisis of 2007 and mounting pressure from influential NGOs and civil society activism, the last decade has seen a cascade in the voluntary adoption of CSR initiatives and instruments by the corporate sector with an increasing focus on non-financial reporting. While reporting is an essential part of corporate accountability, reporting alone is insufficient to elicit consistently sustainable behaviour from corporations, even if reporting is legally obligatory. Reporting is merely reporting, it is not action directly in support of sustainability.

The formula captured by the phrase 'protect, respect and remedy' stands in contrast to the more limited notion of 'report or explain' prevalent in the corporate sector. The literature on environmental accounting and sustainability reporting took off in the 1990s in response to the exponential growth of corporate sustainability reporting practices by the business sector, and a growing body of empirical research on the effects of sustainability accounting and corporate sustainability reporting has subsequently developed (Lamberton, 2005; Roca and Searcy, 2012). Reflecting a social appetite for greater clarity and accountability for the social and environmental impact of business, John Elkington coined the term 'triple bottom line' (Elkington, 1997) to promote corporate reporting on economic, social and environmental impacts (Correa-Ruiz and Moneva-Abadía, 2011). More recently, the notion of 'corporate sustainability reporting' has emerged to refer to the expanded scope of a corporation's reporting responsibilities beyond what it owes shareholders alone in the areas of financial and non-financial reporting (Ballou *et al.*, 2006).

This shift from CSR to corporate sustainability reporting reflects the recognition, harkening back to the 'social conscience' of corporations aired in the 1950s, that the operations of corporations have profound social impacts and that responsible public discourse on the role of corporations in society begins with disclosure of information about the activities of corporations affecting society, community and environment. While sustainability reporting may include non-environmental aspects of corporate conduct and performance, green and environmental accounting are sometimes used interchangeably with this term and speak to the predominantly environmental focus of this instrument (Choudhuri and Chakraorty, 2009; Roca and Searcy, 2012).

However, reporting as it is currently practiced has serious limitations. The absence of a clearly defined and mutually agreed framework (Othman and Ameer, 2009) means that corporate sustainability reporting continues to be 'plagued by [a] lack of uniformity, consistency and comparability' (Sherman and DiGuilio, 2010). Recent studies have identified that a vast discretion in reporting indicators together with the lack of standardization has led to uneven disclosure in corporate sustainability reporting across all sectors and jurisdictions (Roca and Searcy, 2012). Major limitations include the lack of comparability of the content of sustainability disclosures through the variety of reports produced under the existing instruments, the overwhelming emphasis on addressing the interests of business and investor stakeholders in guiding the development and implementation of these existing instruments, and the lack of independent assurance and reliability of corporate sustainability disclosures. These significant gaps and weaknesses in the existing international corporate sustainability reporting framework obstruct accessibility to comparable and reliable reports that provide comprehensive and digestible information on the social and environmental impacts of corporate activities for analysis and critique by civil society, hindering the role of corporate sustainability reporting in enhancing the transparency and accountability of corporate behaviour.

More generally, the voluntary approach to CSR does not and cannot be expected to produce significant sustainability benefits.[1] First and foremost, from the reigning neo-liberal perspective corporations are obligated to maximizing value for shareholders, and those advocating social and environmental obligations must always make the 'business case' for CSR. Under the intense competition of today's globalized capitalism, as Reich has pointed out (2007), no firm can afford to sacrifice profits in one area of operations for taking actions to benefit the common good unless those actions also increase profits overall – in which case this behaviour is not motivated by a sense of social responsibility, but rather is the very profit-oriented behaviour for which the firm was created in the first place. CSR may be providing firms with new opportunities to furbish their images and increase profits, but it will not have systemic effects; such lasting effects require political decisions and policy instruments and cannot rely on the goodwill of private economic institutions.

As a practical matter, voluntary initiatives, however much fanfare accompanies them, must sell themselves as a service to corporations in order to attract participation. If the service isn't potentially profitable, businesses will not invest. There are well over 60,000 multinational corporations operating in the world today (Gabel and Bruner, 2003). The Global Compact currently has approximately 8000 businesses that participate (Global Compact, 2014), while the Global Reporting Initiative (GRI) has about 6800 participants who use its guidelines (GRI, 2014). While these numbers may reflect early days as more businesses join these initiatives, the trend is not encouraging.

While the impacts of these initiatives may not be negligible, it would be a great exaggeration to claim that the Global Compact, the GRI and similar instruments taken together form a global regime for corporate social responsibility.

They remain what they have always been: voluntary instruments that some businesses will adopt with varying degrees of compliance depending upon their perceptions of self-interest, while other businesses – most, we argue – ignore such initiatives because they perceive it to be in their interests to remain fully unaccountable to other stakeholders, at least in the international arena. In addition to the majority of multinationals that do not join initiatives such as GRI and the Global Compact, even those that do may not adhere to the relatively light reporting requirements of these instruments. For instance, the Global Compact has delisted roughly 3000 firms that failed to submit performance reports after first joining. According to Ethical Corporation, those firms did not reapply (Ethical Corporation, 2012).

Conclusion: towards corporate accountability after Rio +20

The Rio+20 conference produced ambiguous results in the area of corporate accountability. A coalition of corporate and civil society actors had attempted to codify the voluntary approach to reporting through a multilateral instrument that would have mandated that corporations issue sustainability reports or explain why they did not, thus leaving in place the discretion of CSR while covering it with a veneer of CA. The initiative failed to gain traction, leaving the world of CSR/CA in limbo, with a recognition that the voluntary approach has gone about as far as it can go, but that more is needed, yet without a solid coalition backing a more regulatory approach at this time.

The CSR movement and the resulting array of voluntary instruments, from individual corporate codes of conduct to sector-wide standards and global codes of conduct and reporting initiatives have fundamentally changed the discourse on the role of corporations in society and the global economy. Even corporations that don't walk-the-walk often talk-the-talk, because the general public expects multinational corporations to conduct their business ethically and to social and environmental standards and goals in addition to making money for their shareholders and contributing to economic growth. However, the experience of the past 20 years has also made apparent the limits to voluntarism, with limited participation, evasion of standards, low standards, incompatible reporting, partial reporting and sheer confusion over the multiplicity of standards, guidelines, principles and initiatives as common complaints among stakeholders. A corporation that claims to be socially responsible may or may not be, with the general public having no consistently reliable means of knowing whether claims are valid and justified. Regulatory frameworks are needed, not to replace voluntary initiatives in all cases but to supplement and vitalize them as well as set new and higher standards and ensure that corporations cannot evade their responsibilities through non-participation.

After the failure of 'report or explain' to gain sufficient traction to lead to a new instrument at Rio+20 or afterwards, and the exhaustion of the CSR approach, the movement for corporate accountability is in need of a renewed and more ambitious effort. The role of multinational corporations in economic development will only grow in the coming decades, and the associated social and environmental impacts and risks cannot help but motivate stakeholders to seek a more regulated regime for investors. The movement towards mandatory approaches is gaining momentum. In 2014 both the EU and India introduced mandatory corporate reporting laws. India's law goes further than reporting, requiring domestic and international companies operating in India to demonstrate that their CSR expenditures equal at least 2 per cent of their profits. At the national level, regulatory cultures and traditions can shape the approach taken, from a rules based approach to corporate governance as is practiced in the United States to the United Kingdom and Germany's more flexible 'comply or explain' tradition. Another promising option is to modify corporate governance along the lines of 'enlightened shareholder value', which could require directors of companies to take a long-term view of corporate financial sustainability within the context of social and environmental concerns over against short-term profits. Currently enshrined in weak form in corporate law in the United Kingdom under the 2006 Companies Act (Williams, 2012), the enlightened shareholder value argument could serve as a foundation for re-evaluating and reformulating the role of the corporation in society.

Regional and national approaches, however, still leave gaps and especially do not address the needs of the most vulnerable people and ecosystems in least developed countries, where governance is often poor. The UN Human Rights Council has voted in favour of a resolution to develop a legally binding instrument regulating the human rights obligations of multinational corporations. However, more is needed. Specifically, a more comprehensive approach, in the form of a framework convention on corporate accountability, would solve two of the main problems facing stakeholders and decision makers in this arena: the fragmented nature of responsibility/accountability regimes and the difficulty of negotiating binding rules, especially beyond the issue of reporting. A framework convention would set out the general parameters of the social and environmental obligations of corporations in legally binding form, and yet leave the particular rules for future negotiations in the form of protocols, as is often done in the development of environmental regimes. A framework convention can be prescriptive in some areas, such as reporting, and aspirational in other, politically more challenging aspects.

Note

1   This does not mean that CSR initiatives are cynical, but rather that the structural constraints of the current market system and the framework of corporate law governing corporations severely limits the potential of all such instruments. For instance, while instruments such as the Dow Jones Sustainability Index, the FTSE4GOOD and other social and sustainability stock indexes that attempt to measure the sustainability performance of corporations and provide responsible investors with tools to guide their decisions, these indexes play a marginal role in the investment world, and cannot directly influence corporate behaviour of the vast majority.

References

AccountAbility. 2012. *The AA1000 standards*. URL: www.accountability.org/standards/index.html [accessed 29 March 2012].

Ballou, B., Heither, D. L. and Landers, C. E. 2006. The future of corporate sustainability reporting: a rapidly growing assurance opportunity. *Journal of Accountancy*, December: 65–74. URL: www.journalofaccountancy.com/Issues/2006/Dec/TheFutureOfCorporate SustainabilityReporting [accessed 29 March 2012].

Burke, E. 1788. *At the trial of Warran Hastings*. URL: http://joseignaciogutierrezarrudi. e.telefonica.net/documentacion/tij03.pdf [accessed 26 April 2012].

Business Action for Sustainable Development (BASD). 2002. *"Lekgotla" – Business day; Johannesburg Business Pledge for Action*. URL: http://basd.free.fr/activities/lekgotla_ pledge.html [accessed 26 April 2012].

Carroll, A. B. 1999. Corporate social responsibility: evolution of a definitional construct. *Business and Society*. 38(3): 268–95.

CERES. 2010. *The Ceres Principals*. URL: www.ceres.org/about-us/our-history/ceres-principles [accessed 29 March 2012].

Choudhuri, A. and Chakraborty, J. 2009. An insight into sustainability reporting. *The Icfaian Journal of Management Research*. 8(4): 46–53.

Clapp. J. 2005. Global environmental governance for corporate responsibility and accountability. *Global Environmental Politics*. 5(3): 23–34.

Clean Clothes Campaign (CCC). 1998. *Codes of conduct for transnational corporations: an overview*. URL: www.cleanclothes.org/resources/ccc/corporate-accountability/code-implementation-a-verification/574 [accessed 15 May 2012].

Cohen, S. D. 2007. Multinational corporations and foreign direct investment. *Oxford Scholarship Online*. URL: www.oxfordscholarship.com/view/10.1093/acprof:oso/97801951 79354.001.0001/acprof-9780195179354-chapter-12v [accessed 29 March 2012].

Correa-Ruiz, C. and Moneva-Abadía, J. M. 2011. Special issue on social responsibility accounting and reporting in times of sustainability downturn/crisis. *Spanish Accounting Review*. 14(1): 187–211.

Davis. K. 1960. cited in Carroll, A. B. 1999. Corporate social responsibility: evolution of a definitional construct. *Business Society*. 38(3): 268–95.

Deardorff, A. 2004. 'Who makes the rules of globalization?' Paper presented at CESifo Venice Summer Institute 2004 Globalization Workshop, 21–22 July 2004.

Elkington, J. 1997. *Cannibals with forks: the triple bottom line of 21st century business*. Oxford: Capstone.

Forest Stewardship Council (FSC). 2012. *History of FSC*. URL: www.fsc.org/history. html [accessed 29 March 2012].

Frederick, W. C. 1994. cited in Moir, L. 2001. What do we mean by corporate social responsibility? *Corporate Governance* 1(2): 16–22.

Friends of the Earth. 2005. *Briefing: corporate accountability*. London: Friends of the Earth.

Gabel, M. and Brunner, H. 2003. *Globalinc: an atlas of the multinational corporation*. New York: The New Press.

Glac, K. 2010. *The influence of shareholders on corporate social responsibility; history of corporate responsibility project*. Working paper No. 2. Minneapolis, MN: Center for Ethical Business Cultures.

Global Compact. 2014. *Website consulted for updated participation information*, December, 2014. URL: www.unglobalcompact.org/ParticipantsAndStakeholders/Index.html [accessed 26 April 2012].

Global Reporting Initiative (GRI). 2012. *Report or explain campaign forum*. URL: www. globalreporting.org/network/report-or-explain/Pages/default.aspx [accessed 26 April 2012].

Global Reporting Initiative (GRI). 2014. *Website consulted for updated participation information,* December, 2014. URL: www.globalreporting.org/Pages/default.aspx [accessed 26 June 2014].

Greenpeace. 2002. *Bhopal principals on corporate accountability.* URL: http://archive.greenpeace. org/earthsummit/docs/bhopalpr.pdf [accessed 29 March 2012].

Guay, T., Doh, J. P. and Sinclair G. (2004). Non-governmental organizations, shareholder activism, and socially responsible investments: ethical, strategic, and governance implications. *Journal of Business Ethics* 52: 125–39.

Hohnen, P. and Potts, J. (ed.). 2007. *Corporate social responsibility: an implementation guide.* Winnipeg, Canada: International Institute for Sustainable Development.

Human Rights Council (HRC). 2008. *Human Rights Council, Eight session, agenda item 3; Promotion and protection of all human rights, civil, political, economic, social and cultural rights, including the right to development; protect, respect and remedy: a framework for business and human rights; report of the special representative of the Secretary-General on the issue of human rights and transnational corporations and other business enterprises, John Ruggie.* URL: www. reports-and-materials.org/Ruggie-report-7-Apr-2008.pdf [accessed 16 May 2012].

International Labour Organization (ILO). 2006. *Tripartite declaration of principles concerning multinational enterprises and social policy.* 4th edition. Geneva, Switzerland: International Labour Office.

International Labour Organization (ILO). 2012. *Social protection floors for social justice and a fair globalization.* Geneva, Switzerland.

International Labour Organization (ILO). 2012a. *Origins and history.* URL: www.ilo.org/ global/about-the-ilo/history/lang-en/index.htm [accessed 15 May 2012].

International Organisation for Standardization (ISO). 2010. Guidance on social responsibility. *ISO Standard 26000.* URL: www.cnis.gov.cn/wzgg/201405/P020140512224950899020. pdf [accessed 29 March 2012].

International Organisation for Standardization (ISO). 2011. *ISO 26000:2010.* URL: www.iso. org/iso/catalogue_detail?csnumber=42546 [accessed 29 March 2012].

Khor, M. 2002. *The fight for WSSD's commitment to corporate accountability.* Third World Network. URL: www.twnside.org.sg/title/twr145c.htm [accessed 25 April 2012].

Kolk, A. and van Tulder, R. 2002. *International codes of conduct: trends, sectors, issues and effectiveness.* Rotterdam, The Netherlands: Erasmus University, Department of Business-Society Management.

Kolk, A. and van Tulder, R. 2005. Setting new global rules? TNCs and codes of conduct. *Transnational Corporations.* 14(3): 1–28.

Kolk, A., van Tulder, R. and Welters, C. 1999. International codes of conduct and corporate social responsibility: can transnational corporations regulate themselves? *Transnational Corporations.* 8(1): 143–80.

KPMG Advisory N.V., United Nations Environment Programme, Global Reporting Initiative and Unit for Corporate Governance Africa. 2010. *Carrots and sticks – promoting transparency and sustainability; an update on trends in voluntary and mandatory approaches to sustainability reporting.* URL: www.kpmg.com/ZA/en/IssuesAndInsights/ArticlesPublications/Advisory-Publications/Documents/Carrots_Sticks_2010.pdf [accessed 26 June 2012].

KPMG International Cooperative. 2011. *KPMG international survey of corporate responsibility reporting 2011.* URL: www.kpmg.com/ru/en/issuesandinsights/articlespublications/ pages/international-survey-of-corporate-responsibility-reporting.aspx [accessed 25 April 2012].

Lamberton, G. 2005. Sustainability accounting – a brief history and conceptual framework. *Accounting Forum.* 29(1): 7–26.

Leon H. Sullivan Foundation. 2012. URL: www.marshall.edu/revleonsullivan/principled/ global.htm [accessed 2 November 2012].

Moir, L. 2001. What do we mean by corporate social responsibility. *Corporate Governance: The International Journal of Business in Society.* 1(2): 16–22.

Moneva, J. M., Archel, P. and Correa, C. 2006. GRI and the camouflaging of corporate unsustainability. *Accounting Forum.* 30(2): 121–37.

Office of the United Nations High Commissioner for Human Rights (OHCHR). 2005. *Human rights resolution 2005/69: human rights and transnational corporations and other business enterprises, 20 April 2005.* URL: www.unhcr.org/refworld/docid/45377c80c.html [accessed 10 July 2012].

Office of the United Nations High Commissioner for Human Rights (OHCHR). 2007. *International covenant on economic, social and cultural rights.* URL: www2.ohchr.org/english/law/cescr.htm [accessed 14 May 2012].

Organization for Economic Cooperation and Development (OECD). 1995. *OECD negotiations on a multilateral agreement on investment.* URL: www.oecd.org/dataoecd/57/32/43389907.pdf [accessed 11 May 2012].

Organization for Economic Cooperation and Development (OECD). 1998. *Multilateral agreement on investment – report to the Ministers,* April, 1998. URL: www.oecd.org/document/4/0,3343,en_2649_33783766_1933060_1_1_1_1,00.html [accessed 11 May 2012].

Organization for Economic Cooperation and Development (OECD). 2011. *OECD guidelines for multinational enterprises,* (2011 edn). ParisOECD Publishing. URL: http://dx.doi.org/10.1787/9789264115415-en [accessed 21 May 2012].

Othman, R. and Ameer, R. 2009. Environmental disclosures of palm oil plantation companies in Malaysia: a tool for stakeholder engagement. *Corporate Social Responsibility and Environmental Management.* 17(1): 52–62.

Principals for Responsible Investment (PRI). 2012. *About us.* URL: www.unpri.org/about/ [accessed 29 March 2012].

Reich, R. 2007. *Supercapitalism.* New York: Vintage Books.

Robins, N. 2006. *The corporation that changed the world: how the East India Company shaped the modern multinational.* Ann Arbor, MI: Pluto Press.

Roca, L. C. and Searcy, C. 2012. An analysis of indicators disclosed in corporate sustainability reports. *Journal of Cleaner Production.* 20(1): 103–18.

Sauvant, K. 2015. The negotiations of the United Nations Code of Conduct on Transnational Corporations: experience and lessons learned. *The Journal of World Investment and Trade.* 16: 11–87.

Shell. 2006. *Shell General Business Principles.* [No publication information].

Sherman, W. R. and DiGuilio, L. 2010. The second round of G3 reports: is triple bottom line reporting becoming more comparable? *Journal of Business and Economics Research.* 8(9): 59–77.

Social Accountability Accreditation Services (SAAS). 2012. *Who we are and what we do.* URL: www.saasaccreditation.org/about.htm (accessed 29 March 2012).

Social Accountability International (SAI). 2012. *SA8000 standard.* URL: www.sa-intl.org/index.cfm?fuseaction=Page.ViewPage&PageID=937 [accessed 29 March 2012].

Social Accountability International (SAI). 2013. URL: www.saasaccreditation.org/certfacilities.htm [accessed 26 July 2013].

SRI World Group, Inc. (SRI) 2012. *Social investment timeline.* URL www.socialfunds.com/media/timeline.cgi [accessed 29 March 2012].

The Equator Principals Association (TEPA). 2011. *About the equator principals.* URL: www.equator-principles.com/index.php/about-the-equator-principles [accessed 29 March 2012].

United Nations (UN). 1948. *Universal Declaration of Human Rights.* UN General Assembly. [No publishing information].

United Nations (UN). 1966. *International covenant on economic, social and cultural rights*. UN General Assembly. [No publishing information].

United Nations Conference on Trade and Development (UNCTAD). 2010. *World Investment Report*. URL: http://unctad.org/en/docs/wir2010_en.pdf [accessed 29 March 2012].

United Nations Department of Economic Social Affairs, Division for Sustainable Development (UNDESA DSD). 2004. *Johannesburg declaration on sustainable development*. URL: www.un.org/esa/sustdev/documents/WSSD_POI_PD/English/POI_PD.htm [accessed 29 March 2012].

United Nations Department of Economic Social Affairs, Division for Sustainable Development (UNDESA DSD). 2005. *Johannesburg plan of implementation*. URL: www.un.org/esa/sustdev/documents/WSSD_POI_PD/English/POIToc.htm [accessed 29 March 2012].

United Nations Department of Economic Social Affairs, Division for Sustainable Development (UNDESA DSD). 2009. *Agenda 21, Section III strengthening the role of major groups, Chapter 30 strengthening the role of business and industry*. URL: www.un.org/esa/dsd/agenda21/res_agenda21_30.shtml [accessed 29 March 2012].

United Nations Environment Programme Finance Initiative (UNEP FI). 2012. *Work streams; sustainability reporting*. URL: www.unepfi.org/work_streams/reporting/index.html [accessed 22 May 2012].

United Nations General Assembly (UNGA) 2011. Human Rights Council, 17th session, agenda item 3. *Promotion and protections of all human rights, civil, political, economic, social and cultural rights; including the right to[. . .]*. URL: www.ohchr.org/documents/issues/business/A.HRC.17.31.pdf [accessed 15 May 2012].

United Nations Global Compact (UNGC). 2006. *UN global compact and global reporting initiative form strategic alliance; move to further advance corporate citizenship*. URL: www.unglobalcompact.org/newsandevents/news_archives/2006_10_06.html [accessed 2 May 2012].

United Nations Global Compact (UNGC). 2010. *Blueprint for corporate sustainability leadership*. [no publishing location]: UN Global Compact.

Utting, P. 2008. The struggle for corporate accountability. *Development and Change*. 39(6): 959–75.

United Nations Human Rights Council (UNHRC). 2011. *Promotion and protection of all human rights, civil, political, economic, social and cultural rights, including the right to development: protect, respect and remedy: a framework for business and human rights report of the special representative of the Secretary-General on the issue of human rights and transnational corporations and other business enterprises*, prepared by John Ruggie. Geneva. Switzerland.

United Nations Office at Geneva (UNOG). 2011. *UN human rights council endorses new guiding principals on business and human rights*. URL: www.unog.ch/unog/website/news_media.nsf/(httpNewsByYear_en)/3D7F902244B36DCEC12578B10056A48F?OpenDocument [accessed 15 May 2012].

United Nations Office of the High Commissioner for Human Rights (UNOHCHR). 2013. *Extractive industries and indigenous peoples: report of the special rapporteur on the rights of indigenous peoples*, Report A/HRC/24/41. Geneva, Switzerland.

Williams, R. 2012. Enlightened shareholder value in UK company law. *University of New South Wales Law Journal*, 35(1): 360–77.

World Bank. 2007. *Global economic prospects: managing the next wave of globalization*. Washington, DC: The World Bank.

World Business Council for Sustainable Development (WBCSD). 2012. *Overview*. URL: www.wbcsd.org/about/overview.aspx [accessed 7 May 2012].

2 Corporate human rights risk
Reconciling law and firm behaviour

Audrey Mocle[1]

Introduction

This chapter begins from the premise that human rights as a political discourse is valuable to society. The doctrine and language of human rights has become a fixture in domestic and international legal orders alike due to its notable success in 'sustaining the struggle of ordinary people against oppressive social practices' (Ignatieff, 2001).[2] Human rights have been traditionally understood as applying in the first instance to the political institutions of states (Beitz, 2009). This is because states were understood to have the greatest power in society and individuals and groups of persons were understood to be the most vulnerable to this power. As long as this assumption holds, human rights discourse remains a successful tool in preventing the oppression of individual interests. The problem this chapter seeks to address is how to maintain the force and legitimacy of human rights when the assumed dyadic power dynamic between individual and state is disrupted by a third, very powerful, actor – namely the firm. Though they are beneficial in many ways, the commercial activities undertaken by firms can interfere with the full range of interests typically safeguarded by human rights.

The first among the foundational principles of the United Nations Guiding Principles on Business and Human Rights is that:

> States must protect against human rights abuse within their territory and/or jurisdiction by third parties, including business enterprises. This requires taking appropriate steps to prevent, investigate, punish and redress such abuse through effective policies, legislation, regulations and adjudication.
>
> (UNSPRSG, 2011: 3)

The Guiding Principles, which are based on the recommendations of Special Rapporteur on Business and Human Rights, John Ruggie, are representative of a social dynamic wherein the power of firms is checked by human rights norms in the same way as state power is kept in check. It relies on state institutions as the enforcement mechanism to achieve this goal. To date, state institutions have not adequately accomplished this task. This chapter will focus on institutions in the European Union, the United States and Canada as these regions currently house the majority of corporate headquarters (FIDH, 2012). This is not to ignore the fact that emerging economies are increasingly producing powerful firms. It is instead to recognize that the aforementioned regions have both the greatest capacity and opportunity to regulate the lion's share of global business activity.

It is argued that the central impediment to adequate state protection against human rights risk generated by firms is the law's failure to understand and reflect the real nature of these entities, in particular the way in which firms perceive and react to human rights risk. Ideally, firms ought to mitigate idiosyncratic human rights risk to the greatest extent feasible given industry and regional parameters. For example, as with Danzer AG in the Democratic Republic of Congo, natural resources firms operating in a region where police and military forces are known to be prone to violence, the parent company must monitor its subsidiary in the region and prevent the subsidiary from being a cause for police operations (ECCHR, 2014: 2). For firms operating in regions of armed conflict, as Nestlé was in Colombia, a parent company ought to prevent its subsidiary from cooperating with parties to the conflict (ECCHR, 2014: 2). Similarly, apparel companies like Gap should prevent the use of pay slips to fake compliance with legal hours and wages (Kernaghan, 2014: 31). The treatment of the corporation,[3] in both public and private law overlooks ways in which regulatory and liability rules can be used to incentivize improved firm behaviour. It is imperative that legal institutions such as legislators, regulators and adjudicators understand the subject they seek to control so that the rights, duties and incentives accorded to said subject (i.e. the firm) can effectively influence its behaviour. This chapter undertakes this task.

The behaviour of firms is examined using sociological and management theories and studies to uncover the drivers of firm behaviour that encourage the kinds of practices that routinely interfere with the enjoyment of human rights. Part I will examine the external environment of a firm and identify the aspects of this environment that work to prevent firms from incorporating human rights considerations into their strategies. Part II will focus on the internal configuration around which firms are most often constructed. Referring to sociological analyses of perpetration, it will be argued that the structures and roles often found in modern firms create the situational forces that increase a firm's human rights risk. In both parts, legal changes states can implement to help firms minimize human rights risk will be analysed.

Part I: Incentivizing concern for human rights: counteracting the external drivers of human rights risk

Market forces and drivers of human rights risk

In general, firms interacting in specific markets seek stability among their interactions (Fligstein, 2001). Firms are embedded in larger groups of organizations including competitors, suppliers, distributors or owners called organizational fields. Organizational fields promote stability; they are the basic mechanism of external control affecting firms (Fligstein, 2004: 410). The most successful firms are those whose strategy gives them a significant advantage over their competitors (Porter, 1990). In the formulation of their strategy, firms use economic principles to filter information, solve problems and inform their decisions.

This chapter posits three ways in which industry structure and economic reasoning make firms susceptible to either creating or failing to mitigate human rights risk. First, the economic principles that firms use to filter information and guide their problem solving obscure their perception of social ills like human rights violations. Second, dynamics in particular organizational fields can lead to the perpetuation of criminogenic market structures that induce firms in a given industry to adopt harmful business practices. Finally, competitive strategies that focus on lowering costs make firms susceptible to cutting corners and externalizing social costs associated with human rights violations.

Economic rationality obscures human rights risk

Firms operate by solving economic problems such as which goods to produce, how to produce them, with what resources, and what price they should command (Couret Branco, 2009). They approach these problems using a positivistic, 'calculation . . . which arises from the application of the principles of efficiency and rationality, regardless of any value judgment' (Couret Branco, 2009: 97). For example, Bakan documents how Nike breaks down production for its internal calculations:

> Production of a shirt [. . .] was broken down into twenty-two separate operations: five steps to cut the material, eleven steps to sew the garment, six steps to attach labels, hang tags, and put the shirt in a plastic bag, ready to be shipped. A time was allotted for each task, with units of ten thousandths of a second used for the breakdown. With all the units added together, the calculations demanded that each shirt take a maximum of 6.6 minutes to make – which translates into 8 cents' worth of labor for a shirt Nike sells in the United States for $22.99.
>
> (Bakan, 2001: 66)

Meanwhile, the harsh working conditions present in the factories in which these shirts and other products are made are omitted from the calculation. The costs and benefits of human rights are hard, if not impossible, to monetize and consequently harder to handle within the typical cost/benefit computation (Couret Branco, 2009).

While not suggesting that firms wilfully or commonly disregard regulatory compliance (e.g., on international labour standards), the economic logic they employ in pursuit of profit does not in principle incorporate human rights risk into their policy formulations, thus making it more likely that firms will ignore such risks. This reflects a problem referred to as Gresham's law of decision making: quantifiable effects will tend to dominate cost–benefit analyses even when the analysing agent recognizes that qualitative effects may be more important (Ogus, 2004: 160). Therefore, firms need information on potential human rights abuses to supplement their economic analyses, and direction on how to interpret this information so they can better mitigate future human rights risk. This is a role often undertaken by government regulators and third-party monitoring actors like human rights non-governmental organizations (NGOs). Later, this chapter will suggest improvements to domestic and international social regulation likely to facilitate firm sensitivity to human rights risk.

Industries are susceptible to 'criminogenic market structures'

Evidence suggests that organizations in a given industry are susceptible to becoming increasingly similar in their behaviour (Huff, 1982; Spender, 1989). Less-powerful organizations fall into line with dominant organizations for several reasons. The more dependent one organization is on another, the more similar it will become to that organization in terms of its internal structure and behavioural focus. For example, monopolistic firms use service infrastructures to exert common pressures over the organizations that use them (DiMaggio and Powell, 2003: 113–18). 'The Wal-Mart effect' encompasses the ability of a powerful firm with great buying power (like Wal-Mart) to exert a downward pressure on wages, inflation and prices and encourage firms in its field to continuously reduce costs (Fishman, 2006). Similarly, parent companies often impose standardized reporting mechanisms on their subsidiaries that can include specific accounting practices, performance evaluations and budgetary plans to bring them in line with the policies of the parent. Also, firms tend to model themselves after firms they perceive to be more successful (DiMaggio and Powell, 2003: 118). When a new business idea is executed successfully, firms will naturally imitate it (Ekekwe, 2012). For instance, many technology firms have imitated Apple's product range and design style (Yarow, 2012). Finally, firms may conform to dominant practices for fear of threats to their survival since direct challenges to dominant firms can trigger competitive attacks (Fligstein, 2004). All this suggests that firms in a given industry adopt the same values and practices over time.

This practice of isomorphism within industries is not necessarily harmful. Of concern is the potential for a concentrated market structure to instil excessive power in the hands of a few firms who wield it against their suppliers, consumers and competitors to create conditions that induce organizations within their field to engage in activities harmful to the public (Leonard and Weber, 1991). For example, upon examination of the automobile industry, Farberman found that manufacturers created a 'criminogenic market structure' by imposing a pricing policy on new car dealers that required high volume and low per-unit profit (Farberman, 1991: 206). This financial squeeze set in motion a 'downward spiral of illegal activities' on the part of dealers, including fraudulent service operations and illegal 'short-sales' to generate unrecorded cash (Farberman, 1991: 206). Similar patterns exist in the context of human rights violations. Certain industries have forged a 'race to the bottom' by using their influence to drive down best practices in health, safety, environmental and labour protection. For example, when the oil industry first began producing oil in developing countries, they had little regard for the negative impact of their operations on local communities. For these companies, the lack of labour laws or environmental regulation in these countries represented an excellent opportunity to expand operations regardless of impact on human rights (Falola and Genova, 2005: 124). Dominant players have opposed legal and political changes that would undermine the value of this opportunity (Falola and Genova, 2005: 124). When harmful market structures persist, an intervening force is necessary to prevent dominant firms from dictating policies likely to produce human rights risk.

Firms profit from externalizing human rights risk

A firm's goal is to find a position in its industry where it can best defend itself against competitive forces, or influence them in its favour (Porter, 1998). Porter identifies three generic competitive strategies most often used by firms, either alone or in combination: (1) overall cost leadership, (2) differentiation[4] and (3) focus (Porter, 1998: 35).[5] The cost leadership strategy requires vigorous pursuit of cost minimization throughout the firm's activities (Porter, 1998: 35). Firms can profit from the ability to externalize many social costs such that these costs are not reflected in the price of goods, and those harmed by firm behaviour are forced to bear these costs (Perrow, 2003). When industries are driven by a cost-leadership competitive dynamic, firms are much more likely to externalize costs, including those costs that impede the enjoyment of human rights. While reputational risks can influence firms to be more responsible, firms are often too short-sighted for this risk to significantly change their behaviour; present profits are perceived as more important than the potential loss of future profits (Stiglitz, 2010: 18).

Coincidentally, this cost-leadership strategy is commonly found in industries known for human rights risk. For example, in the 1990s, the apparel industry exhibited a migration of its mass production from higher-wage industrial economies to lower-cost labour markets in the developing world, and apparel firms that could not compete with the low cost of manufacturing characteristic of the industry merged with larger firms, diversified or closed (EGI, 2014a). The production of electronic components used in technological devices is also characterized by intense competition (EGI, 2014b). In both the apparel and electronic technology manufacturing industries, sweatshops routinely force employees, sometimes including children, to work long hours for sub-standard wages in unsafe working conditions (EGI, 2014a). Both the mining industry and the oil and gas industry produce commodity products and can sustain competitive advantages only through cost leadership. These industries are known for destroying biodiversity, polluting the ground and disproportionately exposing workers to accidents and health complications (EGI, 2014c).

While the concept of an externality traditionally only refers to economic costs, this chapter argues that market competition should be regulated such that firms are able to both (i) minimize human rights risk before violations occur and (ii) compensate victims for the costs borne by them in the event the firm's activities are harmful. Ideally, it should not be profitable for a firm to violate human rights. Thus, in theory, the price of a given product should reflect the cost of measures necessary for a particular firm to minimize human rights risk. This might include the cost of higher wages, monitoring systems, technology for pollution reduction, among other risk mitigation measures. If such measures are standard industry-wide, even industries based on a cost leadership strategy will not drive firms to externalize the costs of complying with human rights obligations (Fligstein, 2010: 145). Furthermore, firms may even be driven to differentiate themselves on the extent to which they exceed human rights obligations and introduce innovative new means of mitigating risk. It should be noted that all firms are not equally likely to commit or be complicit in human rights abuses. The extent to which legal and regulatory institutions succeed in crafting effective deterrence mechanisms for firm wrongdoing does influence the extent to which firms will take on more or less human rights risk. Furthermore, as will be discussed in Part II, organizational considerations including the way in which a particular strategy is embedded within an organization and across its affiliates can affect the extent of a firm's exposure to human rights risk in practice.

It has been famously argued by Coase (1960) that externalities are not inherently problematic insofar as consumers can negotiate freely and transaction costs are low. He assumed that when individual negotiation among agents is not feasible, courts can use liability rules to allocate costs efficiently and compensate the bearers of externalities. However, the complexity of the modern global economy precludes small-scale, day-to-day negotiations and the practical barriers to instituting private law disputes against firms mean that these externalities persist under current liability regimes.

Barriers to litigation

Cost and inadequate compensation

Speaking generally of all jurisdictions, private law imposes considerable costs on litigants.[6] As a result, human rights obligations are not internalized through private law instruments, and since firms have no economic incentive to adopt such obligations, these misallocations will persist. Of particular concern is that many human rights abuses cannot be adequately compensated through financial restitution. For instance, a complainant whose child has died as a result of lead poisoning can never truly have their loss rectified. For infringements of this nature, *ex post* compensation is not enough; harmful firm behaviour must be curbed *ex ante* (Stiglitz, 2010: 18).

Extraterritorial hurdles

Private law remedies are even more inaccessible when attempting to litigate against a multinational corporation (MNC). MNCs are able to move assets, operations and activities across borders and so beyond the regulatory influence of any single national jurisdiction, borders become incidental to their activities (Catà Backer, 2008: 504). One of the chief obstacles to initiating a private law claim against an MNC is identifying the appropriate entity or entities against which to lodge the claim. Often, subsidiaries located in developing regions are undercapitalized, insolvent or uninsured (FIDH, 2012: 179). Successful claims against parents rely on the claimant's ability to prove, to the requisite evidentiary standard, connections between the alleged violation, the subsidiary's actions and the parent's involvement (Zerk, 2013: 65). Furthermore, the courts and other legal institutions in developing regions may not be favourable to complainants due to inadequate statutory and/or regulatory legislation, and/or corruption. This renders compensation claims against these subsidiaries essentially futile.

Due to the above failures, one might assume the optimal path to corporate legal accountability is via extraterritorial application of the laws of the home state and/or recourse to the courts of the home state. However, rules of private international law generally include flexible recognition and enforcement conditions that permit sophisticated parties to take advantage of differences in legislation between countries (Van Den Eeckhout, 2008: 3). In both the European Union (EU) and Canada, the applicable civil liability law is that of the state in which the damage occurs (Rome II, Art. 4(1); Pitel & Rafferty, 2010; *Tolofson v. Jensen*). This complicates claims against parent companies where a claimant seeks to establish parent liability by initiating a claim in the parent's home jurisdiction, since domestic courts will apply the law of the place where the damage occurred in order to determine the substantive rights and responsibilities of the parent (Zerk, 2013: 74). Because human rights abuses by MNCs mostly occur in the Global South, the law of European countries and Canada is not readily applicable in these cases (ECCHR, 2013a: 5). In the United States, the Alien Tort Claims Act (ATCA) has been a long-time source of extraterritorial accountability of corporations. However, in a recent case the Supreme Court of the United States narrowed the scope of the ATCA such that it applies only when the activities in question have a sufficient connection with the United States beyond the existence of a corporate presence in the host country (*Kiobel v. Royal Dutch Petroleum Co.*; ECCHR, 2013b).[7]

Further legal hurdles include determining which state can claim jurisdiction over a company and securing recognition and enforcement of foreign judgments by a forum court (FIDH, 2012: 216). In her study of corporate liability for gross human rights abuses, Zerk found that many of the cases studied were challenged on jurisdictional grounds and several were dismissed on this basis (Zerk, 2013: 49). In the EU, the Brussels I Regulation stipulates that a legal person may only be sued in the member state in which that legal person is domiciled. This requirement will not be satisfied if a plaintiff attempts to summon a non-European subsidiary before a member state court (Van Den Eeckhout, 2012: 184). Complainants making claims in countries with a common law tradition will have lengthy procedural struggles due to the doctrine of *forum non conveniens*[8] by which national courts can reject cases if they deem a foreign court provides a more suitable forum (ECCHR, 2013a: 4). The criteria for *forum non conveniens* are not coherent (ECCHR, 2013a: 8), and the doctrine has been used by firms in their jurisdictions of incorporation as grounds for dismissing cases alleging human rights abuses.[9] In order for claimants to clear the procedural hurdle of *forum non conveniens*, they must prove which decisions contributing to the impugned harm were made by the parent company in its home jurisdiction, which is difficult to establish in fact (Rogge, 2001).

All of these extra hurdles increase the cost of litigation, impede the likelihood of successful liability claims against firms and ultimately prevent firms from internalizing the social costs their activities impose on claimants and feeling the resulting incentive to mitigate their human rights risk. When a market failure is accompanied by a private law failure, as is the case when the cost of human rights violations is externalized and the legal system is not an adequate source of redress for those affected, there is a prima facie case for regulatory intervention on public interest grounds (Ogus, 2004: 28).

Regulating respect for human rights

Regulatory mechanisms to mitigate the drivers of human rights risk

Mitigating the above-mentioned environmental drivers of business human rights risk requires making changes to the way firms interact and interpret information. In particular, firms need help gathering and interpreting information regarding potential human rights abuses and incentives in order to act in a human rights-risk-averse manner. The legal environment surrounding firms can affect many aspects of their behaviour (DiMaggio and Powell, 2003: 115). The different levels of state governments and international institutions draw the boundaries of appropriate firm behaviour by defining how markets are constructed (Fligstein, 2004: 409). By limiting the realm of possible choices, governments can encourage firms to innovate and find new courses of action within new limits (Fligstein, 2004: 412). There are several regulatory mechanisms governments can use to this end, including 'command and control' standards, information disclosure rules, comply or explain and economic incentives.

The monitoring associated with command and control standards means that regulators adopt the burden of gathering and interpreting information on human rights risk instead of firms. These standards provide firms with operational boundaries within which they can employ their economic reasoning. Furthermore, sanctions associated with these standards, if properly formulated, act as a deterrent for criminogenic market structures and externalizing behaviour. Disclosure of human rights impacts give regulators the opportunity to provide firms with information regarding their human rights risk that they may have been unable to gather using traditional economic analyses.[10] By equipping socially responsible buyers and investors with this knowledge, they can begin to exert influence against criminogenic market structures. The buyers and investors who react to this information by changing their habits will send market signals to externalizing firms in the form of reductions in sales and/or share value. Economic incentives can also help remedy the three drivers of business human rights risk. By assigning an economic value to undesirable behaviour (i.e., taxation) or desirable behaviour (i.e., subsidization), regulators can encourage firms to indirectly incorporate human rights concerns into their decision making in the form of tangible costs and/or benefits. They can also influence firms to avoid the creation of criminogenic market structures by dis-incentivizing harmful business practices among the dominant firms. Finally, Pigovian taxes applied consistently across industries can discourage firms with a cost-reduction strategy from externalizing the costs associated with preventing human rights abuses.[11]

Strategies for spearheading regulatory change[12]

Rather than overhauling the regulatory institutions of each jurisdiction, legislators could begin a process of incorporating consideration of human rights risk into the regulatory process at various levels of government so that the existing areas of business regulation – financial regulation, securities, trade and competition, labour standards, environmental standards and health and safety, among others – incorporate mechanisms for mitigating the human rights violations related to the areas of the business environment they already govern.

Regulation is an iterative and dialogic process at both domestic and global levels. Whereas it might be presumed the state is the locus of regulatory control, in practice policy-making involves a wide array of public and private actors from different levels and functional areas of government and society (Schmidt, 2004: 276), and business. Schmidt refers to domestic regulatory relationships as networks governed by an interdependence of actors, enduring relations and strategic action. Courts also play an important role in the regulatory process by settling important questions of statutory interpretation. Astute interest groups use reviewing courts as a check on the regulatory process by arguing for various grounds for review. In effect, the regulatory process is a continual feedback loop between the behaviour of interest groups and policy makers responsible for the current legal and policy environments (Schmidt, 2004: 277, 283–91).

Regulation of global business activity is more nebulous than domestic regulation, but still has considerable transformative capacity. Braithwaite and Drahos' research reveals that regulatory processes grounded in dialogue between the regulator and regulated parties are often more influential than those using direct control (Braithwaite and Drahos, 2000: 551). It is vital that the principles underlying human rights are routinely used to contest principles reinforcing the economic status quo in all substantive areas of regulation, and civil society groups are well equipped to do this. They are often willing to bear monitoring costs and have better information about compliance and enforcement than do states and firms (Braithwaite and Drahos, 2000: 574).

There are several strategies civil society groups use to shift regulatory policies. 'Dividing and conquering' firms is a way for groups to attract strategic allies for regulatory reform (Braithwaite and Drahos, 2000: 616). It is easier to garner support from firms that already adhere to a particular standard on a voluntary basis since regulation will offer them protection from competition from non-complying firms who are able to price their products more cheaply (Ogus, 2004: 172); see for example the creation of the Montreal Protocol.[13] Although firms are prone to focusing on the short-term costs and benefits associated with improved standards, rather than the longer-term benefits of innovation, leading management doctrine recognizes that firms should aim to meet or exceed standards since doing so presents an opportunity to move early to upgrade products and processes. In a world where concern for social welfare is increasing, buyers will appreciate products that are safer and cleaner (Porter, 1990). Civil society groups can use this logic to persuade regulators and firms to exploit this strategic opportunity. Firms that have embraced higher standards have an interest in catalysing their early-mover advantage by encouraging other states to improve standards (Braithwaite and Drahos, 2000: 616). Finally, civil society groups can also engage directly with firms to change their practices. History suggests it is more common for the globalization of regulatory standards to follow the globalization of a new business practice than vice versa (Braithwaite and Drahos, 2000: 615). Given the isomorphic tendencies of industries, change agents can begin change initiatives with the dominant firms who effectively dictate industry practice. As management practice and domestic and global regulation embrace the practice of continuous improvement, increasingly wider adoption of changes in practice should induce global adoption of human rights norms.

Part II: Incentivizing improvement of human rights compliance: counteracting the internal drivers of human rights risk

The preceding section discussed ways in which regulation can influence a firm's external environment to encourage it to incorporate human rights considerations into its competitive strategy. However, a firm's internal environment may nevertheless impede the success of these strategic improvements. This section will begin by identifying the internal configuration around which firms are most often constructed. Adopting a structural analysis, it will consider the roles within a corporation and the structures in which these roles are performed (Perrow, 1971: 2). Drawing on sociological analyses of perpetration, it will be argued that these structures and roles create situational forces that exacerbate human rights risk.[14] It will conclude with suggested changes to corporate liability rules aimed at influencing firms to adapt their internal organization to mitigate these forces.

Bureaucratic structure and situational forces contributing to human rights risk

Most modern firms are structured according to what Mintzberg calls 'the divisionalized form'. This is a market-based structure with a central headquarters overseeing a set of divisions, each charged with serving its own markets

(Mintzberg, 1980: 335). It permits a large number of divisions to report up to one central headquarters without the need for close coordination. An important concern of the headquarters is to find a mechanism to coordinate the goals of the divisions with its own, without sacrificing divisional autonomy. The mechanisms most often used are standardized outputs, performance control systems and monitoring (Mintzberg, 1980: 335). In effect, each division is driven to employ what Mintzberg calls 'machine bureaucracy', i.e. using highly specialized, routine operating tasks, very formalized procedures and large-sized units in its operating core (Mintzberg, 1980: 332).

While the organizational map of some corporations has evolved from a pyramid to a network, many conventional firms remain committed to the idea of ultimate authority located at the top (Silbey and Agrawal, 2011: 70). 'Management systems', which consist of distributed roles, standardized rules and prescribed procedures (often linked through information technology), have become the preferred means of assuring compliance with internal rules in many organizations. Like the standard bureaucratic form, management systems also decentralize responsibility while inscribing roles, rules and routines (Silbey and Agrawal, 2011: 74). Divisions may be bureaucratized to a greater or lesser extent based on the internal incentives for performance control used by headquarters to evaluate the divisions (Wintrobe, 1982: 650; Goold and Campbell, 1987). The cost of control and monitoring increases with firm size (as measured by its number of employees), and therefore, an increase in firm size leads to an increase in the level of bureaucratization (Wintrobe, 1982: 661–2). This means that multinational firms will be bureaucratized to a greater extent, which in turn diminishes their capacity to recognize and mitigate human rights risk.

While subsidiaries and supply chain affiliates are not divisions of a corporation per se, headquarters must nevertheless use many of the same tactics to coordinate the operations of these entities with their own. Within corporate groups, the parent corporation has *de jure* control over subsidiaries as a result of equity ownership and can direct the operations of subsidiaries in many of the same ways as it does its own divisions. With respect to suppliers, firms often exert de facto control, for instance, in requiring compliance with certification standards.[15] Most MNCs fit the description of what Baudry and Gindis call the 'V-network form': a vertical form of network organization of firms in which a 'hub firm' coordinates regular essential operations such as the provision, production and distribution between legally independent firms (Baudry and Gindis, 2005: 1–2). The hub-firm's influence on network members is typically the result of the resources it offers, including brand name, reputation, good will and a market niche (Baudry and Gindis, 2005: 10). In practice, the V-network form uses bureaucratic methods such as standardized outputs and performance control systems throughout its network.

Whatever form of bureaucratic control characterizes large complex businesses, they produce situations likely to generate or tolerate human rights risk. Zimbardo has identified situational forces that beget harmful behaviour by otherwise ordinary individuals whereby 'the behavioral context . . . has the power, through its reward and normative functions, to give meaning and identity to [an] actor's roles and status' (Zimbardo, 2007: 445–6). Similarly, Perrow writes that people's attitudes are shaped at least as much by the organization in which they work as by their pre-existing attitudes (Perrow, 1971: 4). According to Zimbardo, 'deindividuation' and 'dehumanization' are situational forces that contribute to the likelihood that an otherwise conscientious individual will cause harm or be indifferent thereto. It is argued that both these forces are endemic to the bureaucratic behavioural context of firms. Using the example of supply chain human rights compliance strategies, it will be shown how even firms who make it their objective to mitigate human rights risk are nevertheless inherently susceptible to such risk as a result of their internal configuration.

De-individuation leads to systemic lack of responsibility for human rights risk

Zimbardo posits that de-individuation occurs whenever a situation makes people feel anonymous, 'as though no one knows who they are or cares to know' and reduces an individual's sense of personal accountability (Zimbardo, 2007: 301). Anonymity is something that can be conferred on others by treating an individual as an 'undifferentiated "other" being processed by the System' (Zimbardo, 2007: 301). The hallmark of a bureaucracy is the existence of positions with formal duties. When an individual holds a position, it is not the individual that has the power, but the position itself (Weber, 1946: 196–8). Several sociological experiments document this phenomenon.[16] Essentialized roles encourage the people occupying them to behave in accordance with what the role requires. This treats individuals as 'undifferentiated others'. Formal positions affect the behaviour of those occupying the position and those subject to their authority. An individual working in a firm feels the need to justify her actions according to the internal logic of the firm, and this makes her less sensitive to the interests of individuals outside the firm than she would be in her life separate from the firm (Coleman, 1974: 98). A sense of accountability for the corporation's actions as a whole is overshadowed by performance monitoring and incentives that emphasize responsibility for only a narrowly defined set of tasks. This suggests routine consideration of human rights risk will not occur if it is not made an essential part of an individual's role within the corporation or incentivized in any way. This is problematic since the responsibility for actions necessary to human rights mitigation is often spread across various units and roles without a specific person being assigned the responsibility to monitor and report risks and violations (Wachenfeld et al., 2012: 57). If the majority of roles include no mandate or incentives to consider and prevent human rights risks or if the corporate culture of the firm is not otherwise reformed to promote sensitivity to human rights risk, deindividuation on a large scale will occur.

To illustrate, human rights problems are more prominent in supply chains than any other facet of operations (Wachenfeld et al., 2012: 6). Traditional corporate sourcing strategies and purchasing practices have been identified as primary impediments to adequate human rights standards for supplier stakeholders (Global CSR, 2011: 20). It is common for parent or hub firms to employ structured incentives and sanctions as a means of performance control throughout their supply chain. These bureaucratic tactics are also applied to the firm's ethics, human rights and labour standards. Literature on the topic has revealed how the traditional approach to compliance has rendered the factory inspection and audit process overly bureaucratic:

> Auditors arrive with lengthy, detailed checklists aimed at exposing record-keeping lapses and easy to detect code violations rather than discovering the sources or root causes of these various workplace problems. Managers, in turn, 'learn' to be inspected by better preparing (sometimes doctoring) their records and do the absolute minimum to remain 'within compliance' of the buyers' codes of conduct.
>
> (Locke *et al.*, 2008: 15)

This 'box ticking' approach to human rights risk management is likely to overlook contextual and external factors that impact the likelihood of human rights abuses along a supply chain. In order to better assess and manage human rights impacts, human rights risk ought to be integrated into existing management systems (Wachenfeld *et al.*, 2012: 44). Embedding human rights risk as a strategic concern requires headquarters to provide a clear definition of how roles across the hierarchy are to take action on human rights, and the individuals occupying the various functional roles within each unit must receive coherent policies and be trained and incentivized to act in ways that support these policies (Wachenfeld *et al.*, 2012: 44).

De-humanization leads to failure to account for human rights risk

According to Zimbardo, de-humanization is the process by which the humanity of potential victims is effaced, thus devaluing them in the eyes of the perpetrator (Zimbardo, 2007: 295). There are certain features of corporate bureaucracy that precipitate this phenomenon. Since performance against the goals of bureaucratic divisions must lend themselves to quantitative measure, the impact of corporate behaviour on human life becomes reduced to a kind of economic calculus.[17] Indeed, there is a noted practice of calculating the costs and benefits of addressing human rights risk in various business relationships. Firms will identify the cost of bringing business partners up to their standards, calculate the cost of delays and other negative effects of human rights problems, and assign costs only to human rights issues that could lead to legal liability (Wachenfeld *et al.*, 2012: 59). Reducing impact on human life to a 'cost of doing business', is arguably akin to effacing the humanity of potential victims of human rights abuses in that their 'value' becomes economic, capable of being weighed against other costs and benefits. This arguably results in the kind of devaluation of human life that Zimbardo suggests is a precursor to perpetration. Firms governed by a financial control strategy are likely to have a higher prevalence of this phenomenon given their focus on financial targets above all else.

The structure imposed by the divisionalized form makes it difficult to transmit information about the real effects of firm activity on human rights throughout the firm. Even if firms appoint designated human rights compliance officers or subunits to deliberately gather information about human rights risk, the nature of large firms is such that implementation of a given action is undertaken by an agent other than the one who determined its governing policy. Furthermore, these agents are likely to be far removed from one another in the organizational structure (Coleman, 1974: 98). Returning to the example of supply chain management, firms make supply chain decisions under conditions of uncertainty about supply chain performance. In many cases, controlling firms are not even aware of the full range of actors in their supply chain.[18] For actors of which they are aware, data on human rights risk will come from various decentralized sources such as self-monitoring suppliers and third-party auditors (Shift Project, 2012: 5–6). Thus, given the organizational distance between the individuals in a firm dictating a human rights policy and the individuals it is meant to protect, dehumanizing forces are likely present.

Even firms with genuine commitments to preventing human rights abuses within their operations will likely find their efforts impeded by the organizational structure and procedures that otherwise facilitate operational efficiency. Fortunately, improvements to organizational design and management systems to combat situational forces leading to human rights risk can elicit improvements.[19] All roles within a firm's organizational chart ought to be assigned some responsibility for the firm's human rights impact, and compliance information must better reflect impact on human suffering.

Liability rules fail to correct internal forces exacerbating human rights risk

Like other social phenomena, the structure of firms is conditioned by legal institutions and the definitions and boundaries of liability used by courts (Meyer and Rowan, 2004: 89). Regrettably, the global legal status quo has contributed to the institutionalization of a firm structure that obviates human rights risks through the legal fiction of limited liability between corporate groups and the weak deterrent effects of corporate civil and criminal liability.

There are two characteristics of legal personality that contribute to impunity for corporate abuses of human rights. The first is the autonomy of every corporate actor, and the second is that one legal person may own another (Català Backer, 2008: 505). Because of this it is possible to construct large and complex networks of legally autonomous persons owned by shareholders of a parent or controlling entity. Firms can thus disperse operations globally but in a way that significantly delinks the liability of the entire enterprise for the actions of any of its parts (Català Backer 2008, 499). In broad terms, a parent company may participate in human rights abuses committed by its subsidiaries or supply chain either by commission of the abuse – taking part in the decision leading to the harm – or omission – failing to act despite an ability to prevent the harm (FIDH, 2012: 235). However, except on the rarest of occasions, a parent company will only be held legally responsible for the actions and omissions carried out through its directors or officers, not for the actions of its subsidiaries or affiliates (Müller-Hoff, 2011: 25). By constructing corporate law in such a way that corporations controlled by the same individuals are treated as having autonomous agency, the legal system signals to firms that headquarters need only incorporate a new entity to shield itself from liability. Without a sense of responsibility for the actions of all the corporate entities they control, the management of parent companies will not be motivated to ensure compliance throughout their operations in the manner required to mitigate the situational forces discussed above.

Failed deterrent effects of corporate liability

The individual legal personality of corporate entities makes it very difficult to bring civil compensation claims against parent corporations for actions taken by any of their subsidiaries or affiliates. This difficulty is compounded by the substantive legal doctrine underlying civil liability regimes.[20] Claimants will generally have to prove who within the firm knew what about a given harmful practice and when they knew it (Zerk, 2013: 44). Bringing claims against sub-entities is also made difficult by weak judicial institutions in the developing regions in which they often operate. Again, this signals to firms that decentralizing operations and diffusing responsibility for human rights risks mitigates liability.

There have been some recent cases before common law courts where it was held that parent companies, on the facts of the case, owe a duty of care to the employees of their subsidiaries (Zerk, 2013: 46).[21] However, unless this doctrine of parent duty of care is properly crafted, it may lose its deterrent effect. For instance, while the recent UK decision in *Chandler v. Cape Plc*[22] has made inroads by extending responsibility to parent firms where evidence of *de facto* control exists, the likely effect of this doctrine is to further encourage ignorance of human rights abuses committed by subsidiaries and affiliates by the parent. For responsibility to be established, complainants must show that the parent (i) had or ought to have had superior knowledge of some relevant aspect of the harm in the particular industry; (ii) knew or ought to have known that its subsidiary's system of work is unsafe; and (iii) foresaw that the subsidiary or its employees would rely on it using its knowledge for protection (*Chandler v. Cape*: para 80). Petrin notes that *Chandler* may lead to misguided incentives for future firm behaviour since, in terms of its liability exposure, Cape plc. could have possibly escaped liability had it not taken any steps to ascertain the health risks of its business (Petrin, 2013: 618). It is perverse that, according to this doctrine, firms might escape liability by *not* embedding concern for human rights throughout their structures. The law should aim to encourage responsibility and deter indifference, not the other way around.

The available remedies for breaches of civil liability also propagate corporate impunity. Even when financial penalties are ordered, they do not have a strong deterrent effect in practice (ECCHR, 2013a: 6). Evidence suggests fines are viewed by offenders as nothing more than a 'cost of doing business' (Zerk, 2013: 39). Despite ever-increasing corporate fines and awards in damages,[23] corporate human rights abuses and recidivism continue. For example, Total, Bayer and the Shell-Group – all Global 500 companies – appear at least five times each in recorded proceedings, and are together involved in more than one quarter of all recorded proceedings (ECCHR, 2013a: 6). This suggests firms emerge relatively unscathed from civil liability suits and (large) profits can be made while breaching standards of civil responsibility.

While the stigma and sanctions of the criminal law typically offer greater deterrence, the peculiarities of corporate personality still limit the criminal law's check on firm power (Pieth and Ivory, 2011: 4). Establishing jurisdiction can be a significant obstacle in cases where the alleged human rights abuses took place or the damage arose in another jurisdiction (Zerk, 2013: 68). In order to identify the appropriate jurisdiction for the case, claimants must determine whether a corporation or individual director of the parent company may be held criminally liable in a particular forum court (FIDH, 2012: 286). States wishing to under-take claims requiring the assertion of extraterritorial jurisdiction must be able to justify its use in the circumstances against one or more permissive principles, such as active personality principle, passive personality principle or universality (Zerk, 2013: 68). The forum court's legislation and other principles of extra-territoriality may also impede criminal liability of a legal person (FIDH, 2012: 286). While most states consider themselves to have jurisdiction as of right over cases involving defendants incorporated under their laws, in common law states like the United States, Australia, New Zealand and Canada, courts may elect not to exercise jurisdiction if they are satisfied that a more convenient forum exists (Zerk, 2013: 68).[24]

Corporate crime cannot be combatted effectively through the commonly used 'identification' approach to criminal liability (Arthurs, 2008: 65). According to this method, the acts and intentions of corporate officers and senior managers are 'identified' with the firm such that those acts and intentions are treated as having been those of the firm itself (Zerk, 2013: 33). Even if prosecutors have established without a doubt that a criminal offence has been committed by, and in the interest of, a corporation, complex organizational structures discussed above make it difficult or impossible to ascertain with sufficient certainty the individual offender(s) (Arthurs, 2008: 65). All of the requisite elements of the criminal offence may not be the *de jure* or *de facto* responsibility of any specific, identifiable individual or group of individuals within a firm (Zerk, 2013: 33).

Furthermore, national laws generally avoid the question of how to deal with offences committed by a corporation that is part of a group of firms (FIDH, 2012: 277). As with civil liability, to establish a parent's criminal liability for crimes committed by its subsidiaries and subcontractors abroad, an adequate causal link must be proven between the parent's participation and the commission of the offence (FIDH, 2012: 278). While a parent company may be charged with complicity for acts committed abroad by a subsidiary, if the interference of the parent in the management of its subsidiaries is minimal, the distinction between the various legal persons will limit the charges of co-liability against the parent (FIDH, 2012: 278). Again, like the rule in *Chandler*, this may encourage parent companies to avoid interfering in the management of its subsidiaries since doing so would open them up to liability (Coffee, 1999: 12). As such, it too signals to firms that they need only incorporate another entity in order to act criminally with impunity.

In sum, the aspects of the legal system discussed above institutionalize indifference, impunity, and a general lack of responsibility for the harmful actions of firms. These legal rules offer no incentive for firms to combat the situational forces of de-individuation and dehumanization that propagate human rights risk. However, since bureaucratic organizations engage in thorough formal and long-range planning, their behaviour is more likely to be influenced by future judicial decisions. Furthermore, a decision that brings about a change in internal structure is highly likely to have lasting effects on the organization's future behaviour. Thus, there exists an opportunity for courts to have lasting and desirable effects on the future conduct of firms (Dan-Cohen, 1985: 14). The following section will outline adaptations of corporate liability that, if instituted, could provide firms with the impetus to improve the internal structural characteristics that contribute to human rights risk and better hold them accountable when this risk materializes into human rights violations.

Organizational liability models may encourage improvements to internal structure

The above analysis suggests corporations cannot be directed to better behaviour by legal challenges posed to the organization as a whole. Instead, the legal system must put an increasingly direct focus on the processes of corporate decision making (Stone, 1975: 120–1; Parker and Gilad, 2011: 170). Ideally, the law would engage internal management capacity to make corporations responsible for and responsive to external social goals like respect for human rights (Parker and Gilad, 2011: 171–2). A firm's fault should lie in its failure to institute protective mechanisms that would have prevented harm from occurring.

Aggregative corporate criminal liability

Aggregative or organizational models of criminal liability treat corporations as capable of committing crimes through 'established internal patterns of decision-making or, in other words, through corporate culture or (dis)organization' (Pieth and Ivory, 2011: 5). Consequently, the corporation is treated as the principal offender in a way that adds together the different acts, omissions, and states of mind of individual stakeholders, particularly corporate officers and senior managers (Pieth and Ivory, 2011: 5). Central to the understanding of corporate criminal responsibility in this way is a company's organogram, its internal regulations and the procedures that reflect the corporation's particular organizational culture (Pieth and Ivory, 2011: 31–2). Unlike the civil and criminal liability regimes discussed in the preceding section, this model does not encourage inaction and indifference by shielding the corporation or its management from liability if they were not directly involved in the commission of human rights abuses. Taking corporate culture into account increases the breadth of application of corporate criminal liability substantially and in so doing increases a corporation's incentives to improve internal controls, since a failure to do so will increase its risk of prosecution (Arthurs, 2008: 61).[25]

While no statutory aggregative liability provisions to date directly allow for the corporate veil between a parent and its subsidiary to be pierced, conceptually these provisions may pave the way for judicial acceptance of challenges to limited liability within corporate groups since they focus attention on the actual process of corporate decision-making, rather than on the formal legal structure of these groups. This could give rise to new understandings of the physical elements of offences, and even to the creation of an offence of failing to adequately supervise corporate subsidiaries and suppliers. Furthermore, there is no conceptual reason why an aggregative model of liability could not extend to actions committed by contractors acting as agents of the corporation (Arthurs, 2008: 79). This would not only encourage preventive action with respect to compliance within each individual corporation, but of parent companies for their subsidiaries and subcontractors.

Additionally, incorporating corporate culture factors in sentencing allows for close attention to the organizational deficiencies that permit the impugned conduct and for the imposition of more sophisticated remedial measures, such as the adoption of improved compliance systems and employee education that goes beyond the traditional 'box ticking' approach (Arthurs, 2008: 62). In effect, it may be possible to use the criminal law to 'rehabilitate' offending corporations, thus preventing future harm (Pieth and Ivory, 2011: 25). Special exculpatory rules relating to the existence and effectiveness of compliance systems would incentivize good faith attempts at instituting said systems. For example, in the United States, corporations are able to mitigate their punishment or avoid indictment on the basis of the adequacy of their compliance systems (Pieth and Ivory, 2011: 33). U.S. prosecutors have used their discretion in sentencing as leverage to incite organizational change to deter future harm (Hechler Baer, 2009: 972). To avoid heavier sentences, firms should define their particular human rights risk profile and design tailor-made compliance systems to meet those needs (Pieth and Ivory, 2011: 3).

Enterprise risk theory of civil liability

The enterprise risk doctrine of vicarious liability[26] is a more comprehensive notion of vicarious liability that can base corporate civil liability on harm caused by systemic organizational problems. It is currently found notably in the jurisprudence of Canada and the United Kingdom.[27] According to this principle, a firm should be held strictly liable for a given loss because its enterprise created the risk that materialized into loss (Ataner, 2006: 81). The requisite test examines the connection between the harm suffered and risks inherent in the enterprise. The aim of such a principle is 'to regulate or control employers' risk-taking activities, in particular, their manner of hiring, training, supervising and otherwise dealing with employees', and it is thought to support both the deterrence and compensation rationales for civil liability (Ataner, 2006: 81). Because it targets risk created by typical features of bureaucratic organizations, enterprise risk theory is capable of accounting for fault derived from systemic organizational problems and encouraging better embedding of human rights concerns into structural roles and employee training.

Applied to corporate groups, enterprise risk theory could entail integrated corporate groups being understood as a single economic enterprise under common management. This has been said to imply that members of such a group should be held jointly and severally liable for harm arising from their fellow members (Zerk, 2013: 47). Courts have rejected arguments in favour of this theory as it creates uncertainty as to when a parent's involvement in the activities of a subsidiary is within what is considered a 'typical parent–subsidiary relationship' or 'becomes so close as to justify a finding of liability against the parent itself' (Zerk, 2013: 50). One way to escape this charge would be to amalgamate enterprise risk theory with the duty of care analysis established in *Chandler*. The rule in *Chandler* bypassed the need to establish the existence of a common economic enterprise by stipulating that a parent company owes a duty of care directly to employees of its subsidiaries in the event of a 'special relationship' wherein the parent has 'relevant control' of the subsidiary's business. Control was held to represent an assumption of responsibility that satisfies the proximity requirement of a typical duty of care analysis (*Chandler v. Cape*: para. 62). Furthermore, the *Chandler* test could avoid its aforementioned incentive problems by instead imputing liability from the failure to take steps to minimize human rights risk, much in the same way as enterprise risk theory. A hybrid of the two doctrines avoids their inherent problems and creates a liability regime that targets organizational risk.

Another problem raised in the preceding section concerns appropriate penalties. It was argued that financial penalties have a weak deterrent effect in practice. Alternatives already put in place by some domestic legal systems include: placing restrictions on the ability of the offending firm to operate in certain economic areas, banning the firm from procurement opportunities, requiring the firm to publicize the judicial ruling, confiscation of property and compulsory winding up (Zerk, 2013: 39). Of course, adequate compensation to victims of human rights abuse should remain a priority for courts. Alternative penalties ought to be combined with compensatory damages awarded to claimants.

Conclusion

It is understood to be part of the state's duty to protect human rights that they use their legislative, regulatory and adjudicative powers to hold private actors like firms accountable to human rights norms. Firms are unique in that they are both market actors and bureaucratic organizations, and legal institutions must acknowledge this empirical reality if they aim to adequately hold them accountable. Although drivers of the firm's external market environment obscure and sometimes impede their ability to recognize and mitigate human rights risk, regulators at all levels of government can use existing business regulatory regimes to signal risky behaviour and deter firms from harmful choices through sanctions and/or incentives. This approach is advantageous as it does not require extensive institutional redesign, it supports a multi-pronged method of regulation that works to consistently ratchet standards upwards over time, and it makes use of the specialized expertise of regulators in various substantive areas of business regulation.

Firms that aim to implement strategies to minimize human rights risk may nevertheless fail to do so unless these concerns are properly embedded throughout their operations. By envisioning liability more holistically, organizational liability models can motivate firms to embed human rights compliance throughout the entire organization to avoid liability or lessen penalties. What aggregative criminal liability and enterprise risk doctrine have in common is the ability to derive fault from organizational problems. As previously established, human rights risk is propagated by situational forces that are natural consequences of the corporate bureaucratic form. At the same time, some industries and regions are inherently more risky than others. In these cases, attention should be directed to identifying patterns of risk and mitigating the likelihood of this risk materializing into human rights abuses. In the absence of liability schemes that account for these forces, victims of human rights abuses will not have the opportunity to be compensated for harms that materialize from them, and firms will not receive adequate incentives to improve their internal operations. These organizational models of liability can also be paired with alternative sentences and penalties and theoretically expanded to account for liability among corporate groups. As a result, they are capable of equipping domestic courts with the tools to shape future firm behaviour for the better.

Further research into the application and compatibility of the regulatory and liability models discussed here with existing domestic regimes is necessary. The role of civil society groups and organizations has been noted, in law reform efforts, advocacy, information collection and relaying claims to the relevant prosecutorial authorities. Still, there remains much to be done in better understanding and supporting their potential for action on human rights, as partner and arbitrator (with business and government), as and drivers of social improvement and reform. While some research exists on organizational liability models,[28] there is still much to be done to uncover best practices, synthesize case law and share information across jurisdictions. Due to the globalized nature of the economy, efforts in law reform are more likely to shift systemic forces in the short term if they are internationally coordinated with the involvement of firms and governments. Although it will be a slow and iterative process, bringing legal institutions into harmony with the way firms operate in practice is the first step to turning firms into rights-respecting social actors.

Notes

1 The author is grateful to Professor Daniel Weinstock for the guidance and inspiration he provided throughout the completion of this chapter.
2 When the term 'human rights' is used, it is to denote a place in a given socio-legal order for the protection of fundamental human interests above other policy considerations. Although people may disagree about the content of human rights, they may agree about the role of human rights in practical reasoning about the conduct of global political life (Beitz, 2009).
3 In this chapter 'firm' is used to refer to business organizations and 'corporation' is used to refer to the legal form firms adopt to benefit from limited liability and other legal protections.
4 In order to differentiate their product or service, a firm must create something that is perceived industry-wide as being unique in terms of design, brand image, technology, features, customer service, dealer network, or other dimensions. For the greatest success, the firm will differentiate along several dimensions. This strategy is not compatible with commodity-producing firms since the nature of their business is to produce a fungible product (Porter, 1998).
5 The focus strategy entails applying either cost leadership or differentiation approaches to a particular buyer group, segment of the product line, or geographic market (Porter, 1998 at 38).
6 Noted practical and financial barriers to pursuing litigation in the event of human rights abuses include: limited availability of legal aid or other viable funding options, 'loser-pays' rules, a lack of access to suitably qualified and experienced legal counsel, the non-availability of collective action arrangements, corruption and political interference, fear of reprisals and intimidation of witnesses, difficulties accessing the information necessary to prove a claim or complaint, and the insufficiency of damages or enforcement problems (Zerk, 2013: 64).
7 See, for example, *Al Shimari et al. v. CACI Premier Technology* where the Court of Appeal found the *Kiobel* threshold was met on the grounds that the acts of torture were alleged to have been committed by U.S. citizens employed by an American corporation with corporate headquarters in the United States, and the alleged torture occurred at a military facility operated by United States government personnel (p 25).
8 *Trans. 'Forum not agreeing'.*
9 In *Sinaltrainal et al. v. Coca Cola Company et al.*, the claim was dismissed on the grounds that the complainants had failed to prove the existence of a sufficiently close link uniting the paramilitary security forces and the Colombian government, the defendants' involvement with the Colombian government in carrying out acts of torture, and the existence of an armed conflict to begin with. In *Sequihua v Texaco, Inc.*, Ecuadorian citizens who felt that Texaco's operations were causing air, water and soil pollution filed suit in U.S. courts under the ATCA. A New York federal court dismissed the suit on appeal, on the basis of *forum non conveniens* arguing that 'Ecuador is an adequate and available forum even though it may not provide the same benefits as the American system' (p 64). Sequihua demonstrates how easily dismissal for inconvenient forum could be justified on the basis of public policy (Rogge, 2001). In *Recherches Internationales Québec v Cambior Inc.*, the Quebec Superior Court rejected jurisdiction on the grounds that the mere fact that the impugned corporation was domiciled in Quebec did not constitute a special link in assessing the appropriateness of the jurisdiction. The court also rejected the complainant's argument that Guyana's judicial system failed to guarantee the right to a fair trail. A claim against Cambior Inc. was subsequently brought in Guyana, but it was dismissed by the Guyanese court, and the victims were ordered to pay for the expenses Cambior incurred during the trial. In *Assoc. canadienne contre l'impunité (A.C.C.I.) c Anvil Mining Ltd.*, the Quebec

Court of Appeal denied jurisdiction for a case alleging corporate complicity in a military repression of an insurrection in the DRC on the grounds of *forum non conveniens*. Despite the fact that the case failed to yield an equitable result in DRC courts, the Quebec court dismissed the claimants' request to hear the case on the grounds that Anvil Mining's Canadian office had not been open long-enough to be implicated in the impugned incident.

10 For example, Canada's primary securities regulator, the Ontario Securities Commission, requires continuous disclosure of company risk factors and recently issued a notice against Chieftain Metals Corp for failing to disclose high levels of contaminants, conflicts with a local indigenous group long-term environmental liabilities and ongoing violations of its waste discharge permit (MiningWatch Canada, 2014). Similarly, recent revisions to the UK Companies Act require all UK-quoted companies to include in their annual reports information about human rights issues, including information on the effectiveness of company policies (CORE *et al.*, 2014). Furthermore, the draft Modern Slavery Bill seeks to enforce further disclosure requirements on United Kingdom companies such as information on the policies and processes they undertake to identify and address the risks and incidences of slavery and forced labour in their supply chains and the effectiveness thereof (CORE *et al.*, 2014).

11 Pigovian tax is a tax applied to a market activity that is generating external costs for somebody else.

12 It should be noted that the global nature of the economy complicates business regulation. A given government's monitoring capacity may not be sufficient to regulate the entire extent of a firm's supply chain, especially in the case of large MNCs. Requiring firms to disclose information regarding their suppliers is helpful, but research shows that many are actually unaware of the full extent of subcontractors contributing to their production processes (Shift Project, 2012: 7). Nevertheless, attempts at regulation are warranted. Mitigating business human rights risk is an iterative process and requires the cooperation of many levels of government, states and international organizations.

13 This protocol, which governs the production of certain substances harmful to the ozone layer, was spearheaded by a coalition of environmental NGOs and DuPont, Inc. who was eager to make large profits from producing chlorofluorocarbon substitutes (Ogus, 2004: 166).

14 The analysis referred to in this paper understands an act of perpetration to include a "role in creating, sustaining, perpetuating or conceding to the conditions that contribute to delinquency, crime, vandalism, teasing, bullying, rape, torture, terror, and violence (Zimbardo, 2007: 6–7). This paper focuses on any subset of these activities that instigate or perpetuate abuses of human rights.

15 Examples include SA8000 (social responsibility and labour), ISO9001 (quality management), ISO14001 (environmental management) and the forthcoming ISO26000 (for social responsibility and sustainability).

16 In his famous Stanford Prison Experiment, Zimbardo observed how ordinary university students readily and quickly adopted the randomly assigned roles of guards and prisoners, with the guards employing violent and demeaning means of control over the prisoners (2007: Chapter 10). A further illustration is the experiment conducted by Milgram in which two out of three volunteers administered shocks up to 450 volts to other persons, in spite of their cries of pain, because the volunteers were told to do so by someone they perceived as a figure of authority (Zimbardo, 2007: 271).

17 "Problems of a cost-benefit kind can only be solved when all the elements of the problems are treated as belonging to the realm of the calculable and the predictable. Hence the executive is always under pressure to treat the social world as predictable and calculable and to ignore any arbitrariness involved in so doing" (MacIntyre, 1992: 185).

18 Recent developments in supply chain human rights compliance employ techniques that replace or lessen the quantification and operational distance characteristics of traditional compliance schemes that can in turn reduce the situational forces of perpetration. For example, one firm hired an outside auditor to conduct a paper audit of its supply chain, and the results revealed that only one out of the firm's ten suppliers knew who its subcontractors were (Shift Project, 2012: 7).

19 See e.g. the "commitment approach" (Locke *et al.*, 2008: 27).

20 "In both common and civil law jurisdictions, findings of negligence turn on the questions of whether the damage suffered by the claimant was "reasonably foreseeable" to the defendant and, if so, whether the defendant had acted in a reasonable way given the risks . . . In common law jurisdictions, these ideas find expression as duties and standards of care. To make out a successful claim for negligence, the claimant must show first, that there was a duty of care; second, that this duty of care was breached; third that breach of the duty resulted in damage or loss to the claimant, and finally, the damage suffered was not too remote to justify compensation in the circumstances" (Zerk, 2013: 44).

21 See e.g. CSR v Wren; Choc v Hudbay Minerals Inc.

22 The court in *Chandler* held that, in appropriate circumstances, the law may impose on a parent company responsibility for the health and safety of its subsidiary's employees.

23 From 1991 to present, the largest corporate fines ranged from USD 900 million to 246 billion (Benoit and Grocer, 2013).

24 The use of *forum non conveniens* in the United Kingdom has been circumscribed by European Union law. Following the European Court of Justice (ECJ) case *Owusu v. N.B. Jackson et al.*, the doctrine of *forum non conveniens* is not allowed under the Brussels I Regulation, which applies to the United Kingdom (Magnus and Mankowski, 2007: 7). The ECJ found that Article 2 of Brussels I, which stipulates that persons domiciled in a Member State shall be sued in the courts of that State regardless of their nationality, is mandatory in nature and thus insulated from any deviation unless the Convention does so explicitly. Since the application of *forum non conveniens* would require, at times, deviating from this rule, the ECJ deemed it no longer applicable in the United Kingdom (*Owusu v. N.B. Jackson*).

25 This feature currently exists in Australian federal criminal law: a corporation may avoid liability for misconduct of its "high managerial agents" by proving that it exercised due diligence to prevent said misconduct. See *Criminal Code Act 1995* (Cth), s 12.3(3).

26 Vicarious liability more generally is the doctrine through which liability for wrongful conduct may be imposed on a party that is not itself at fault, and is most commonly used in the case of the employer of the immediate wrongdoer (Ataner, 2006: 64). It is based on the notion that firms can control the conduct of their agents and assumes that assigning liability to firms will reduce legal violations by encouraging firms to better influence agent behaviour (Buell, 2011: 87).

27 See Bazley v. Curry; Jacobi v. Griffiths; London Drugs Ltd. v. Kuehne & Nagel International Ltd.; Lister v. Hesley Hall Ltd.

28 See e.g. Arthurs, 2008; Pieth & Ivory, 2011; Fanto, 2010; Hechler Baer, 2010.

References

Papers

Ataner, A. 2006. How strict is vicarious liability? Reassessing the enterprise risk theory. *University of Toronto Faculty of Law Review* 64(2), pp. 63–103.

Catà Backer, L. 2008. Multinational corporations as objects and sources of transnational regulation. *ILSA Journal of International and Comparative Law* 14(2), pp. 499–524.

Coase, R. 1960. The problem of social cost. *Journal of Law and Economics* 3(1), pp. 1–44.

Couret Branco, M. 2009. Economics against human rights: the conflicting languages of economics and human rights. *Capitalism, Nature, Socialism* 20(1), pp. 88–102.

Dan-Cohen, M. 1985. Bureaucratic organizations and the theory of adjudication. *Columbia Law Review* 85(1), pp. 1–37.

Fanto, J. 2010. Organizational liability. *Journal of law and social policy* 19(1), pp. 45–54.

Goold, M. and Campbell, A. 1997. Managing diversity: strategy and control in diversified British companies. *Long Range Planning* 20(5), pp. 42–52.

Hechler Baer, M. 2009. Governing corporate compliance. *Boston College Law Review* 50(4), pp. 949–1019.

Hechler Baer, M. 2010. Organizational liability and the tension between corporate and criminal law. *Journal of law and social policy* 19(1), pp. 1–14.

Huff A. S. 1982. Industry influences on strategy reformulation. *Strategic Management Journal* 3(2), pp. 119–31.

Mintzberg, H. 1980. Structure in 5's: a synthesis of the research on organization design. *Management Science* 26(3), pp. 322–41.

Müller-Hoff, C. 2011. Strategic human rights litigation: can it be used effectively against transnational corporations? *Aportes DPLF* 24. Available at: www.dplf.org/sites/default/files/1323186935_0.pdf [Accessed: 4 September 2014].

Petrin, M. 2013. Assumption of responsibility in corporate groups: Chandler v Cape plc. *Modern Law Review* 76(3), pp. 603–19.

Porter, M. 1990. The competitive advantage of nations. *Harvard Business Review* (March-April 1990), pp. 73–93.

Rogge, M. 2001. Towards transnational corporate accountability in the global economy: challenging the doctrine of *forum non conveniens* in *in re: Union Carbide, Alfaro, Sequiha, and Aguinda*. *Texas International Law Journal* 36(2), pp. 299–314.

Silbey, S. and Agrawal, T. (2011). The illusion of accountability: information management and organizational culture. *Droit et société* 77, pp. 69–86.

Van Den Eeckhout, V. 2012. Corporate human rights violations and private international law. *Contemporary Readings in Law and Social Justice* 4(2), pp. 178–207.

Wintrobe, R. 1982. The optimal level of bureaucratization within a firm. *The Canadian Journal of Economics* 15(4), pp. 649–68.

Books

Bakan, J. 2001. *The corporation: the pathological pursuit of profit and power*. Toronto, Canada: Simon & Schuster.

Beitz, C. 2009. *The idea of human rights*. Oxford: Oxford University Press.

Braithwaite, J. and Drahos, P. 2000. *Global business regulation*. Cambridge: Cambridge University Press.

Coleman, J. 1974. *Power and the structure of society*. New York: WW Norton & Company.

Falola, T. and Genova, A. 2005. *The politics of the global oil industry: an introduction*. Westport, CT: Praeger.

Fishman, C. 2006. *The Wal-mart effect: how an out-of-town superstore became a superpower*. London: Penguin.

Fligstein, N. 2001. *The architecture of markets: an economic sociology of twenty-first century capitalist societies*. Princeton, NJ: Princeton University Press.

Magnus, U and Mankwoski, P. 2007. *European commentaries on private international law, brussels i regulation*. Munich, Germany: Sellier.

Ogus, A. 2004. *Regulation: legal form and economic theory.* Oxford: Hart Publishing.

Perrow, C. 1971. *Organizational analysis: a sociological view.* London: Tavistock Publications.

Pieth, M. and Ivory, R. 2011. *Corporate criminal liability: emergence, convergence, and risk.* New York: Springer.

Pitel, S. and Rafferty, N. 2010. *Conflict of laws.* Toronto, Canada: Irwin Law.

Porter, M. 1998. *Competitive advantage: creating and sustaining superior performance.* New York: The Free Press.

Spender J. C. 1989. *Industry recipes: an enquiry into the nature and sources of managerial judgement.* Oxford: Blackwell.

Stone, C. 1975. *Where the law ends: the social control of corporate behavior.* New York: Harper & Row.

Weber, M. 1946. *From Max Weber: essays in sociology.* New York: Oxford University Press.

Zimbardo, P. 2007. *The Lucifer effect.* New York: Random House.

Chapters of books

Buell, S. 2011. Potentially perverse effects of corporate civil liability. In: Barkow, A. and Barkow, R. (eds). *Prosecutors in the boardroom: using criminal law to regulate corporate conduct.* New York: New York University Press, pp. 87–109.

Coffee, J. 1999. Corporate criminal liability: an introduction and comparative survey. In: Eser, A. Heine, G., Huber, B. and (eds). *Criminal responsibility of legal and collective entities.* Freiburg, Germany: Ius crim, p. 9ff.

DiMaggio, P. and Powell, W. 2003. The iron cage revisited: institutional isomorphism and collective rationality in organizational fields. In: Handel, M. (ed.). *The sociology of organizations: classic, contemporary, and critical readings.* Thousand Oaks, CA: Sage, pp. 243–53.

Farberman, H. 1991. A criminogenic market structure: the automobile industry. In: Galliher, J. (ed.). *Deviant behavior and human rights.* Englewood Cliffs, NJ: Prentice Hall, pp. 205–20.

Fligstein, N. 2004. From the transformation of corporate control. In: Dobbin, F. (ed.) *The new economic sociology: a reader.* Princeton, NJ: Princeton University Press, pp. 407–32.

Fligstein, N. 2010. Lessons from Europe: some reflections on the European union and the regulation of business. In: Balleisen, E. and Moss, D. (eds). *Government and markets: toward a new theory of regulation.* Cambridge: Cambridge University Press, pp. 143–63.

Ignatieff, M. 2001. Human rights as politics. In: Guttman, A. (ed.). *Human rights as politics and idolatry.* Princeton, NJ: Princeton University Press, pp. 3–52.

Leonard, W. and Weber, M. 1991. Automakers and dealers: a study of criminogenic market forces. In: Galliher, J. (ed.). *Deviant behavior and human rights.* Englewood Cliffs, NJ: Prentice Hall, pp. 193–204.

MacIntyre, A. 1992. Utilitarianism and cost-benefit analysis: an essay on the relevance of moral philosophy to bureaucratic theory. In: Gillroy, J. and Wade, M. (eds). *The moral dimensions of public policy choice: beyond the market paradigm.* Pittsburgh, PA: University of Pittsburgh Press, pp. 179–94.

Meyer, J. and Rowan, B. 2004. Institutionalized organizations: formal structure as myth and ceremony. In: Dobbin, F. (ed.). *The new economic sociology: a reader.* Princeton, NJ: Princeton University Press, pp. 86–110.

Parker, C. and Gilad, S. 2011. Internal corporate compliance management systems: structure, culture and agency. In: Parker, C. and Nielsen, V. (eds). *Explaining compliance: business responses to regulation.* Cheltenham, UK: Edward Elgar, pp. 170–98.

Perrow, C. 2003. Markets, hierarchies, and hegemony. In: Handel, M. (ed.). *The sociology of organizations: classic, contemporary, and critical readings*. Thousand Oaks, CA: Sage, pp. 288–94.

Schmidt, P. 2004. Law in the age of governance: regulation, networks, and lawyers. In: Jordana, J. and Levi-Faur, D. (eds). *The politics of regulation: institutions and regulatory reforms for the age of governance*. Cheltenham, UK: Edward Elgar, pp. 273–95.

Stiglitz, J. 2010. Government failure vs. market failure: principles of regulation. In: Balleisen, E. and Moss, D. (eds). *Government and markets: towards a new theory of regulation*. Cambridge: Cambridge University Press, pp. 13–51.

World Wide Web pages

Baudry, B. and Gindis, D. 2005. *The v-network form: economic organization and the theory of the firm*. Available at: http://papers.ssrn.com/sol3/papers.cfm?abstract_id=795244 [Accessed: 4 September 2014].

Benoit, D. and Grocer, S. 2013. *Where J.P. Morgan's settlement sits in history of corporate fines*. Available at: http://blogs.wsj.com/moneybeat/2013/10/19/where-j-p-morgans-settlement-sits-in-history-of-corporate-fines/ [Accessed: 4 September 2014].

CORE, Anti-Slavery International, Hausfiedl & Co. LLP and Traidcraft. 2014. *Submission to the parliamentary joint committee on the draft Modern Slavery Bill*. Available at: http://corporate-responsibility.org/wp-content/uploads/2014/07/Submission-to-Joint-Cttee-on-draft-Modern-Slavery-Bill_CORE-Coalition_10-February-2014_final-with-logos3.pdf [Accessed: 4 September 2014].

ECCHR: European Center for Constitutional and Human Rights. 2013a. *European cases database: analysis*. Available at: www.ecchr.de/publications-592.html [Accessed: 4 September 2014].

ECCHR: European Center for Constitutional and Human Rights. 2013b. *Kiobel case: ECCHR supports victims of corporate abuse before US supreme court*. Available at: www.ecchr.de/publications-592.html [Accessed: 4 September 2014].

ECCHR: European Center for Constitutional and Human Rights. 2014. *The responsibility of European corporations for human rights violations abroad: to what extent does corporate due diligence extend to subsidiaries?* Available at: www.ecchr.de/publications-592.html [Accessed: 4 September 2014].

Ekekwe, N. 2012. *When you can't innovate, copy*. Available at: http://blogs.hbr.org/2012/05/when-you-cant-innovate-copy/ [Accessed: 4 September 2014].

FIDH: International Federation for Human Rights. 2012. *Corporate accountability for human rights abuses: a guide for victims and NGOs on recourse mechanisms*. Available at: www.fidh.org/en/globalisation-human-rights/business-and-human-rights/Updated-version-Corporate-8258 [Accessed: 4 September 2014].

Locke, R., Amengual, M. and Mangla, A. 2008. *Virtue out of necessity? compliance, commitment and the improvement of labor conditions in global supply chains*. Available at: http://papers.ssrn.com/sol3/papers.cfm?abstract_id=1286142 [Accessed: 4 September 2014].

MiningWatch Canada. 2014. *OSC forces chieftain metals to correct 2013 AIF and retract corporate presentation*. Available at: www.miningwatch.ca/news/osc-forces-chieftain-metals-correct-2013-aif-and-retract-corporate-presentation [Accessed: 4 September 2014].

Shift Project. 2012. *Respecting human rights through global supply chains*. Available at: www.shiftproject.org/publication/respecting-human-rights-through-global-supply-chains-shift-workshop-report-no-2 [Accessed: 4 September 2014].

Van Den Eeckhout, V. 2008. *Competing norms and European private international law – sequel to promoting human rights within the union: the role of European private international law* Available at: http://papers.ssrn.com/sol3/papers.cfm?abstract_id=1259334 [Accessed: 4 September 2014].

Wachenfeld, M., Hodge M., Zimmerman, V., Lehr, A., St. Dennis, H. and several staff of IHRB and GBI. 2012. *State of play: the corporate responsibility to protect human rights in business relationships.* Available at: www.ihrb.org/pdf/state-of-play/State-of-Play-Full-Report.pdf [Accessed: 4 September 2014].

Yarow, J. 2012. *The most blatant examples of companies stealing Apple's design.* Available at: www.businessinsider.com/apple-copy-cats-2012–1?op=1 [Accessed: 4 September 2014].

Reports

Arthurs: Arthurs Allen Robinson. 2008. *'Corporate culture' as a basis for the criminal liability of corporations.* United Nations Special Representative of the Secretary General for Business and Human Rights.

Global CSR: Global CSR & Copenhagen Business School. 2011. *Changing course – a study into responsible supply chain management.* Copenhagen, Denmark: Danish Ministry of Foreign Affairs.

Kernaghan, C. 2014. *Gap and Old Navy in Bangladesh: cheating the poorest workers in the world.* Pittsburgh, PA: Institute for Global Labour and Human Rights.

Zerk, J. 2013. *Corporate liability for gross human rights abuses: towards a fairer and more effective system of domestic law remedies.* Geneva, Switzerland: Office of the High Commissioner of Human Rights.

Encyclopedias

EGI: *Encyclopedia of Global Industries.* 2014a. 4th edn. 'Apparel'. Gale Virtual Reference Library.

EGI: *Encyclopedia of Global Industries.* 2014b. 4th edn. 'Electronic Components'. Gale Virtual Reference Library.

EGI: *Encyclopedia of Global Industries.* 2014c. 4th edn. 'Mining, Metal. Gale Virtual Reference Library.

Jurisprudence

Al Shimari *et al.* v. CACI Premier Technology, Inc *et al.*, 758 F.3d 516.

Assoc. canadienne contre l'impunité (A.C.C.I.) v. Anvil Mining Ltd., 2012 QCCA 117, 228 ACWS (3d) 394 (Can.).

Bazley v. Curry, [1999] 2 SCR 534 (Can.).

Chandler v. Cape Plc, [2012] EWCA Civ 525, [2012] 3 All ER 640 (U.K.).

Choc v. Hudbay Minerals Inc., [2013] ONSC 1414 (Can.).

CSR v. Wren, (1997), [1998] 44 NSWLR 463 (Austr.).

Jacobi v. Griffiths, [1999] 2 SCR 570 (Can.).

Kiobel v. Royal Dutch Petroleum Co., 621 F. Supp. 3d 111 (2013).

Lister v. Hesley Hall Ltd., [2001] 2 WLR 1311 (U.K.).

London Drugs Ltd. v. Kuehne & Nagel International Ltd., [1994] 3 SCR 299 (Can.).

Owusu v. N.B. Jackson *et al.* [2005] ECR 1–1383.

Recherches Internationales Québec v. Cambior Inc., [1988] QJ No 2554 (Can.).
Sequiha v. Texaco, Inc., 847 F. Supp. 61 (1994).
Sinaltrainal *et al.* v. Coca Cola Company *et al.*, 256 F. Supp. 2d 1345.
Tolofson v. Jensen, [1994] 3 SCR 1022, 120 DLR (4th) 289 (Can.).

Legislation

Alien Tort Claims Act, 28 U.S.C. § 1350.
Criminal Code Act 1995 (Cth) (Austr.)

International Materials

Brussels I: Council Regulation (EC) No 44/2001 of 22 December 2000 on jurisdiction on the recognition and enforcement of judgments in civil and commercial matters, E.U., 22 December 2000, OJ L 12/1.
Rome II: Regulation of the European Parliament and of the Council of 11 July 2007 on the law applicable to non-contractual obligations, E.U., 11 July 2007, OJ L 199/40.
Universal Declaration of Human Rights, G.A. Res. 217 (III) A, U.N. Doc. A/RES/217(III) (10 December 1948).
UNSPRSG: Special Representative of the Secretary General, *Guiding Principles on Business and Human Rights: Implementing the United Nations "Protect, Respect and Remedy" Framework*, Human Rights Council, U.N. Doc. A/HRC/17/31 (16 June 2011).

Part 2

Community interests and responsibility

3 A space of isolation

Entrepreneurship in a time of crisis in Italy

Michele Filippo Fontefrancesco

Introduction

We may regard responsibility as arising from a sense of attachment and interconnection with others. What happens in the context of economic decline?

'The crisis has left us alone, and they left us with only our pants'. Arturo was about 50 years old. He was an entrepreneur, a builder, who had worked for over 30 years in the field. He had experienced the impact of the economic crisis just as many of his colleagues. The crash of the real estate market, the halt of new construction projects, the shrinking of new contracts, in particular those from public institutions – all of these had left his firm of over 50 employees in 2005 with only 12 in 2012. They still had a large fleet of vehicles and plenty of machinery, but most lay idle now. His words express his anger against the situation of the market, but above all against the state and society at large. In his view, they had abandoned the entrepreneurs in the face of the crisis. What was left was the sense of solitude that, Arturo concluded, pushed every entrepreneur to 'do the best one can just to survive'. Arturo was not an isolated voice. In the research I conducted from 2012 to 2014 in the province of Alessandria in northwestern Italy, many entrepreneurs, in particular those who ran small and medium firms, shared the same sentiment and used the same rhetoric of abandonment and isolation.

Using an analytical approach taken from the anthropology of rhetoric (Carrithers, 2005), this chapter investigates the way of expressing the entrepreneur's experience of isolation in a context of economic recession. In particular, the research interrogates this feeling of isolation in order to understand the sense of (corporate) responsibility perceived and pursued by the entrepreneurs and how far it extends. This ethnography, thus, sheds light on the very way in which entrepreneurs understand their existence in the world, their place in society and the changes the crisis has caused. These are the fundamental cultural elements needed to understand the possibility of future, sustained development.

The chapter opens with a presentation of the disciplinary angle taken in this chapter. It then introduces the particular area investigated during the research, followed by the main features of the fieldwork conducted. This chapter then presents the ethnographic data collected, followed by an analysis of the entrepreneurs' sense of isolation. This then helps us understand their disengagement from society, and the consequences for their sense of corporate responsibility. Conclusions follow.

Approaching rhetoric

It is an ancient teaching. Since Aristotle, a number of scholars have suggested that language and poetry are ways in which human beings can express their individuality and in so doing shape the space that surrounds them, giving things meaning (Fergusson, 1961). The works of Shotter (1996), Katz and Shotter (1996), and Cunliffe (2002) have explored how meaning is created between people as they utilize discursive resources in imaginative and improvisational ways. In this respect, Herzfeld (1997: 139–45) suggested the analysis of 'social poetics' representing an ethnographic field of research able to illuminate new aspects of a society and re-think anthropological interpretative schemata. Following this heuristic tradition, Carrithers (2005: 579) pointed out that the study of rhetoric, that is, the arts of arguing and convincing, 'lays open to study that feature of social life that is so difficult to capture, its historicity, its eventfulness'. In fact, he follows, 'Rhetoric adds to [. . .] previous depiction[s] of human sociality a more vivid sense of (1) the moving force in interaction, (2) the cultural and distinctly human character of that force, and (3) the creation of new cultural forms in social life' (Carrithers, 2005: 579). The rhetoric dimension is not only an ambient 'reducible to speech alone' (Carrithers, 2005: 582), but a complex occurrence of speech and gestures moved by a communicative intent. Thus, its analysis should not encompass only the speech alone, but also a study of the social relations that are conveyed, built and effected through the employment of discursive objects.

In the past 10 years, this approach has been tested to explore different contexts and situation, from agriculture in Britain (Carrithers et al., 2011), policies of integration in Germany and the United States (Carrithers, 2009) and the building of roads in Nepal (Campbell, 2010). Above all, it also proved to be particularly effective in bringing to the fore the worldviews of the community, and the set of values, expectations, and fear a community shares and lives. In particular, as Gudeman (2009) showed, this approach can offer a new insight on the making of economy by highlighting the very ways in which an economic context is perceived and the ethical and moral basis that drives the economy. It is from these examples that this research flows.

The field

The Alessandria province is at the centre of the Italian north-west: the area surrounding the so-called industrial triangle of Genoa, Milan and Turin. The province, whose capital is the city of Alessandria, extends for over 3,500 square kilometres and has a population of 440,000 inhabitants. This territory was chosen for its socioeconomic representativeness of national and regional economic trends within Italy (see Fontefrancesco, 2013b).[1]

While the economic development of Turin, the most important city in the region where Alessandria lays, was based on the hegemonic presence of one big firm, the Fiat car company, the province of Alessandria has instead followed a path of development that mixed the presence of big industrial plants and firms, such as Montedison and Michelin in Alessandria, Italsider in Novi and Eternit and Buzzi in Casale Monferrato (hereafter M.to), with the creation of specialized industrial districts of small and medium firms in Valenza (jewellery industry), Casale M.to (refrigeration industry) and Tortona (logistics) (Fondazione Gianfranco Pittatore and The European House Ambrosetti, 2011). While these sectors, dominated by big often multinational firms, met their first crisis in the 1980s, the industrial districts experienced steady growth until the 2000s.

Aside from the manufacturing, the entire province has since the 1990s experienced a profound transformation in the service sector. International and national chains of supermarkets and malls have opened their establishments in the area, turning the province of Alessandria into one of the areas of higher concentration of malls per inhabitant in Italy, and large investments were made in the tourism industry, in particular, restaurants, small hotels and bed and breakfast (B&B) services. One of the most important achievements of these economic efforts was the recognition of the Monferrato hills as one of UNESCO's world heritage sites in 2014.

In the past decade, the entire province experienced a period of economic decline, most markedly after 2008, when the recession reached its peak. Between 2009 and 2013, the unemployment rate in Alessandria province doubled with general unemployment rising from 5.8 to 11.7 per cent, and youth unemployment hitting 30 per cent. To this end, the province has followed the general trend of north-west Italy (Assessorato al Lavoro, 2011). While large firms survived by reducing their personnel, small firms did not survive the crisis. An example of this impact is the case of Valenza. In this small city of about 20,000 inhabitants, in 2005 about 7,500 people worked in the jewellery industry, in an industrial district that counted over 1,100 firms; in 2013, the number employed in the industry had dropped to 3,500 and the firms to fewer than 800 (Fontefrancesco, 2013a). The data published by the Chamber of Industry and Commerce of Alessandria in the past three years (2011–2014) suggests a radical transformation of the entrepreneurial landscape corresponding to the shrinking of the average size of local businesses and a substantial rise of one-man enterprises: in June 2014 these micro-enterprises accounted for over 60 per cent of all the firms in the Province (27,280 firms out of 44,840) (Bocchio, 2014).

The regional government tried to counter the social effects of the small and medium-size enterprise (SME) crisis. In particular, they mostly focused their action on the problem of employment. Since 2009 the regional council has financed a special social cushion dedicated to the SMEs' redundant workers, who are excluded by the regular national mechanism of welfare. Most recent data shows that between 2009 and 2012, the Regional Council has financed 12,872 cases of redundant workers (De Vincenzi and Iadevaia, 2014) investing, according to data provided by the regional government, about €60 million every year in these measures.[2] Moreover, the regional government drew on the European Regional Development Funds to implement innovation measures aimed at strengthening the competitiveness of local firms and expand the number of workers.[3] However, while the business organizations requested substantial cuts in taxation, no main action has been taken in this direction. These data highlight the direction taken by the public institutions, but also, as will become clear, a substantial mismatch between what the entrepreneurs asked for and the decision taken by the policy-makers. It is within this policy context that the experiences of the entrepreneurs of the Alessandria province are located. While these local trends are consistent and mirror the more general dynamics that Italy and in particular its 'affluent' north have experienced in the past five years (Perulli and Picchieri, 2010), they have also turned the province into a case study in how one understands entrepreneurship among SMEs in Italy.

The fieldwork

The data presented in this chapter were collected during a field research that lasted from 2012 to 2014. The research aimed at investigating the changes in the entrepreneurial culture caused by the prolonged recession. The work continued previous research concerning the impact of an economic downturn in the district of Valenza (Fontefrancesco, 2013a) and among youth in the province (Fontefrancesco, 2013b), building on that research by investigating in particular the experience of the crisis among SMEs.

The research involved comprehensive interviews with 87 entrepreneurs, only eight of which were conducted with owners and executive managers of large enterprises. At 12 firms, moreover, I conducted focused ethnographies (Knoblauch, 2005) that encompassed fieldwork studies lasting from one to four weeks at the individual enterprise. In the selection of informants I covered the main forms of enterprises present in the province (stock companies, partnerships, cooperatives, one-man companies) and the main economic sectors of the province (Table 3.1).

The interviews were conducted according to the history of life method (Bertaux, 1999; Grimaldi and Porporato, 2012) aimed at reconstructing the entrepreneurial experience and describing the worldview that underpins it.

Bourdieu (1999), in his seminal study of the social life in Paris *banlieue*, showed that histories of life of ordinary individuals can offer positive evidence for understanding the ways of being in the world that distinguishes the members

Table 3.1 Scope of the study

Sector	N. Study Subjects
Agriculture	13
Manufacturing	23
Building	21
Service	30

of a society, offering a realistic reconstruction of the society and its change that resists a sterile objectification of social complexity. The ethnographic presentation of the reality that emerges from the research draws from this example to build a narration of the transformations of the economic landscape in the Alessandria province and the social impact of the change.

A space of solitude

The quantitative data concerning the economic transformation of the Alessandria province outline an erosion of the entrepreneurial milieu and the shrinking of the number of workers and firms (Tables 3.2 and 3.3).

The local newspapers, as well as the political debate, have been focusing their attention mainly on the numerical dimension of the phenomenon: titles such as 'Negatività stabile per le imprese,'[4], 'Colpo d'accetta sull'edilizia: dimezzati i posti di lavoro',[5], 'Artigianato futuro nebuloso'[6] are examples of this trend. In this public discourse, the term 'isolamento' (isolation) has been one of the key expressions used both by entrepreneurs and workers. 'Do not abandon us' was a recurrent sentence during demonstrations and strikes. Banners with this motto dominated the façades of occupied public offices, such as the Alessandria city council-owned enterprise AMIU in September 2013, as well as factories, such as *Cerutti* establishment in Casale M.to The same claim was voiced by entrepreneurs in public assemblies and conferences, such as Confederazione Nazionale Artigiani's (hereafter CNA) meeting in April 2013 in Valenza.

This sense of isolation has pervaded the human landscape of the province. 'We are alone, left on our own' was the comment of Carlo, 35 years old. He was an entrepreneur in the marketing sector. In 2003 he opened a small enterprise: four employees (two designers, one communication expert and an accountant) and a studio based in Alessandria. They worked with small and medium firms, mainly in the food industry. The enterprise seemed to thrive until 2009 when the crisis began. In 2010 he had to ask his workers to opt for a part-time contract. This was not enough to cope with the loss of customers. In December 2013 the enterprise closed down. In 2014 Carlo opened a new firm, this time a one-person enterprise.

Table 3.2 SMEs in Alessandria province[7]

SMEs 2009	SMEs in 2011	SMEs in 2013
13.317	12,993	12,241

Table 3.3 Unemployment rate in Alessandria Province[8]

Unemployment rate 2009	Unemployment rate 2011	Unemployment rate 2013
5.8%	6.7%	11.7%

We are alone and the market is killing us. Nobody seems to care much. Where is the state? It asks for more and more taxes and does nothing for us. People don't realize that the death of small firms is [Italy's] key problem.

Carlo's experience echoes the testimony of other informants. Despite the difference of industry and size of the enterprises, the entrepreneurs I met lamented a similar situation. They see themselves as actors in what should be a mutually supportive relationship with both the state and communities, operating in a social context of economic and political trade-offs.

Within this context, the entrepreneurs assess their condition considering not only the actual revenues of their firms, but also on the basis of their possibility of influencing political decisions. While the downturn eroded economic relationships, the entrepreneurs also pointed out the weakening of their political voice locally and nationally. They lamented on a local level the futility of the meetings and workshops promoted by the City Council and the business associations since 2009, and on a national level pointed out the inactivity of the government in key areas for the jewellery industry such as taxation on luxury goods, and trade mark regulation and protection. The sense of solitude is directly linked with this perception of disempowerment.

'People don't care if we thrive or close. There are even people who would be happy if we drowned. We asked help from the state and the answers were more taxes, some social benefits for our employees, but nothing more', Arturo pointed out. He was underlining what he perceived as the unwillingness of government to put in place any measures to support entrepreneurship through stimuli or tax reliefs, or launch any measures promoting or protecting production during the five-year period. On the contrary, as Arturo, and many other entrepreneurs pointed out, SMEs have struggled with increasing austerity measures; the real rise of taxation (Centro Studi CNA, 2014) that SMEs experienced in the past five years, have furthered the effects of the downturn. In this context, he recognizes that 'it seems as if we were all mute. Our voices are not heard, but they do produce sound, don't they? It seems to me nobody cares about us, not even our associations'. The difficult relationship between these small businesses and both the state and communities also now extends to the relationship of the firms with their associations. While business associations have often offered legal and accounting services to their members, they have also been the main political tool for SMEs to influence national and local politics in Italy (Constantelos, 2004; Gaggio, 2007). However, in the eyes of entrepreneurs, the associations had lost their political relevance.

'The associations offer some services to us and we pay for them, but for the rest they are not so useful. It seems they weren't able to provide much help in these years'. These are Giulio's comments, a builder in his fifties. He has spent 35 years in construction, of which 25 were spent in the province of Alessandria. When he opened his firm, in 1989, he joined one of the main associations and was happy to use their accounting services.

They offered a good and cheap service. But for me the association was more ... it was a reference point. When I had a problem or a doubt they were able to answer my questions. However, they were powerless in the face of the crisis. I am still happy to be part of it, but somehow they have lost [political] ground and us with them.

The experience of Giulio highlights the difficulties the business associations have had to cope with during the past five years. The crisis undoubtedly contributed to a substantial loss of affiliates; many of them just closed their establishments, others left the associations looking for cheaper solutions for their management needs. Despite this economic change, the associations had to cope with a qualitative change in the demands of their members. As the director of a local branch of one of the main business associations commented:

In the past, [the affiliates] came here asking for tax deductions and financial resources. Today when they are not asking us how to close their firms down, they are asking technical questions about foreign markets. They hope to find prospective customers beyond the Alps which they do not find in this country. Often we have no answer to their questions; however, the solution is not abroad. The problem is in the structure of many of these firms; they know, they knew, but never acted to better their situation. Now they consider themselves victims, but ... it's too late.

While existing business associations seem not to answer the new demands of entrepreneurs, in the past five years no experiment of new mutualism has been realized. Many entrepreneurs lamented the worsening of the relationship between enterprises, and the increasing competition that is often perceived as unfair. Marco, a Valenza jewellery producer and the owner of a small studio in the city concluded: 'You know the proverb: give [other firms] a finger and they will take your arm ... this is what happens'. This prejudicial attitude is shared by other informants. The general trend that has emerged from the research indicates a reduction of partners and suppliers not only to internalize production, but also to exclude rivals. The crisis, thus, seems to have undermined the bond of trust that linked the firms in the area: trust that underpinned the social capital of each enterprise, on the one hand, and on the other motivated a policy of social responsibility.

'Why should my firm be responsible for society? Leave me alone. After all these years, what remains to us is isolation in a hostile world ... nothing more ...' is the concluding remark of Marco.

Inside the isolation

Considering the words of my informants, it appears that 'isolation' is a recurrent theme in the ways of describing their daily life. 'Isolation' does not refer to social exclusion, but rather a sense of abandonment profoundly rooted in the economic experience. In particular, it highlights the difficulty that entrepreneurs experience in relating to the state, their peers, business associations and communities. This effect suggests an erosion of that strong social capital that historically characterised the SME in Italy.

The seminal work of Piore and Sable (1984) has pointed out the peculiar structure of Italian industrialism, which is mainly based on agglomerations of SMEs that dominate local industry. These agglomerations, named 'industrial districts' after Alfred Marshall's theory of local industry (Becattini *et al.*, 2009), have been at the centre of a heated debate that have involved economists, geographers and social scientists. Scholars have investigated the connection between firms and communities that characterize these local systems 'where a community of people live and work, with a great deal of persistently overlapping experiences' (Becattini, 1978). The entrepreneurs' social capital, which is the capacity of being embedded in a tangled network of relationships with other firms and institutions, has been central to the development and thriving of these agglomerations. A large bibliography has documented this (for a comprehensive discussion of the theme see Becattini, 2006) and pointed out the role of business associations as fundamental bridges between the state and the entrepreneurs: key players in policy-making. A vivid example of the role of business associations has been discussed by Gaggio (2007) in his analysis of the main Italian jewellery districts and in particular Valenza and its production milieu. Gaggio shows that up until the 1970s local business associations were able to influence local and national policy-making and be the drivers of important economic initiatives. The present experiences of entrepreneurs testify to the loss of this social role. Business organizations are now perceived as just administrative and financial service centres. The political role played by business organizations at a local and national level is no longer valued by my informants who prefer not to be involved in the events or initiatives promoted by these groups, which are seen as inefficient and ineffective in changing the economic context. Similarly, entrepreneurs do not recognize their representative roles in the national parties and their local branches. The experiences of the entrepreneurs describe a new profoundly different scene from that politicized world described by Blim (1990), Pardo (1996) and Gaggio (2007).

An impolitic social body

Now there is a human landscape distinguished by an ethos of public and political disengagement. Thus, it is clear that a crisis is not merely a slowdown or an interruption in the exchange of goods and capital, but a collective moment for reconsidering the very idea of being a community. The erosion my informants testify to corresponds to the rise of a new politically and socially disengaged body of entrepreneurs.

The notion of a 'body impolitic' was used by Herzfeld (2004) to describe the incapacity of local artisan entrepreneurs in Crete to create a stable alliance among them in order to develop a political presence in order to lobby locally and nationally. While Herzfeld finds the roots of this phenomenon in the very social process of training and becoming an artisan and an entrepreneur in Crete, the 'impolitisation' among entrepreneurs in Alessandria is rooted in the context of the downturn.

While as Martini and Quaranta (2014) suggested present dissatisfaction could be seen as the result of long-term trends, such as poor economic performance nationally in the form of unemployment and inflation, the downturn that started in 2008 is perceived as a turning point; the discontent and retreat of entrepreneurs from political engagement has been sharpened by the worsening of the general economic situation. This response follows a general anthropological trend noted by Ferguson (1999) that links economic recession with the phenomenon of social disintegration. In particular, as Ferguson (1999) suggests, an economic crisis is a crisis of meaning 'in which the way that people are able to understand their experience and to imbue it with significance and dignity has (for many) been dramatically eroded' (Ferguson, 1999: 14). The experience expressed by Alessandria's entrepreneurs suggests that their erosion of political engagement is tied up with a sense of not feeling any responsibility towards a wider community, the state and even the same local entrepreneurial milieu to which they belong.

The experience of the economic crisis is linked with a new way among entrepreneurs of being and feeling in the world. Social scientists have often noticed a substantial politicization of entrepreneurs in Italy. In particular, anthropologists such as Shore (1990), Blim (1990) and more recently Muehlebach (2012) have documented a widespread solidarity and attitude towards aggregation and collaboration through which they were able to lobby for enforcing policies and reforms. This literature often looks at the period of the 1970s to 1990s while the last decade, and in particular the last five years, have been scarcely investigated from this perspective.[9] The experiences collected in the field suggest that this solidarity has been giving way to a rising individualism among entrepreneurs.

Scholars (e.g. Harvey, 2010; Graeber, 2011; Connerton,2009; and Hart *et al.*, 2010), reviewing the economic and social transformation of the past 30 years, have recognized the emergence of a new ethos fostered by the so-called neo-liberalism. The rise of neo-liberalism on the one hand has unleashed free market innovations, but on the other hand has increased social inequality. It has nourished an individualistic ethos among entrepreneurs and workers, eroding a sense of community and belonging to collective entities. This selfish model of the entrepreneur does not adequately characterize the behaviour of entrepreneurs in Alessandria.

Arguably, the shift in their entrepreneurial attitudes towards individualism is less due to the influence of a neo-liberal market philosophy and more a defence against the rapid crumbling of local social and economic links as businesses failed under financial crisis; cooperative relationships these entrepreneurs relied on to access markets and organize production workflows.

Experiencing a steep downturn, the demands on business associations during the downturn also changed as finding ways of discovering new markets or tools for marketing products became especially urgent. SMEs now saw their business associations and also the state as 'the last shore where to find help', but the both the associations and the state bodies seemed to lack the capacity or will to answer. The limitations presented by these public and private bodies seemed to mark the gradual rise of a widespread sense of disillusion, solitude and isolation that grew stronger during the worsening of the economic context.

The feeling of isolation thus corresponds to a sense of loss of direction in the face of the economic changes that these entrepreneurs experienced. Nesi (2010) suggests the crisis was a tragic realisation by the entrepreneurs of the Italian industrial weakness in the context of the complexity of the global market, and that the responsibility for this weakness lay on the shoulders of the state and the business associations who embraced the dream of globalization in the 1990s without preparing the county and its entrepreneurs for the challenges that globalized markets brought Similarly, my informants, mostly working in the manufacturing business, shared this conviction, growing from being a minority view in 2012, to a commonly held opinion in 2014. They lamented the failure of both the government, and the professional associations to give tools, help and information to help overcome the downturn, thus their substantial solitude in face of the crisis: feeling powerless, and of being alone against forces that overshadow them.

Reconsidering responsibility

Considering closely the rhetoric of the entrepreneurs, we notice that the local and global economies appear as an imminent, metaphysical machine in which local entrepreneurs appear as subjects of its dehumanized running, rather than its actors and motors. Thus, this interpretation of the economy ushers in a new anthropological understanding of the role of entrepreneurs in society. The sense of empowerment and prowess felt by entrepreneurs in the 1990s and early 2000s described by Bovero (1992), Garofoli (2004) and Gaggio (2007) led these entrepreneurs to a new understanding of their social role. Local entrepreneurs now portray themselves as victims of global transformations, innocent subjects who have to cope with a steep market downturn, finding themselves unable to face this change. This phenomenon emerges not just in Alessandria but across the entire nation (Bonomi 2013; Nesi, 2010), and this mode of understanding reflects a sense of powerlessness that erupted in entrepreneurs' everyday lives, cracking the mask of self-reliance, boldness, virility and swiftness that commonly distinguishes entrepreneurship in Italian culture (Molé, 2012): a crack that in other parts of Italy, as scholars (Bonomi, 2013; Bortolussi, 2012) and even the international press has reported,[10] has ended up with extreme acts, such as small business owners committing suicide.

If the particular vision of the world economy portrayed by the entrepreneurs does subordinate the local to the global, then the agency and, consequentially, any responsibility for driving change can no longer be attributed to local actors. On this basis, entrepreneurs are renegotiating their position in the world and in particular their sense of responsibility towards the rest of society. In other words, in light of their now diminished status, entrepreneurs began to reconsider their responsibilities towards society, and to ask for more protection from the state and the society against the effects of the downturn. In particular, from the interviews it emerges that the radius of the sphere of SME responsibility has shrunk. In his seminal work, Sahlins (1972) pointed out that the methods of reciprocity were directly linked with spatial and kinship distance. Thus, an individual's sense of responsibility toward others decreases when spatial distance increases and social intimacy decreases. In the early interviews the discourse of responsibility among the entrepreneurs encompassed social spaces such as the parish and the neighbourhood and a strong emphasis was given to the welfare of suppliers and clients. In more recent interviews, the discourse had profoundly changed and the commitment of the entrepreneurs was described in more limited terms, only to their employees and the entrepreneurs' families. Their rhetoric paints a landscape marked by a profound sense of danger and difficulty, such as that of the forager who must hunt in a hostile forest in order to provide food to the family.

Conclusion

This chapter opened with a question: what happens to business responsibility in a context of economic crisis? This ethnographic analysis suggests the erosion and transformation of the cultural foundations of business or corporate responsibility towards society. The transformation lies in the isolation described by entrepreneurs of the Alessandria province. This rhetoric describes a relational space between entrepreneurs and society at large in which the bonds among actors are weakening. Although entrepreneurs suggest the emptiness of social relationships that fill this space is a product of systemic transformation, the weakening of social bonds is the result of a twofold process. First, the inability of the state, professional associations and civil society at large to answer the demands of entrepreneurs, making them feel 'isolated' in facing transformations of the international and national market. Second, the very process of entrepreneurs feeling powerless has accentuated their own marginalization, and thus their inability of finding answers for their needs in other actors.

After the mid-2000s scholars, mostly economists, have focused on this ongoing transformation and identified a reorganization in the structure of industrial districts and SMEs in Italy (e.g. Bianchi, 2009; Rabellotti *et al.*, 2009; Ramazzotti, 2008). Some transformations of national and international markets[11] have led to a progressive marginalization of those (generally small) firms not provided with the managerial tools, some competitive advantage (e.g. recognizable brands and direct access to the market) and financial resources for competing in the global market (Gereffi, 2007). While scholars have focused on the economic basis for the marginalization of SMEs in Italy, the analysis here of the rhetoric of entrepreneurial isolation shows the marginalisation processes as comprising both political and social dimensions. The SMEs seeing themselves as being subordinated to economic forces they are unable to govern or modify (rather than as economic motors of change) feeds a sense of disempowerment shared by the entrepreneurs that makes them perceive themselves as subjects of the market and consequentially free from responsibilities to society at large. The economic crisis thus not only causes an economic decline and shrinking of enterprises but also marks a social involution of entrepreneurs' sense of social responsibility, who no longer see their roles carrying any responsibility towards society at large, only to the restricted sphere of their families and their employees. Thus, the 2009–2014 period leaves behind an economic and social landscape in which the social capital and the very social prominence of SMEs have been eroded. The ongoing social phenomena this research has highlighted leads to a political and economic system in which entrepreneurs are turning into passive subjects unable to become a pressure group in the political domain.

The present holds a space of silence and at the moment it is difficult to imagine that a new sound that fills this emptiness can originate from marginalized entrepreneurs. In order to better understand the future of SMEs, their sense of marginalization as outlined in this chapter has to be further explored.

In the past SMEs have thrived thanks to the ability of using social capital to create vast production networks. While the crisis has all but destroyed entrepreneurial social capital and eroded their sense of social responsibility, the question that emerges is about exploring methods to rekindle the sense of responsibility and strengthen social capital among entrepreneurs. Further, how can we reignite their passion for creating economic and social value? Moreover, this research has focused primarily on the business community. While entrepreneurs do play a fundamental role in shaping an economy and its social fabric, other actors have also to be scrutinized. In particular, what role can civil and civic societies play in breaking the isolation of the entrepreneurs? In the answers to these questions we may find the sounds to pierce the silence.

Notes

1 For a detailed explanation: Fontefrancesco, 2013b.
2 www.regione.piemonte.it
3 An example of these initiative is the ERDF regional operative programme 2007–2013 of the Activity 1.3 'Innovation and SMEs' of the Axis I "Innovation and production transition" (http://www.regione.piemonte.it/industria/). Overall, the Regional Council has financed the Axis I actions with €497,985,496 over the seven years.
4 'Stable negativity for the enterprises', *Il Piccolo*, 24 April 2013, p. 12.
5 'Building industry slashed: job positions halved', *Radiogold*, 27 November 2014, www.radiogold.it.
6 'Artisan industry: clouded future', *Il Monferrato*, 8 January 2013, p. 8.
7 Data from Confartigianato's *Compendio dati statistici artigianato piemontese* July 2009, July 2012, 2014
8 Data from Istat's online database, *Unemployment rate – provincial level*, (http://dati. istat.it), last access 30/11/2014
9 For a detailed review of the current literature about SME and industrial districts in Italy: Fontefrancesco, 2013.
10 For example. Elisabetta Povoledo and Doreen Carvajal, 'Increasingly in Europe, suicides 'by economic crisis'" *The New York Times*, 14 April 2012.

11 Such as the disappearance of competitive advantage secured by protectionist measures and devaluation policies adopted by the Italian government from the 1950s to the late 1990s, and the intensifying competition in national and international markets (Gereffi, 2007).

References

Assessorato al Lavoro, 2011, *Articolouno 6: avanti piano* (Provincia di Alessandria, Alessandria, Italy).

Becattini G, 1978, 'The development of light industry in Tuscany: an interpretation' *Economic Notes* 7 (2–3): 107–23.

Becattini G, 2006, 'Industrial district', in J Beckert, M Zafirovski (eds), *International encyclopedia of economic sociology* (Routledge, London).

Becattini G, Bellandi M, De Propris L, 2009, *A handbook of industrial districts* (Edward Elgar, Cheltenham, UK).

Bertaux D, 1999, *Racconti di vita. La prospettiva etnosociologica* (Franco Angeli, Milan, Italy).

Bianchi P, 2009, 'Crisi economica e politica industriale' *Quaderni Deit* 21.

Blim M, 1990, *Made in Italy: small-scale industrialization and its consequences* (Praeger, New York).

Bocchio A, 2014, *Torna a crescere il numero delle imprese* (Camera di Commercio, Alessandria, Italy).

Bortolussi G, 2012, *L'economia dei suicidi : piccoli imprenditori in crisi* (Marcianum Press, Venice, Italy).

Bonomi A, 2013, *Il capitalism in-finito. Indagine sui territori della crisi* (Einaudi, Turin, Italy).

Bourdieu P, 1999, *The weight of the world* (Polity Press, Cambridge).

Bovero S, 1992, *Vivere a Valenza: Mondo Orafo e Disagio Urbano* (Unità Socio-Sanitaria Locale N.71, Valenza, Italy).

Campbell B, 2010, 'Rhetorical routes for development: a road project in Nepal' *Contemporary South Asia* 18 (3) 267–79.

Carrithers, M, 2005, 'Why anthropologists should study rhetoric' *Journal of the Royal Anthropological Institute* 11 (3) 577–83.

Carrithers M, 2009, *Culture, rhetoric, and the vicissitudes of life* (Berghahn Books, New York).

Carrithers M, Bracken L J, Emery S, 2011, 'Can a species be a person? A trope and its entanglements in the Anthropocene era' *Current Anthropology* 52 (5) 661–85.

Centro Studi CNA, 2014, *Comune che vai fisco che trovi* (Osservatorio permanente CNA sulla tassazione delle Piccole Imprese in Italia, Rome).

Connerton P, 2009, *How modernity forgets* (Cambridge University Press, Cambridge).

Constantelos J, 2004, 'The Europeanization of interest group politics in Italy: business associations in Rome and the regions' *Journal of European Public Policy* 11 (6) 1020–1040.

Cunliffe A L, 2002, 'Social poetics: a dialogical approach to management inquiry' *Journal of Management Inquiry* 11 (2) 128–46.

De Vincenzi R, Iadevaia V, 2014, 'Modelli di governance regionale per la gestione degli ammortizzatori sociali in deroga e apprendimenti istituzionali'. Paper for the Espanet Conference *Sfide alla cittadinanza e trasformazione dei corsi di vita: precarietà, invecchiamento e migrazioni*, Università degli Studi di Torino, Torino, 18–20 Settembre 2014. Online: http://isfoloa.isfol.it/handle/123456789/934. Last accessed 6 January 2015.

Ferguson J, 1999, *Expectations of modernity: myths and meanings of urban life on the Zambian Copperbelt* (University of California Press, Berkeley, CA).

Fergusson F, 1961, 'Introduction', in F Fergusson (ed.), *Aristotle's Poetics* (Hill and Wang, New York).

Fondazione, G P and The European House Ambrosetti, 2011, *2° Forum: La Valorizzazione Del Monferrato Per Lo Sviluppo Della Provincia Di Alessandria* (Fondazione Cassa di Risparmio di Alessandria, Alessandria, Italy).

Fontefrancesco M F, 2013a, *The end of the city of gold? industry and economic crisis in an italian jewellery town* (Cambridge Scholars, Newcastle upon Tyne, UK).

Fontefrancesco M F, 2013b, 'Accesso al lavoro al tempo della Crisi: un'etnografia di esperienze e cambiamenti'. *Narrare i Gruppi* 7 (1): 64–77.

Gaggio D, 2007, *In gold we trust: social capital and economic change in the Italian Jewelry Towns* (Princeton University Press, Princeton, NJ).

Garofoli G, 2004, *Il distretto orafo di Valenza: tendenze evolutive e prospettive* (Franco Angeli, Milan, Italy).

Gereffi G, 2007, 'La catena del valore dell'ro e del gioiello nel distretto di Valenza' *Newsletter dell'Osservatorio del Distretto di Valenza* 1 (1) 20–44.

Graeber D, 2011, *Debt: the first 5,000 years* (Melville House, New York).

Grimaldi P, Porporato D, 2012, *Granai della memoria: Manuale di Umanità 2.0* (Università degli Studi di Scienze Gastronomiche, Pollenzo-Bra, Italy).

Gudeman S, 2009, *Economic persuasions* (Berghahn Books, New York).

Hart K, Laville J-L, Cattani A D, 2010, *The human economy* (Polity, Cambridge).

Harvey D, 2010, *The enigma of capital and the crises of capitalism* (Profile, London).

Herzfeld M, 1997, *Cultural intimacy: social poetics* (Routledge, London).

Herzfeld M, 2004, *The body impolitic: artisans and artifice in the global hierarchy of value* (University of Chicago Press, Chicago, IL).

Katz A M, Shotter J, 1996, 'Hearing the patient's "voice": towards a social poetics in diagnostic interviews' *Social Science Medicine* 43 (6) 919–31.

Knoblauch H, 2005, 'Focused ethnography' *Forum Qualitative Social Research* 6 (3) 1–14.

Martini S, Quaranta M, 2014, 'Finding out the hard way: uncovering the structural foundations of political dissatisfaction in italy, 1973–2013' *West European Politics* 38 (1) 28–52.

Molé N J, 2012, *Labor disorders in neoliberal Italy : mobbing, well-being, and the workplace* (Indiana University Press, Bloomington, IN).

Muehlebach A K, 2012, *The moral neoliberal : welfare and citizenship in Italy* (University of Chicago Press, Chicago, IL).

Nesi E, 2010, *Storia della mia gente* (Bompiani, Milan, Italy).

Pardo I, 1996, *Managing existence in Naples: morality, action, and structure* (Cambridge University Press, Cambridge).

Perulli P, Picchieri A, 2010, *La crisi italiana nel mondo globale* (Einaudi, Turin, Italy).

Piore M, Sable C F, 1984, *The second industrial divide* (Basic Books, New York).

Rabellotti R, Carabelli A, Hirsh G, 2009, 'Italian industrial districts on the move: where are they going' *European Planning Studies* 17 (1) 19–41.

Ramazzotti P, 2008, 'Industrial district and economic decline in italy' *Quaderni del Dipartimento di Istituzioni Economiche e Finanziarie* 45 2–32.

Sahlins M D, 1972, *Stone age economics* (Aldine, Chicago, IL).

Shore C, 1990, *Italian communism: the escape from Leninism : an anthropological perspective* (Pluto, London).

Shotter J, 1996, 'Living in a Wittgensteinian world: beyond theory to a poetics of practices' *Journal for the Theory of Social Behaviour* 26 (3) 293–311.

4 Locating local community interests between government's assurances and investor's expectations

Ciprian N. Radavoi

What community wants – does it really matter?

From a stakeholder theory perspective, the myriad codes of conduct at company, industry and United Nations level, recommending 'stakeholder engagement' and 'community engagement', suggest that local residents have a strong say in an investment affecting their community. The status of the local community has apparently evolved during the last three decades, if we think that local community was not even listed in the stakeholder chart in Freeman's foundational book (Freeman 1984: 56), and it was only briefly mentioned as a dependent stakeholder in another influential work building upon Freeman's in the 1990s (Mitchell *et al.* 1997: 865). The yearly quantity of studies dedicated to community engagement also seems to confirm that the 'Principle of Who or What Really Counts' (Freeman 1984) has gathered momentum over time: from one study in 1984 and less than five per year until 2000, there have been over 30 up to around 2010 (Bowen *et al.* 2010: 301). As for the investors, commitments like 'obtaining local community support is an important goal'[1] are commonplace in their corporate responsibility statements. But from scholars to companies or governmental officials, everybody seems shy about asking a simple question: What happens when the community denies support, and their refusal is for environmental reasons?

In approaching this matter, we examine two recent and similar cases of foreign investment in which the local community has tried to have a say. These cases suggest the difficulty of balancing economic growth, social needs and environmental protection; that is, of adopting a sustainable path of development. The examples are by no means extraordinary, but their temporal and geographical proximity highlight the scope of the local community for influencing the final investment decision between the economic and environmental arguments.

Rosia Montana is a commune in the north-west of Romania, comprising 16 villages. The area also holds over 17 million ounces of gold, according to Gabriel Resources,[2] the Canadian investor who has been struggling for years to begin its exploitation, in spite of initial authorizations from the Romanian government. The final strike in the heart of the project was given by the Romanian Parliament, in November 2013, rejecting a proposed law that would have given a green light to the project. The stated reason for this rejection was the public opinion's vehement opposition to the project, mainly for environmental reasons.[3] The use of cyanide to extract gold is a topic to which Romanians are extremely sensitive after the Baia Mare disaster in 2000,[4] so hundreds of Romanians took to the streets in most of the major cities, exerting a strong pressure on the authorities. Interestingly, the local community offered strong support for the project: a field research undertaken by specialists from Exeter University in 2011 revealed that some 80 per cent of the locals were in favour of the project.[5] Opposition was found only at the level of non-governmental organizations (NGOs) (Adey *et al.* 2011), who were putting out appeals to an already sensitive national public opinion and exerting an intense presence in the national and international media.

Only some 300 kilometres to the east, on the other side of the Carpathians, Pungesti is a village in north-eastern Romania. In April 2014, the US-based energy giant Chevron began exploring for shale gas in spite of fierce protests by virtually all the local community, from peasants to priests and local administration. Similarly to the Rosia Montana case, Chevron had initially obtained the necessary permits from the government (in October 2013) but immediately after, more than 800 locals, priests and activists gathered in front of the empty lot where Chevron was planning to install the well, fearing that chemicals used in the fracking process would damage their environment.[6] After several clashes between the locals and the riot police, in which tens of villagers were allegedly beaten,[7] the government managed to eliminate the protests so Chevron could resume operations.

Looking at the two cases in parallel, the sad irony is that in the first one the locals will not get the project, although they wanted it, while in the second they got it, although they fought hard against it. Seen in a national perspective, these cases highlight the tensions between the community's interest and what the government or the majority sees as national interest. These cases also raise the human rights issue of the community's right to protest.

However, when put in an international context, these cases also shine a light on the frailty of another right: the doctrine of investor's legitimate expectations. Basically, the doctrine establishes that the investor should be able to rely in good faith on government assurances and consequently allocate resources in the host country, and should be protected against sudden and unilateral changes of the 'rules of the game'.

Investor's 'legitimate expectations' and local community opposition

The second of the scenarios above has been presented in several cases of international investment arbitration when the host government, unlike in Romania, chose to halt the investment.

Bilateral investment treaties (BITs) are entered into, from the perspective of the capital exporting states, in order to secure safe conditions for their investors.

An often put forward argument is that since the investors bear the commercial risk, it is fair to have them protected from the political one, that is, the risk of having its investment damaged by injurious actions by the host authorities or third parties in the recipient country (Salacuse 2010: 109). Of most concern for investors are, according to MIGA-EIU Political Risk Survey 2013,[8] adverse regulatory changes, breach of contract and civil disturbance. A local community mobilizing against an investment in its vicinity, plus consequences such as termination of contract by the government, may qualify for all the three circumstances most feared by investors. Investors are protected against such events by the doctrine of 'legitimate expectations', even when they did not have a contract but mere assurances from the authorities. In the last decade this doctrine has become widely used by arbitral tribunals in the field of international investment law.

Under BITs, a breach of the vague and omnipresent standard of 'fair and equitable treatment' (FET) owed to the investor can be found by investment arbitral tribunals when the host government fails to meet the investor's legitimate expectations. This is because from being a mere interpretive tool rarely used in investment arbitration, the legitimate expectations principle has lately become a self-standing subcategory and independent basis for a claim under the fair and equitable standard (*Thunderbird*, Separate Opinion of Thomas Wälde, para. 37). Investor's legitimate expectations can be derived 'from general legislation and regulations, any undertakings or representations made explicitly or implicitly by the host State, or even of a mixture of these factors' (Dolzer and Schreuer 2008: 134). More specifically, there are three types of scenarios in existing case law: first, when the government takes some contractual commitments, for example issuing a permit; second, expectations are derived from unilateral declarations of the host state, for example assurances that such a project has governmental support; and third, expectations are created by the existence of the regulatory framework per se (Potestà 2013: 90). The first two, differentiated only by the level of formality, are of relevance for this chapter.

The increased criticism (e.g., Zeyl 2011; Sornarajah 2010)[9] lately directed against the use of 'legitimate expectations' in international investment arbitration does not seem to have affected court practice, where virtually all awards make some reference to this concept. One may, however, sympathize with judges: they are given, in BITs, a standard comprising two words, *fair* and *equitable*, that could mean anything and they have to operationalize it somehow. While the main critique against legal judgments translating 'fair and equitable' as 'meeting the investor's legitimate expectations' was that it represents an arbitrary importation of a doctrine from the administrative law of a limited number of countries (see e.g., Zeyl 2011), other authors argue that we should not be bothered by this aspect, since 'in extrapolating a general principle of law from rules of municipal law one need not establish actual universality of application of identical rules' (Snodgrass 2006: 21). In fact, the doctrine's origin was actually never mentioned in arbitral awards. Rather, it is seen by investment law professionals (Dolzer and Schreuer 2008: 122) as encompassing good faith and partly overlapping with the notion of *non venire contra factum proprium* (no one may set himself in contradiction to his own previous conduct, also known as the principle of estoppel): since the host willingly created some expectations in order to induce the investor to commit resources, the investor relied on the host's representations, making the latter bound by its promises or inducements, however vaguely given. Moreover, the idea of stability, expressly tied to 'fair and equitable treatment' in some treaties,[10] apparently reconfirms that 'legitimate expectations' can be seen as part of the 'fair and equitable treatment'.

So the problem should be its application, rather than its origin. Here, the criticism raised by scholars (Spronk and Crespo 2008; Chodhury 2008) and international NGOs[11] is the severe restriction on the host's freedom of action in times of economic crisis,[12] or more generally, action to protect legitimate general interests like preservation of the natural environment.[13] The balance between host government's right to vary policy in fields like environmental protection, on the one hand, and the investor's right to be compensated when such actions interfere with their business, on the other, is extensively debated in case law or legal and political theory (for an overview of the issue see Chodhury 2008: 792–6). But the weight that should be afforded local community views (especially their objections) that may have initiated reversals in government policy is not established. Courts, as seen below, prefer to avoid the topic of community protest, unless the scale of protest and violence forces their hand.

Local community action and arbitral tribunals

The cases in which local protests over environmental issues have played a decisive role in an investment failure are not numerous. This scarcity reflects the host governments' willingness to deal with these protests, as in the Romanian Pungesti case, in a manner desired by the investor, or 'legitimately expected' from the investor's perspective,[14] and very often supported by arbitral tribunals. In the few cases existing, the awards refer to the community protest either *en passant* (*Metalclad*) or in a belittling way (*Tecmed*), as examined below. In another case where there was a large-scale community mobilization, the tribunal chose to not refer at all to community action (*Gallo*). These cases highlight that merely reading the body of the arbitral decision can be misleading. In order to better understand the facts in their real context, one needs recourse to a variety of sources, such as newspaper articles or NGO reports.

Metalclad, award in 2000: largely ignoring the community protest

'Demonstrators impeded the "inauguration", blocked the entry and exit of buses carrying guests and workers, and employed tactics of intimidation against Metalclad' (*Metalclad*, para. 46). The quote refers to actions having occurred in March 1995, and is the only reference made in the 2000 NAFTA arbitral award acknowledging the local community voicing its discontent in the case. Metalclad had bought the Mexican company COTERIN in 1993 with the intention of continuing to operate its waste management business and landfill, so the strong opposition of the local community, loudly voiced as early as 1991,[15] should have been relevant in the case. In the end, the project succumbed as the local authorities stood by the community and refused to issue the permits. The fact that, as asserted by Metalclad, the investor was given assurances by the state environmental agency 'that the responsibility for obtaining project support in the state and local community lay with the federal government' (*Metalclad*, para. 34) was the determining factor in the tribunal's ruling in favour of the investor:

> Metalclad was entitled to rely on the representations of federal officials and to believe that it was entitled to continue its construction of the landfill. In following the advice of these officials, and filing the municipal permit application on November 15, 1994, Metalclad was merely acting prudently and in the full expectation that the permit would be granted.
>
> (*Metalclad*, para. 89)[16]

As one scholar observes, had the tribunal taken into consideration the circumstances, that is, the local residents' constant opposition and the project's history, Metalclad's application would not have looked so prudent and reasonable as expectations:

> The tribunal made little mention of the troubles that gave rise to the local populace's opposition to Metalclad's operation. Yet this local opposition entirely was foreseeable given the hazardous way in which Metalclad's predecessor, COTERIN, had managed hazardous waste (. . .) The tribunal would not admit that local resistance to the operation of the facility on public health grounds . . . could not have caught Metalclad by surprise.
>
> (Schneiderman 2008: 84)

As Schneiderman highlights, the tribunal would not entertain the idea that Metalclad should have known about the local opposition, perhaps because to do so would go beyond the scope of the doctrine. The tribunal mentions Metalclad's expectations in other several instances, using formulations such as 'reasonably-to-be-expected economic benefit of property' (para. 103) or 'an investor of a Party acting in the expectation that it would be treated fairly and justly' (para. 99). The latter formulation suggests some sort of relation between investor's expectations and the FET standard of protection, but not the strong link – almost equivalence – that was to be established in *Tecmed*, and constantly used thereafter.

Tecmed award in 2003: belittling the community protest

In *Tecmed*, the tribunal on the contrary permanently had in focus the community's opposition to the landfill of hazardous waste that Cytrar, a subsidiary of a Spanish corporation, had already been operating for one year. Noting that '[t]he community's opposition to the Landfill, in its public manifestations, was widespread and aggressive, as evidenced by several events at different times' (para. 108), the tribunal goes on to describe the events in several paragraphs, to conclude that 'one of the essential causes for which the renewal of the Permit was denied was its proximity and the community pressure related thereto' (para. 117). Aside from the alleged toxic spills and other landfill misuse, what enraged the local populace was its location: only 8 kilometres from the city, although the law required a minimum of 25 kilometres.

The tribunal then states that it will perform an examination of the proportionality between such social pressure and the government reaction, in order to decide upon the expropriatory character of the denial of permit renewal. When putting these on the balance, the protest dimension is presented as less impressive than it looked in the previous paragraphs, as if the tribunal looks now through the opposite end of the binocular:

> Even after having gained substantial momentum, community opposition, although it had been sustained by its advocates through an insistent, active and continuous public campaign in the mass media, could gather on two occasions a crowd of only two hundred people the first time and of four hundred people, the second time out of a community with a population of almost one million inhabitants, '. . . which makes it the city with the highest population in the state of Sonora'. Additionally, the 'blockage' of the Landfill was carried out by small groups of no more than forty people. The absence of any evidence that the operation of the Landfill was a real or potential threat to the environment or to the public health, coupled with the absence of massive opposition, limits 'community pressure' to a series of events, which, although they amount to significant pressure on the Mexican author-ities, do not constitute a real crisis or disaster of great proportions, triggered by acts or omissions committed by the foreign investor or its affiliates.
>
> (*Tecmed*, para. 144)

This paragraph is largely ignored in later jurisprudence or the literature referring to this arbitral case, but is highly relevant to the present discussion, as it inadvertently sets a threshold above which a community may veto a project due to environmental concerns. According to the judges in *Tecmed*, the opposition needs to be 'massive' (which seems to be determined by calculating the fraction the protesters represent in the total population of the city), to lead to 'a real crisis or disaster of great proportions', and to originate in some investor's wrongful acts or omissions. Obviously, such standard, similar to a state of necessity defense threshold (or even above, given the requirement of the investor's fault) is very difficult to meet by any local environmental protest.

The tribunal made history, however, by being the first one clearly linking the FET standard to the protection of investor's legitimate expectations, using the good faith as cement to tie the two notions together:

> [T]he commitment of fair and equitable treatment (. . .), in light of the good faith principle established by international law, requires the Contracting

Parties to provide to international investments treatment that does not affect the basic expectations that were taken into account by the foreign investor to make the investment (. . .) The foreign investor also expects the host State to act consistently, i.e. without arbitrarily revoking any preexisting decisions or permits issued by the State that were relied upon by the investor to assume its commitments as well as to plan and launch its commercial and business activities.

Having found that the local community pressure was not above the threshold it determined (possibly unconsciously), the tribunal ruled that the non-renewal of the permit as a reaction to this pressure was an arbitrary decision, and so upheld Tecmed's claim for compensation.

Gallo award in 2011: community protest seen as irrelevant

The tribunal in *Gallo* was luckier, as the circumstances in the case allowed it to find a lack of jurisdiction without any need to count the number of Aboriginals having attended the environmental protests that led to the alleged expropriation. The investment came soon after a highly controversial decision of Toronto city council allowing shipping of more than 20 million tonnes of garbage over 20 years to the abandoned Adams Mine, almost 400 kilometres north, in the lands of the First Nations. Prior to and after the decision, the Natives have shown their opposition in various ways, from rallies to railroad blockades,[17] the protests culminating 'in the largest act of civil disobedience in Ontario history' (Anderson and Grusky 2007: 10). It is under these circumstances that in 2002, the investor purchased the Adams Mine, which already had certain administrative approvals required for its use as a waste disposal site. In 2004 however, the Ontario legislature passed the Adams Mine Lake Act, prohibiting the disposal of waste at the Adams Mine. The tribunal found that the investing company was, in fact, Canadian, since the alleged American investor 'has failed to marshal convincing evidence that at the time of enactment of the AMLA he [Mr. *Vito Gallo*] was the owner of the Enterprise' (*Gallo*, para. 336) so it accepted the respondent's objection to jurisdiction. It did that without having to examine the relation between local protests on the one hand, and the investor's expectations being frustrated by the governmental prohibition, on the other.

Rosia Montana and the question of 'who' constitutes the local community

In the above cases, the investor probably knew that the local community's opposition to the project is at a scale that leaves no room for negotiation or mitigation, and still carried on, based on governmental assurances of various kinds. While it is generally admitted that the investor's diligent conduct is relevant to the application of the legitimate expectations doctrine (Potestà 2013: 118), situations of this kind are not among those in which arbitral tribunals found the expectations as unreasonable. Rather, the due diligence seems to refer to a general analysis of the broad 'political, socio-economic, cultural and historical conditions prevailing in the host state' (*Duke*, para. 340); even when the claim of legitimate expectations failed in circumstances related to citizens pressuring for environmental protection, the failure was not based on some unfulfilled requirement to consult with the community, but because the 'Claimant was operating in a climate that was becoming more and more sensitive to the environmental consequences of open-pit mining' (*Glamis*, para. 767), which led to changes in the country's legal framework.

Reasonableness is the core element in a claim of legitimate expectations breach, as 'legitimate expectations cannot be solely the subjective expectations of the investor' (*EDF*, para. 219). When weighing reasonableness, arbitral tribunals tend to focus indeed on wider economical, social and political aspects that define the host's general level of development. Arguably, in cases of deep, violent and notorious local opposition to a particular project, there is no reason not to include it among the accepted limits to legitimate expectations. Whether reasonableness is assessed objectively (requiring a diligent and prudent investor) or subjectively (expectations required to not conflict with other knowledge the investor had about the representations made by the host state – Snodgrass 2006: 41), carrying on a project to which community opposition is fierce and notorious seems to be stepping beyond the limits of the legitimate expectations principle.

But assessing the reasonableness of expectations may be difficult in some circumstances, as the recent case of Rosia Montana shows. If it makes it to ICSID arbitration, this case will probably be also decided by application of the 'legitimate expectations' doctrine, and it may lead to a record US$4 billion compensation if one is to believe the bellicose statements of the investor's chief executive officer (CEO).[18] As shown before, governmental assurances were in this case in line with the local community's support for the project, and it was only the mobilization of the national and international civil society that pressured the country's leadership to stepping back and halting the project. This case illustrates the difficulties of establishing what is the local community. Geographically speaking, the term *fenceline* communities, proposed by Friends of the Earth (2006), is a suggestive description of the local community consisting of people in the immediate location of an investment project – although one may ask how far from the project site should we draw this fence, as neighbouring and even further regions may also be affected. But even accepting that this imaginary border can be accurately located, numerous variables within the 'fence' make identification of the 'community' a difficult task. Aside from being members of that local community, individuals have a multitude of other identities (Calvano 2008: 794) – jobseekers, consumers, parents, educators and other groups – which may generate divergent attitudes towards an investment affecting their environment.

Moreover, the initiation of an open conflict and its success may depend on another variable, namely the degree of community organization, sometimes stimulated by external factors such as NGOs or even competitors of the investors.[19]

Evolutions in governmental responsibility, and their impact on 'legitimate expectations'

Cases of widespread and violent opposition rarely make it to investment arbitration, as noted before, and this may be a justification for courts to bypass the topic of local protest and resolve the claims through other legal or contractual provisions (as in *Metalclad* or *Gallo*). But what if the investor was under an obligation to assess the local community support for their project, prior to committing any resources? In such a scenario, all cases of immitigable opposition would be known in advance, and not only the notorious ones. Would it still be legitimate for the investor to rely on governmental assurances that the project can be implemented?

The answer may come from China and its 'Guidelines for Environmental Protection in Foreign Investment and Cooperation' (GEPFIC), jointly launched in 2013 by the Ministry of Commerce and the Ministry of Environmental Protection, and rather ignored by corporate responsibility scholars. As early as 2008, one scholar noted that 'expectations that investors should be good corporate citizens and respect the emergent principles of international corporate social responsibility (. . .) represent a benchmark by which the conduct of multinational enterprises will increasingly be judged in the future' (Muchlinsky 2006: 535). In building a strategy of host country defence against a FET claim based on the investor's conduct, the author pointed to international codes of conduct, especially the OECD Guidelines for Multinational Enterprises, and to corporate and industry codes as a source of standards against which to assess the investor's conduct: a general duty to obey the law, to pay taxes, to act in accordance with fundamental labour standards and to observe human rights principles.

To the extent that the principles contained in these documents become widely accepted, they may indeed be incorporated in a defence against a FET claim. Both the ICJ Statute, in article 38,[20] and the Restatement (Third) of the United States, in Section 102(4)[21] provide for that defence, but universal adoption may be frustrated by the so called North-South divide in terms of 'the conceptual and practical gap existing between the developed and developing countries in relation to corporate social responsibility' (Gugler and Shi 2009: 3). To take the example of labour standards, China for instance has not ratified four, out of the eight international conventions seen as fundamental by International Labour Organization (ILO).

However, since China adopted the environmental guidelines in 2013, we may observe changing attitudes to environmental responsibility. Acknowledging its difficulties in dealing with labour or human rights issues against Western standards, China 'decoupled' the environment in its guidelines for overseas investors (Radavoi and Bian 2014), thus bringing at least this field in line with international norms. The OECD Guidelines for Multinational Enterprises have now a Chinese counterpart in the environmental field (GEPFIC), and this is an extraordinary step towards convergence of standards, since the OECD countries and China represent the home countries of the huge majority of investors.[22] By sending the same message as the OECD, China contributes to one of the main requirements of customary international law making: repetition. As one specialist put it some decades ago, 'the recalling of guidelines adopted by other apparently concurrent international authorities, recurrent invocation of the same rules formulated in one way or another at the universal, regional and more restricted levels, all tend progressively to develop and establish a common international understanding' (Dupuy 1991: 424–26).

One of the common standards established by the two guidelines is the requirement that the foreign investor makes timely contact with communities likely to be affected by the investment. In article 20 of the Chinese document, investors are advocated to

> . . . establish a way of communication and dialogue mechanism for enterprises' environmental social responsibilities, take the initiative to strengthen their contacts and communications with their communities and relevant social groups, and take opinions and suggestions with respect to environmental impacts of their construction projects and operation activities through forums and hearings according to requirements of laws and regulations of the host country.

As for the OECD Guidelines, the chapter on environmental concerns provides that enterprises should '[e]ngage in adequate and timely communication and consultation with the communities directly affected by the environmental, health and safety policies of the enterprise and by their implementation' (OECD Guidelines 2011: 42). Once we admit that governmental responsibility does evolve, through convergence of rules[23] and constant practice,[24] towards some form of customary soft law, the aforementioned 'Caveat Investor' must be updated to include the obligation to consult the community, and from here, the inference that in cases of fierce and beyond mitigation opposition, the investor knew these circumstances, or at least ought to have known.

Significantly both guidelines require timely engagement with the local community: the OECD is explicit on this matter, while in the Chinese text, this can be inferred from its purpose, namely to 'take opinions and suggestions'. But timing is also critical to the legitimate expectations doctrine as applied in arbitral disputes on foreign investments, according to numerous and convergent tribunal judgments. For example, *Enron v. Argentine* speaks about 'expectations derived from the conditions that were offered by the state to the investor at the time of the investment' (*Enron*, para. 262), while *Duke v. Ecuador* makes it clear that '[t]o be protected, the investor's expectations must be legitimate and reasonable at the time when the investor makes the investment' (*Duke*, para. 340). Even admitting that time of the investment is not a clear-cut notion, especially in investments made in several steps (Schreuer and Kriebaum 2010), it appears that before committing considerable resources pursuant to government representations, investors should be aware they are on a potentially dead-end road.

We should be minded that the expectations are legitimate when government representations, be they contractual or mere verbal assurances, were given in order to induce the investor to commit. Courts speak of inducement, in formulations like 'clear and explicit representations made by or attributable to the NAFTA host State in order to induce the investment' (*Mobil*, para. 152) – but since the investor knew, or should know, the situation in the field at an early stage, can they be like Snow White innocently accepting the poisonous apple from the government? This situation where an investor is tempted by government inducement, but aware there is beyond-mitigation opposition at the location of proposed operations, invites a reconsideration of the limits of legitimate expectations.

For *Tecmed*, *Metalclad* or *Gallo*, the fact that locals are not willing to negotiate over their environment should have been known, as it was notorious. But from now, with the emerging requirement that investors gain local support becoming universal in governmental guidelines for investors, the notoriety of the conflict should not matter any longer: all cases of immitigable local opposition on environmental grounds are supposed to be known to the investor. By application of the rule that the investor must take the host country as he finds it, if he decides to carry on with the investment in spite of a volatile or hostile environment, the risks he assumes could be seen as business rather than political.

This scenario inevitably brings the analysis to the field of good faith as far as the investor actions post-contact with community are concerned. From a contract theory perspective (contract as accepted promise, where the promise is the governmental representation, and the acceptance is the initial allocation of investor's resources), distinction should be made, according to Barak-Erez (2005), between expectation damages (compensating financial loss incurred due to frustration of the expectation to profit from the contract) and reliance damages (compensating financial loss resulting from costs incurred due to reliance on the contract). The investor, as party to a contract, has a duty to mitigate damages once aware of the other party's inability to perform the contract, therefore said investor could be seen as being entitled to reliance damages only for actions undertaken until the moment when they (the investor) knew, or ought to have known, of the other party's inability. From an economic theory perspective, good faith could bring about a discussion on moral hazard: the investor might be tempted to undertake projects in spite of the insurmountable hindrances, in order to attain profitability in the form of compensation, without any economic efficiency, by mere activation of the 'insurance' provided by the government representations (Bonnitcha 2011).

From a political and governance perspective, the investor may claim that governmental representations override local opposition, and it was not for them to ascertain the legitimacy of the government's assurances. In practice, some governments indeed find a way to impose the contested project if the investor fails to obtain local consent, usually by use of force. One may question the legitimacy, in a plain meaning, of an investor's 'expectation' that the army or the riot police should be employed to impose their project.

Discussion: the right to veto within and beyond the limits of international investment law

Some of the preceding discussion needs revisiting. First, it is too early to speak of a North–South convergence of rules regarding timely engagement with the local community, although the signal coming from the Chinese environmental guidelines is a strong one. Second, one may ask what could be the relevance of an investor's awareness of local opposition, when even expectations conflicting with laws were upheld by arbitral tribunals. There are at least two cases in which courts saw the legitimate expectations of the investor as overriding existing local regulations when these were in conflict with the investment project's aim and scope. In *MTD v. Chile*, the claimant won the arbitration based on legitimate expectations created by the city administration's assurances, although they were in conflict with local regulations on real estate development. In *Tecmed v. Mexico*, the investor knew the law requiring a minimum of 26 kilometres between the waste dump and the city, but again he won because he had obtained a permit to operate the site even though it was only 8 kilometres from the city.

Third, and most important, as long as the discussion is contained to the international investment law field, the BITs system is built like a spider web that makes it difficult for the host government to escape liability. If the legitimate expectations principle is found inapplicable for the reasons highlighted in the previous sections, the investor has other avenues for their claims. For instance, courts may find a breach of the full protection and security (FPS) standard, traditionally designed for the physical protection and security but lately increasingly applied in its widest meaning, as a duty 'to ensure the foreign investment can function properly on a level playing field, unhindered and not harassed by the political and economic domestic powers' (Wälde 2004: 390). Several recent arbitral decisions confirm this view. For example

> The Arbitral Tribunal adheres to the Azurix holding that when the terms 'protection' and 'security' are qualified by 'full,' the content of the standard may extend to matters other than physical security. It implies a State's guarantee of stability in a secure environment, both physical, commercial and legal. It would in the Arbitral Tribunal's view be unduly artificial to confine the notion of "full security" only to one aspect of security . . .
>
> (*Biwater Gauff*, para. 729)

Community protests, to be effective, will try to somehow hinder the operations, often by blocking access to a site. Under the broader meaning of FPS, the investor does not even need to invoke a breach of his legitimate expectations, when he brings an arbitral claim based on these facts.

Fourth, the three cases described – *Tecmed*, *Metalclad* and *Gallo* – are in the field of waste management. The discussion would be perhaps similar if the concern was a polluting factory, or an oil refinery, but these arguments and defences may not apply to an extractive project. Intuitively the issue appears to be totally different, since natural resources are exploited where they are found, and that reality objectively limits the likelihood of total opposition from the community. This intuition is, however, contradicted by the emergence of the 'social license to operate' (SLO) notion, a concept launched by the Canadian mining executive Jim Cooney in the late 1990s (Prno 2013) and later developed into a complex model, now widely applied by Canadian mining companies and increasingly by mining companies worldwide. The model requires mining companies to obtain from an early stage of exploration, and maintain throughout the exploitation process, local communities' acceptance of both company and its operations (Luning 2012: 208). This requirement seems to make mining the industry in which the community comes closest to having its voice heard. In practice, community engagement for obtaining the SLO is often realized through specialized consulting firms. Interestingly, one of the leading companies in the field, 'On Common Ground, Inc.' has the rare audacity to launch on one of its websites[25] a bold question: 'Can the community fail to grant the license?' Its answer is unfortunately not really an answer, but a gracious way of avoiding it:

Can the community fail to grant the license?

> (. . .) The key to a community's capacity to issue a meaningful Social License is the pattern of social capital it has in its network structure. Without the right patterns of social capital within the community and between the project and the various elements of the community network, it is difficult, if not impossible, to gain and retain a Social License to Operate. Companies that want Social License need to know the patterns of social capital in the network they wish to interact with. With this information, the company knows where to place effort (. . .).

If avoiding a direct answer may be understandable in the case of a company specialized in engagement consulting, it is less so in the case of scholarship. It is troubling that well-publicized episodes of negative interactions with communities in practice are not looked at through the lens of the emerging obligation of engagement. The already referred to systematic review of the community engagement literature by Bowen *et al.* (2010) found only four such studies, examining respectively the following negative forms of engagement: retaliation, neglect, monitoring and buffering (Bowen *et al.* 2010: 311). True, the review was undertaken in 2010, but more recent research remains mainly concerned with recommending ways for obtaining the community agreement, for example by reducing power asymmetries during engagement (Dawkins 2014), by a less defensive and more constructive approach to stakeholder engagement (Owen and Kemp 2012), by establishing functional equity between stakeholders (Kemp and Owen 2013), by building trust (Moffat and Zhang 2014) or by hiring a high percentage of local workforce (Carrington and Pereira 2011). Other articles look at the process from the community side, and recommend ways to improve bargaining power by pressuring more powerful stakeholders (Calvano 2008).

But the literature, be it the general 'stakeholder engagement' or the more targeted 'SLO' for mining, falls short, for now, of addressing the legal and moral consequences of the community denying, or withdrawing, the 'license'; this possibility is only mentioned at times as something to be avoided. In mining, as in all other industries, in the end, the locals have to accept the project.

Practising and theorizing community engagement is laudable, but at least the academic community should be less shy in addressing this uncomfortable question, for now left to civil society and the human rights literature. More specifically, the academic community should explore to which extent the notion of free, prior and informed consent (FPIC), as it is now developed in the field of indigenous rights, could be expanded to any community affected by a noxious investment. True, the basis of indigenous peoples' claim to a right to withhold consent – not yet clearly established, except for the inter-American human rights system – is wider than mere distributive justice, as it encompasses rights like self-determination and (unwritten) property rights. But the logic of the 'C' in FPIC moving from consultation to consent is the same for all communities, regardless of sociological characterizations in terms of ethnicity, race or class: what is the value of being consulted if you cannot say 'no'? In these circumstances, is 'engagement' not just a masquerade, what Dawkins (2014: 286) calls 'the camouflage of benign verbiage', hiding the real motivations of the powerful elite?

Conclusions

Arbitral tribunals have interpreted the 'fair and equitable treatment' standard found in most of the bilateral investment treaties as a host government's duty to act in accordance with the investor's 'legitimate expectations'. The fact that in practice, the government's failure to fulfil these expectations was sometimes motivated by local opposition on environmental grounds did not impress the judges in the few arbitration cases relevant to the topic. This may have happened because until recently, the obligation of contacting and consulting the local community prior to committing resources for an investment project was broadly in keeping with Western standards in that local communities are acknowledged as being a legitimate stakeholder, with interests to be taken into account, and as promoted in the OECD guidelines and the CSR codes of Western companies. But the introduction, in 2013, of the Chinese Guidelines for Environmental Protection in Foreign Investment Cooperation, suggests that the investor's obligation to consult with the local community has been accepted by states with different models of governance, including those that historically paid little attention to the voice of local communities. This chapter argues that under these circumstances, government assurances alone are not any longer sufficient for establishing a breach of the legitimate expectations doctrine, since the investor knew, or should have known, that the local community firmly rejects an environmentally damaging project.

The argumentation tangentially revealed two areas that require stronger scholarly efforts: a specific one – the Chinese guidelines, largely ignored in academia, and a more general one – the right of a local community to say 'no' to an investment project. Has the obligation of the investor to consult the local community any substance, in the absence of the latter's right to deny approval? This is a sensitive question, but still deserving an answer – if not from policy-makers or companies specialized in negotiation between corporations and communities, at least from scholars. Besides, authors such as Goodland (2004) and Banerjee (2011) have already questioned the right to veto being assigned only to indigenous communities. Their suggested wider application of FPIC is still conditioned by some sociological determinants (rural and urban poor), but in light of the universalization of investors' duty to engage local communities in environmental matters, a more vigorous exploration of expanding veto rights to all fenceline communities is necessary.

Emphasizing these gaps in the scholarship is by no means a way of overlooking this chapter's own limitations. Its central thesis is built on two simplifications. First, that the Chinese guidelines are a strong enough commitment to suggest that there is convergence of East–West standards in matters of environmental responsibility, in principle if not (as yet) in practice. Second, that the local community is a homogenous group, not decisively influenced in its actions by any degree of organization or stimulated by external factors (NGOs, pressure groups, competitors of investor). While an answer to the first limitation may be provided only in time, the second one requires further research in order to establish to which extent extrinsic factors play a role in the process of community mobilization – as happened in *Tecmed* according to the judge – and more generally, how does the protest's degree of organization influence its ingenuity and spontaneity, and from here, the fine balance of rights relevant to investor-community environmental conflicts.

Notes

1 A motto used by the International Petroleum Industry Environmental Conservation Association (IPIECA) – the global oil and gas industry association for environmental and social issues. http://www.ogp.org.uk/files/7113/3544/4521/ipiecaogpfactsheetsocial development.pdf
2 Gabriel Resources webpage, http://www.gabrielresources.com/site/projects.aspx
3 *The Globe and Mail*, an influential Canadian newspaper, was reporting that 'the company's plan was . . . building a four-pit monster, one that would blow up two mountain sides, displace about 2,000 villagers and fill an entire valley with waste-rock and cyanide-laced sludge' (18 October 2013).
4 A transboundary spill provoked by a mining joint venture including an Australian investor, and considered by the most affected country (Hungary) among the worst environmental disasters that ever happened in Central Europe, second only to Chernobyl nuclear accident. See Eszter Szamado, 'Cyanide spill is ecological crisis: Hungarian official', Agence France Presse, 12 February 2000.
5 Making it highly similar to another case, recently submitted to ICSID Arbitration (*Infinito Gold v. Costa Rica*). According to the 'Request for Arbitration' in *Infinito*, locals took the streets in favour of the project, a gold exploitation by a Canadian mining company, when the EIA was delayed after a moratorium prohibiting open pit mining.
6 Reuters, 19 October 2013.

7 *The Guardian*, 5 December 2013.
8 World Investment and Political Risk, MIGA 2013 www.miga.org/documents/WIPR13. pdf
9 Zeyl (2011) argues that the current approach to the doctrine as a general principle of law is a misstatement of law; Sornarajah, (2010 p. 114), warns against the perpetuation of the incorrect application of the doctrine.
10 For example, the U.S.–Argentina BIT stipulates that 'fair and equitable treatment of investment is desirable in order to maintain a stable framework'.
11 Some even demand an end of the BITs framework, for being incompatible with democratic governance and state sovereignty. See 'Reclaiming public interest in Europe's international investment policy', a report published by the Transnational Institute on behalf of the Investment Working Group of the Seattle to Brussels Network, Amsterdam, July 2010, available at http://www.tni.org/report/reclaiming-public-interest-europes-international-investment-policy?context=70931
12 See for instance CMS *v. Argentina*, where Argentina failed in the use of 'state of necessity' defence.
13 See for instance the often-quoted para. 72 in *C.D de Santa Elena v. Costa Rica* ('Expropriatory environmental measures – no matter how laudable and beneficial to society as a whole – are, in this respect, similar to any other expropriatory measures . . .').
14 In both of the Romanian cases mentioned in the text, the investors' expectations were created by the issuance of some permits related to the exploration and exploitation of natural resources. When the investors tried to make use of the permits, environmental concerns among citizens have led to national (Rosia Montana) or local (Pungesti) opposition to the projects.
15 'When local authorities ignored the complaints of outraged community members, citizens brandishing machetes mobilized in September 1991, preventing tractor trailers from unloading more toxic wastes.' (Wheat 1995)
16 The strong conviction of investors that local governments would grant them permits just because central governments provides such assurances is in itself an interesting if dangerous presumption. In a globalized world, with sub- and transnational levels of governance emerging as a complement to traditional centralized policy making, a prudent foreign investor would not treat the local government as a mere arm of the central administration and blindly rely on the latter's assurances. Similarly, a democratically elected central government needs to formulate policy that is sensitive to local priorities and preferences.
17 Aboriginal Multi-Media Society (AMMSA), 'Communities United in Opposing Toronto Toxins', available at http://www.ammsa.com/publications/windspeaker/com munities-united-opposing-toronto-toxins-0
18 The Globe and Mail, 30 April 2014. The investor's Irish CEO, Jonathan Henry, threatened to sue the Romanian government for up to US$4 billion 'for multiple breaches of investment treaties.'
19 The complexity of examining the legitimacy of community expectations in relation to foreign direct investment is beyond the scope of this chapter but is important and demands more research attention.
20 Listing 'the general principles of law recognized by civilized nations' among sources of international law.
21 Positing that '[g]eneral principles common to the major legal systems, even if not incorporated or reflected in customary law or international agreement, may be invoked as supplementary rules of international law as appropriate'.
22 Moreover, non-OECD countries of some large investors, like Brazil, consider themselves bound by the OECD Guidelines.

23 A signal of convergence may be seen in the increased interest for the subject 'engaging the community' in the scholarship across emerging economies (Brazil, Russia, India and China). With no source at all approaching this topic prior to 2000, now there are several publications per year, according to the comprehensive survey undertaken by Bowen at el, 2010, 301.

24 Even in the case of Chevron's investment in Romania described in Chapter 1, the representatives of the company approached the locals to collect their opinions, although allegations arose that the process was manipulative, important information being concealed from the interviewees (Environmental Justice Organisations, Liabilities and Trade, http://www.ejolt.org/2013/12/rosia-montana-is-saved-but-fractivists-in-romania-still-under-attack-from-chevron/).

25 http://socialicense.com/definition.html.

Cases

Biwater Gauff (Tanzania) Ltd. v. Tanzania, ICSID Case No. ARB/05/22, Award, 18 July 2008

Duke Energy Electroquil Partners and Electroquil SA v. Ecuador, ICSID Case No. ARB/04/19, Award, 12 August 2008

EDF Services Limited v Romania, ICSID Case No ARB/05/13, Award, 8 October 2009

Enron Corporation and Ponderosa Assets, L.P. v. Argentine Republic, ICSID Case No. ARB/01/3, Award, 22 May 2007

Glamis Gold, Ltd. v. USA, NAFTA/UNCITRAL, Award, 8 June 2009

International Thunderbird Gaming Corporation v. The United Mexican States, NAFTA/UNCITRAL, Award, 26 Jan 2006

Metalclad Corp. v. Mexico, ICSID Case No. ARB(AF)/97/1, Award, 30 August 2000

Mobil Investments Canada Inc. and Murphy Oil Corporation v. Canada, ICSID Case No. ARB(AF)/07/4, Decision on Liability and Principles of Quantum, 22 May 2012

MTD Equity Sdn. Bhd. and MTD Chile S.A. v. Chile, ICSID Case. No. ARB/01/7, Award, 25 May 2004

Técnicas Medioambientales (Tecmed) S.A. v. Mexico, ICSID Case No. ARB(AF)/00/2, Award, 29 May 2003

Vito G. Gallo v. Canada, NAFTA/UNCITRAL, Award, 15 September 2011

References

Adey E, Shaila R and Wall F, 2011, *Roşia Montană Stakeholder Conflict: 'Our mountains bear gold yet we are begging from door to door'*, presentation at the First Seminar on Social Responsibility in Mining, Santiago, Chile.

Anderson S and Grusky S, 2007, *Challenging Corporate Investor Rule*, a joint report of the Institute for Policy Studies and Food & Water Watch.

Banerjee S B, 2011, Voices of the Governed: Towards a Theory of the Translocal, *Organization* 18(3) 323–44.

Barak-Erez D, 2005, The Doctrine of Legitimate Expectations and the Distinction between the Reliance and Expectation Interests, *European Public Law* 11(4) 583–602.

Bonnitcha J, 2011, The Problem of Moral Hazard and its Implications for the Protection of 'Legitimate Expectations' under the Fair and Equitable Treatment Standard, *Investment Treaty News* 3(1) 6–8.

Bowen F, Newenham-Kahindi A and Herremans I, 2010, When Suits Meet Roots: The Antecedents and Consequences of Community Engagement Strategy, *Journal of Business Ethics* 95(2) 297–318.

Calvano L, 2008, Multinational Corporations and Local Communities: A Critical Analysis of Conflict, *Journal of Business Ethics* 82(4) 793–805.

Carrington K and Pereira M, 2011, Assessing the Social Impacts of the Resources Boom on Rural Communities, *Rural Society* 21(1) 2–20.

Choudhury B, 2008, Recapturing Public Power: Is Investment Arbitration's Engagement of the Public Interest Contributing to the Democratic Deficit? *Vanderbilt Journal of Transnational Law* 41(2) 775–832.

Dawkins C E, 2014, The Principle of Good Faith: Toward Substantive Stakeholder Engagement, *Journal of Business Ethics* 121(2) 283–95.

Dolzer R and Schreuer C, 2008, *Principles of International Investment Law*, New York : Oxford University Press.

Dupuy P M, 1991, Soft Law and the International Law of the Environment, *Michigan Journal of International Law* 12(2) 420–35.

Freeman R E, 1984, *Strategic Management: A Stakeholder Approach* (1st edn), Boston, MA: Pitman.

Friends of the Earth, 2006, *Fenceline Communities Speak Out*, www.foe.co.uk/campaigns/cor porates/news/shell_fenceline/index.html [accessed 29 March 2012].

Goodland R, 2004, Free, Prior and Informed Consent and the World Bank Group Sustainable, *Development Law and Policy* 4(2) 66–74.

Gugler P and Shi J Y J, 2009, Corporate Social Responsibility for Developing Country Multinational Corporations: Lost War in Pertaining Global Competitiveness? *Journal of Business Ethics* 87(S1) 3–24.

Kemp D and Owen J R, 2013, Community Relations and Mining: Core to Business but not 'Core Business' *Resources Policy* 38(3) 523–31.

Luning S, 2012, Corporate Social Responsibility for Exploration: Consultants, Companies and Communities in Processes of Engagements, *Resources Policy* 37 205–11.

Ministry of Commerce, 2013, *Guidelines for Environmental Protection in Foreign Investment and Cooperation*, http://english.mofcom.gov.cn/article/policyrelease/bbb/201303/2013 0300043226.shtml [accessed 26 June 2014].

Mitchell R K, Agle B R and Wood D J, 1997, Towards a Theory of Stakeholder Identification and Salience: Defining the Principle of Who and What Really Counts, *The Academy of Management Review* 22(4) 853–86.

Moffat K and Zhang A, 2014, The Paths to Social Licence to Operate: An Integrative Model Explaining Community Acceptance of Mining, *Resources Policy* 39(1) 61–70.

Muchlinsky P, 2006, 'Caveat Investor'? The Relevance of the Conduct of the Investor Under the Fair and Equitable Treatment Standard, *International and Comparative Law Quarterly* 55(3) 527–58.

OECD, 2011, *OECD Guidelines For Multinational Enterprises* (2011 edn), www.oecd-ilibrary.org/governance/oecd-guidelines-for-multinational-enterprises_9789264115415-en [accessed 29 March 2012].

Owen J R and Kemp D, 2012, Social Licence and Mining: A Critical Perspective, *Resources Policy* 38(1) 29–35.

Potestà M, 2013, Legitimate Expectations in Investment treaty Law: Understanding the Roots and the Limits of a Controversial Concept, *ICSID Review* 28(1) 88–122.

Prno J, 2013, An Analysis of Factors Leading to the Establishment of a Social License to Operate in the Mining Industry, *Resources Policy* 38(4) 577–90.

Radavoi C N and Bian Y, 2014, Enhancing the Responsibility of Transnational Corporations: The Case for Decoupling the Environmental Issues, *The Environmental Law Review* 16(3) 168–82.

Salacuse J W, 2010, *The Law of Investment Treaties*, New York: Oxford University Press.

Schneiderman D, 2008, *Constitutionalizing Economic Globalization: Investment Rules and Democracy's Promise*, Cambridge: Cambridge University Press.

Schreuer C and Kriebaum U, 2010, At What Time Must Legitimate Expectations Exist? In Werner J and Ali A H (eds), *A Liber Amicorum: Thomas Wälde Law beyond Conventional Thought*, London: Cameron May.

Snodgrass E, 2006, Protecting Investors' Legitimate Expectations – Recognizing and Delimiting a General Principle, *ICSID Review – Foreign Investment Law Journal* 21(1) 1–58.

Sornarajah, M, 2010, *The International Law on Foreign Investment* (3rd edn), New York: Cambridge University Press.

Spronk S and Crespo C, 2008, Water, Sovereignty and Social: Investment Treaties and the Struggles against Multinational Water Companies in Cochabamba and El Alto, Bolivia, Law, *Social Justice & Global Development Journal* (1), www.go.warwick.ac.uk/elj/lgd/2008_1/spronk_crespo [accessed 26 March 2012].

Wälde T, 2004, Energy Charter Treaty-Based Investment Arbitration, *Journal of World Investment and Trade* 3(5) 390–1.

Wheat A, 1995, Toxic Shock in a Mexican Village, *Multinational Monitor* 16(10), www.multinationalmonitor.org/hyper/issues/1995/10/mm1095_07.html [accessed 26 March 2012].

Zeyl T, 2011, Charting the Wrong Course: The Doctrine of Legitimate Expectations in Investment Treaty Law, *Alberta Law Review* 49(1) 203–36.

Part 3

Reconciling stakeholder expectations

5 Health and well-being vulnerability of the socio-economically disadvantaged
The role of food

Louise Manning

Introduction

The British consumer has seen the benefit of globalisation in lower food prices, wider product choice and the advent of 'convenience' foods (Manning and Baines, 2004). At the same time social developments such as smaller households, women being mobilised into the workforce and easier access to processed food has changed diets at both individual and family levels. These lower monetary prices, the product of fierce competition among food retailers who in turn demand lower prices from myriad suppliers, carry a potentially high social price in the long term for developed economies. Low-income individuals and families in the United Kingdom looking for cheaper food present a significant business opportunity, but one fraught with challenges for policy-makers, the food industry and consumers, affecting the long-term health and well-being of all. These challenges centre on locating responsibility (or its absence) for the quality of food we purchase and consume, and the implications for long-term individual health and well-being. The implications go beyond the individual, carrying workplace, economic and societal consequences. Further, these accountability challenges have some international reach, involving opaque supply chains that mask a cocktail of economic, social and ethical, food safety, production and environmental issues. For example, witness the 2008 melamine contamination of milk in China and the exporting of contaminated milk products, the Chinese government in 2013 banning certain New Zealand exported milk products, due to high levels of nitrate, and the European Union (EU) incident in 2013 where horsemeat contamination mired much of the EU food industry.

The aim of this chapter is to explore the extent to which, in the context of a developed economy, consumers on low income, the government, or the food industry should be held responsible for food consumption choices. For example, should low-income consumers be free to choose what they purchase and consume, should their choices be circumscribed by government intervention through its responsibility for public health, or should the food industry simply produce safe, good quality food. The question is important: on one hand there is need to protect the vulnerable consumer from a global food production system where the economics of food production can seem to override ethical concerns over the nutritional value of food. On the other hand, consumer sovereignty and individual liberty demands that individuals have the freedom to choose, on the assumption that they are also adequately informed, about the choices they have.

The discussion will focus largely on the UK, while drawing evidence from other developed nations in the EU, United States (US) and Australia. By way of providing some background the chapter first examines some trends in the cost of food in the UK, and provides a brief discussion of what constitutes nutritious food. Next, the idea of vulnerability and socio-economic disadvantage is introduced, as a framework for exploring the purchasing habits of low-income consumers, and the potential long-term health outcomes of poor food choices. The discussion then explores the extent to which those other than consumers, namely corporations and government, should take responsibility for the part their actions play in the long-term health of consumers. In particular, whether businesses and/or government have a responsibility to edit food choices of the socio-economically vulnerable, or whether this is an infringement of free choice and individual responsibility.

Background: valuing food

During the last decade food prices around the globe have been rising faster than income with consequences for the affordability of food; a challenge that policy-makers continue to struggling with. At the same time in developed economies, such as the UK, the demand for low-price or economy foods has thrown into sharp relief a distinction between nutrient rich and energy dense foods.

According to the Food and Agriculture Organisation of the United Nations (UNFAO), food prices have more than doubled between 2000 and 2011, pushing millions into poverty or 'food peril' (FAO, 2013). Several factors have been blamed, with up to 50 per cent of the increase being attributed to increasing demand for a Western style meat-centred diet among the growing middle classes of China and India. Other factors include commodity speculation, climate change and the cost of petroleum-based fertilisers. The financial crisis of 2007–2008 saw the British pound weakened against the Euro by about 25 per cent, further pushing up prices for imported food. The *Food Statistics Pocketbook* (FSP, 2011) highlights that between January 2007 and May 2011, UK food prices rose by three times as much as food prices in France.

The global food price crisis that began in 2007 posed major challenges to policy-makers in developed and developing countries alike, affecting the affordability of food, especially in the lowest-income quintile of the population (FAO, 2014). When food prices rose in real terms in 2007 and 2008, low-income households in the United Kingdom were affected disproportionately with a rise of 1.6 to 16.8 per cent of all household spend, compared to 10.8 per cent of household spend for all UK households (FSP, 2011). By 2011 there was a marginal reduction with food representing 16.6 per cent of the household income of those in the lowest

20 per cent by equivalised income (the lowest income quintile) as compared to 11.3 per cent for all households (FSP, 2013). The combination of falling income (after rising housing costs including fuel/energy) and rising food prices further reduced the affordability of food in low-income households (FSP, 2013). This led to a change in the types of food in the shopping basket of low-income households, with less carcase meat, fruit, vegetables and fish, but more flour, cheese and confectionery, non-carcase meat and meat products (FSP, 2013). In essence the contents of this shopping basket tilted away from nutrient-rich foods and further towards energy-dense foods. Nutrient-rich foods (e.g. carcase meat, fruit, vegetables, fish, grains) are associated with better health outcomes but tend to cost more per kilocalorie (kcal) than energy dense foods, the latter being low in fibre and water, and high in fats and sugar (e.g. sweets, refined grains, fried snack foods, and fast food such as fried chicken or cheeseburgers) (Monsivais *et al.*, 2010). Monsivais *et al.* established that the mean price increase for all foods between 2004 and 2008 was 25.2 per cent. Within this overall increase the foods in the lowest quintile of energy density (kcal per gram of food) increased in price by an average of 41 per cent, while the highest energy density foods rose in price by only 12.2 per cent. They highlight that, for a given food basket, nutrient-rich foods rose in price faster than their high-sugar high-fat counterparts. Similarly, Drewnowski and Darmon (2005) and Drewnowski (2010) show that foods with added sugars and added fats are far more affordable than the recommended 'healthful' diets (based on lean meats, whole grains, and fresh vegetables and fruit). They identified an inverse relationship between energy density of foods (kJ/g) and energy cost ($/MJ), such that higher energy-dense foods (grains, fats, and sweets) represent the lowest-cost dietary options to the consumer. As Appelhans *et al.* (2012) observe, the relative affordability of energy-dense over nutrient-rich foods could promote socio-economic disparities in dietary quality and the likelihood of poor health outcomes, such as obesity.

Vulnerability

Vulnerability is the sensibility of individuals who, although intact, are at the same time weak, fragile or biologically ill with an increased predisposition towards supplementary damage (Kottow, 2007 cited by Toader *et al.*, 2013). Similarly, Winston (1999) characterises vulnerable groups as those lacking the ability or power to fully or effectively protect and defend their own interests. Vulnerability in such terms encapsulates fragile integrity and weak consent, and describes individuals or groups having a predisposition to being harmed. Historically, particular consumer groups including babies, just weaned, young children, elderly, pregnant and the immune-deficient have been classified as vulnerable to acute food safety issues, such as pathogens. Food carries risk for food allergen suffers and those expressing food intolerance symptoms. Food risk potentially also encompasses the nutritional and health issues associated with chronic food safety concerns resulting from excessive consumption of sugar, salt, saturated fat, preservatives, additives and other substitutes. Of interest here are groups predisposed to food intoxication on health grounds where they overlap with low-income groups that make food purchasing decisions that then lead to health problems such as type 2 diabetes, heart conditions or strokes. For our purposes we may also include low income households as being defined as vulnerable.

As Goodin (1985) observes, vulnerability can come as a natural and inevitable part of life, or it can be created and sustained by social arrangements whereby the vulnerability of other human beings comes from our individual and collective attitude towards those deemed vulnerable. Large segments of the population, such as low-income households, may be described as vulnerable to rising food prices, particular food ingredients, or health issues. As noted by Defra (FSP, 2011; 2013) the lower the weekly household income then proportionally more is spent on food. Consequently, changes in food prices can have a profound effect on low income households, highlighting their vulnerability to adverse food price movements (Johnson et al., 1981). Since low-income groups are exposed to rising food prices, they are also susceptible to diet related malnutrition; a phenomenon affecting many (3 million in the UK in 2007), costing in excess of £13 billion and corresponding to about 10 per cent of the expenditure on health and social care in that year (Elia and Stratton, 2009). More widely across the EU about 20 million people are affected by diet-related malnutrition, costing EU governments up to €120 billion annually (Freijer et al., 2013). At the same time, Goodin's (1985) observation about the social attribution of vulnerability highlights that those affected by diet-related malnutrition are often regarded as culpable for having a predisposition to obesity, type 2 diabetes and heart disease. They are then often seen as causing their own health problems, and as with smokers and heavy drinkers, generate an avoidable drain on health care resources and therefore deserve societal censure. While culpability implies (poor) choices being freely made by subjects of interest (the vulnerable), often subjects act not from free choice but from a psychological predisposition. According to Packard et al. (2012) personality traits, mental health and general mental approach to life are significant predictors of consumption of fruit and vegetables in the economically deprived group in their study. They conclude that health improvement interventions may be more effective when they are adapted to an individual's personality characteristics and have a specific focus on supporting and enhancing mental well-being.

Nevertheless, stigma and discrimination towards the vulnerable, such as the obese, is pervasive and poses numerous consequences for those individuals' psychological and physical health (Puhl and Heuer, 2010). They identify studies documenting the development of stereotypes that judge 'overweight and obese individuals are lazy, weak-willed, unsuccessful, unintelligent, lack self-discipline, have poor willpower, and are noncompliant with weight-loss treatment' (Puhl and Heuer, 2010:1). Perversely, Toader et al. (2013) argue that vulnerability may be created as a consequence of ill-directed public policies and practices that promote stigmatisation and marginalisation. This can lead to unstable self-esteem, ultimately having an undesirable impact on the health status of individuals, for example by suggesting increased exercise levels for people with high body mass index as a way to lose weight when they live in an area rife with street crime and fear leaving their homes. More broadly, a wide range of public health and social policies and associated legislation, including urban planning, transport, food safety, agricultural policies and global trade rules, can have far-reaching unintended influences on health (Swinburn, 2008). Consider, for example, the shift of manufacturing to countries with lower labour costs, leaving weak opportunities for employment, especially for those of low education or skill levels. Inadvertently, such policies and practices can contribute to higher levels of neuroticism, hopelessness, hostility and depression, nudging individuals towards greater vulnerability.

More broadly, low-income consumer groups may also be regarded as socio-economically disadvantaged. From this view, such groups draw disadvantage not only from low income, but also from educational level, social background, living conditions, social heritage and may be at risk of poverty (Poleshuck and Green, 2008; Cederberg *et al.*, 2009). Moreover, food poverty is a real prospect for low-income groups to the extent that they lack the means to purchase a nutritionally adequate diet, and are exposed to the related impacts on health, culture and social participation (Combat Poverty, 2014). Socio-economic disadvantage is a relative and multi-faceted construct that involves making value judgements about commonly interrelated social dimensions (Posselt, 2000), and psychological traits. For example, Packard *et al.* (2012) see personality traits as being associated with socio-economic status. They argue that low socio-economic status is associated with high levels of neuroticism, hostility and depression and low levels of sense of coherence (SoC) and conscientiousness. As noted earlier, Packard *et al.* (2012) suggest that personality and health behaviours may explain why certain sub-groups of the population experience significantly better or worse health outcomes. This suggests that certain sub-groups of the population, or indeed geographical areas within a location, have a distinct collective personality that promotes traits or dispositions, which, in turn, shape shared health behaviours, including those behaviours that lead to chronic health issues or early death. Nevertheless, the links between collective personality and shared health behaviours can be very difficult to demonstrate. For example, those researching the well-known 'Glasgow effect' (Reid, 2011; Walsh *et al.*, 2010) still cannot fully explain why this city suffers from significantly worst health and life expectancy compared with the rest of the UK and Europe.

Dietary patterns and socio-economic concentration

The range and types of food available locally directly affects dietary patterns and levels of obesity. For example, Larson *et al.* (2009) believe that disparities between neighbourhoods in terms of their dietary options are of great concern because of the implications for obesity. They suggest that residents of low-income, minority and rural neighbourhoods were most often affected by poor access to supermarkets and to healthy (i.e., nutrient-rich) food. Similarly, in their survey of food availability and cost across neighbourhoods in Los Angeles and Sacramento, Jetter and Cassady (2006) found that in areas served by smaller grocery stores, access to whole-grain products, low-fat cheeses and ground meat with less than 10 per cent fat was limited. They conclude that lack of availability of nutrient-rich foods in small grocery stores located in low-income neighbourhoods – and where it was available the higher prices of the healthier food basket – may be a deterrent to healthier eating among very low-income consumers. To make matters worse, the availability of fast-food restaurants and energy-dense foods was found to be greater in lower-income and minority neighbourhoods. Similarly, Celnik *et al.* (2012) identify that fast-food outlets in the UK tend to be located in areas of higher deprivation where people are under greater economic pressure and time stress. In these areas, obesity is more frequent and awareness or concern over the links between food choices and health tend to be low. Insofar as such patterns of supply and demand are due to market forces, one solution would be to encourage more small stores offering healthy foods into such neighbourhoods. Indeed, Bordor *et al.* (2007), from their study in New Orleans, suggest that the provision of fresh produce by small urban food stores located within 100 metres of residences seems to encourage greater uptake of fresh fruit and vegetables. In the UK, the Faculty of Public Health argues that improving access to affordable, good quality foods for those with limited transport would improve health (FPH, 2005). They suggest that such concerns must be considered in the planning and regeneration of town centres and residential areas. In the US, increased fast food purchasing is found to be associated with lower education, being a blue-collar employee, and low-household income (Thornton *et al.*, 2011). Bowman *et al.* (2004) cited in Newman *et al.* (2014), also found that one-third of American children eat fast food on a daily basis. The link with purchasing power is clear: as Newman *et al.* (2014: 2) argues, pricing tactics such as 'lower price ... value' offerings appeal to the economically disadvantaged.

Further, with increased urbanisation and competition for jobs and resources (especially accommodation, security, health, education), financially challenged individuals who have abandoned to others the responsibility for preparing their food place themselves at risk of future health issues by assuming the food retailer will represent their health interests. Forget and Lebel (2001) found a connection between health, factors such as poverty and malnutrition, and the influence of the wider socio-economic environment in which people live. They concluded that in order to effectively improve an individual's health all these factors needed to be addressed simultaneously. Neighbourhoods or communities that lack access to affordable fruits, vegetables, whole grains, low-fat milk and other foods that make up the full range of a healthy diet have been described as 'food deserts' (CDC, 2014). Defra (2006) defines food deserts as geographical areas where access to grocery retail outlets and healthy food is relatively limited, particularly for those on low incomes or without cars, so they can only access the food they can physically carry. Access constraints such as poor distribution of food, or the poor nutritional quality of available food choices increases personal and community vulnerability. Lebel (2003) proposes that rather than the biomedical approach to assessing health there should be an 'ecosystem approach' whereby health is also considered as being influenced by community, environment and the local (and wider) economy. There are many specific elements of poverty that can predispose adults to diabetes and poor diabetes control (Seligman *et al.*, 2011). Their research in the US demonstrates that the inability to afford healthy foods is likely to impact on an individual's ability to consume a glycaemically appropriate diet. Similarly, the Australian study by Williams *et al.* (2012) concluded that people living in the most disadvantaged areas were significantly more likely to develop abnormal glucose metabolism (AGM), compared with those living in the least deprived areas.

Convenience foods: at what cost?

Convenience food can be described as any fully or partially prepared foods in which the preparation time, culinary skills or energy inputs have been transferred from the individual to the manufacturer (adapted from Traub and Odland, 1979). This would include ready meals, ready to heat foods, and ready to cook foods. Convenience food therefore is a label for fast food and take-away food offered by restaurants, as well as meals solutions offered by the retail stores (Olsen *et al.*, 2012). Many of these foods contain salt and sugar as low-cost natural preservatives that minimise the potential for pathogen growth and/or act as a flavour enhancer especially with lower quality ingredients. Contrary to expectations, Cooper and Nelson (2003) found that economy-line foods often have a nutrient composition similar to, and often better than, branded equivalents. In another study Celnik *et al.* (2012) assessed the energy content and nutritional value of a range of ready meals defined as 'normal', 'special', 'healthy/light' and 'value/economy'. They determined at the start of the research that the energy content for a meal should be between 500 and 700 kcal, based on three meals a day. They found 14 out of 15 value/economy meals fell below this energy content level. For all meals ($n =$ 67) they found that only 12 products fell into the 500–700 kcal energy content range with six products being between 750 and 850 kcal. The main factor affecting energy content in value/economy meals was the portion size (300 g), compared to other ready meals at 400g–700g in the 'normal' or 'special' meals. Three out of four value/economy meals had saturated fat levels that were 39–54 per cent of the recommended total daily amount consumed (GDA) and contained 25–37 per cent of the salt GDA (6 g). The 'special' meals had between 33 and 90 per cent of the saturated fat GDA and also 37–52 per cent of the salt GDA. As previously discussed, both saturated fat and salt, if consumed in raised amounts, have been linked with chronic health issues. This study highlights the potentially detrimental impact on an individual's health of consuming ready meals as part of their diet. Seen in light of the success of this market, these findings suggest consumers are not aware of, or attach little significance to, the nutritional trade-offs being made in the name of convenience, whether 'normal', 'special' or 'value/economy'. There is no simple relationship between purchasing power and diet quality as many other factors are at play such as taste, lifestyle and ease of access. While convenience foods are clearly attractive to those with limited time, energy, or interest in preparing meals, Celnik *et al.* (2012) criticise the food industry for exploiting the market by selling 'cheap' food presented as convenience meals.

Competition and food safety

As noted earlier, during the 2007–2008 financial crisis UK food prices rose significantly. In the meat sector especially this contributed to the increase in animal feed prices, pressure by supermarkets on their suppliers to reduce costs and also to provide food at marginal cost in order to support promotions (e.g. buy one get one free). These competitive and macro-economic pressures bear down on food quality. The 'pink slime' public outcry in the US in 2012 led burger retailers and manufactures there to reconsider the use of so called 'beef filler' as consumers were concerned about the wholesomeness of the origin of the protein. The requirement introduced by the UK government as a result of EU legislation in April 2012 to stop producing de-sinewed meat, which until then had been a low-cost source of protein in economy burgers and pies, added to the economic pressure on ingredient cost in so called value products. This led to manufacturers and retailers looking for new legal ways of reducing costs and final retail prices in the fiercely competitive value foods arena. Indeed, the demands for low-end food products, sharpened by the 2008–2011 economic recession, was in stark contrast with increasing production costs for beef related products, as animal feed prices rose (Czinkota *et al.*, 2014). Organisations up and down the supply chain face a strategic and moral dilemma, between seeking new ways of reducing costs in order to remain competitive while meeting, if not exceeding, legislative and regulatory requirements over food safety. Cheng (2012) regards this dilemma as an ethical issue encouraging 'food crime', including food fraud and food substitution (with inferior ingredients). For Cheng (2012) this is 'cheap capitalism', characterised by low price, poor quality products and degraded business morality.

Arguably the prospect of food crime transcends individual or isolated corporate wrongdoing, being the unavoidable result of competition and complex and opaque international supply networks. The European Parliamentary Research Service (EPRS, 2014) in their briefing document 'Fighting Fraud' highlighted the reasons they believe led to the 2013 horsemeat incident in Europe. These include: the financial crisis, rising food prices and the demand for cheap food, complex food supply chains and pressure on control services, low risk of detection, lack of focus on detecting fraud, and lack of a strong deterrent (penalties). This incident shows that substitution of horsemeat for beef was undertaken in products where there was pressure on minimising product cost and final price, where the substitution was least likely to be detected (composite foods) and where tests were not being routinely done as part of quality assurance programmes verifying the origin of the 'meat' source in these products. The European Parliament Draft Report (EP, 2013: 6) concluded that the:

> retail sector has a special responsibility to guarantee the integrity of food products and to demand from its suppliers a safe and secure supply chain;

[and the European Parliament] deplores the pressure on primary producers from retail and other food business operators to produce ever more cheaply.

Safe food is not a luxury but an essential component of food regardless of quality. Nevertheless, Trench et al. (2011) identify several factors driving increasing health risk in 'value food chains':

- shift in consumption patterns including consumption of more high risk foods/processed foods;
- giving up responsibility to others for cooking and preparing food, and for controlling food safety and legality;
- higher demand for 'cheap' food, which has led to an increase in the globalisation of food supply. This has introduced the potential for increased health risk from pathogens (harmful microorganisms) and zoonoses (diseases that can pass from animals to humans such as avian influenza, *Salmonella*) to a wider population;
- increases in urbanisation leading to a reliance on 'anonymous' supply chains. That is, where the producer does not know the consumer, that producer is more likely to prepare or sell food of a poorer standard, even substituting ingredients that can be to their personal detriment. Urbanisation and large-scale food production creates this emotional detachment and a geographic break between food producer and consumer; and
- greater demand for convenience and fast food in city and urban areas.

Consumer choice: free or circumscribed

Should government, advocacy groups and businesses be trying to 'edit' consumer food choices, or should consumer choice be unrestricted, and satisfied on demand, is responsibility for health an individual decision? The Sustainable Development Commission (SDC, 2006) highlighted the idea of 'choice editing', especially with regard to sustainability and improving the environmental footprint of food products that are available to the consumer. Supporters of choice editing advocate shifting the field of choice for mainstream consumers so that certain products are removed from the shelves in favour of those that are considered more 'healthy' and at the same time environmentally responsible. Examples of choice editing can be found in animal welfare (free-range eggs), ethical trade (fair trade tea and coffee), sustainable fishing (the Marine Stewardship Council) and other areas where food quality standards are bound up with social, ethical and/or environmental concerns. Such previously 'niche' products are becoming more mainstream with the resultant pressures on suppliers to deliver volume and appropriate pricing strategies at the point of purchase. In contrast, the widely held belief in consumer sovereignty holds that consumers should be provided with information about social and environmental performance, and be left to choose. Russell and Russell (2010), for example, argue that consumers, through their purchases and consumption of products, are the final judges of corporations' behaviour. This view overstates the capacity and readiness of consumers to make healthy choices, and underestimates the power of government and business to determine what we eat (Maniates, 2010). For example, Cowburn and Stockley (2005) examined 103 published papers, mostly from northern Europe and North America, reporting on consumer understanding of food nutrition labelling. They found that consumers do use simple numerical information to make comparisons between alternative food products, but struggle to make sense of more complex descriptive information. While governments do play a useful role in shaping choices, for example through setting limits on the use in food production of potentially harmful chemical ingredients (e.g., transfats), there is also a danger that in pursuit of ever higher food hygiene standards, government removes choice, for example by outlawing particular foods, such as the EU ban on *casu marzu*, a traditional Sardinian sheep milk cheese (Frauenfelder, 2005). Still, there is always a black market for foods in demand and where supply is weak this drives the potential for food associated crime.

Instead, according to Lang (in Maniates, 2010), government, food manufacturers and retailers should take responsibility for shaping choices on behalf of consumers. Although both Maniates and Lang are concerned with the impact of consumer choice on environmental sustainability, their arguments apply equally well to the impact of consumer choice on health. Governmental policy-making is often criticised for being paternalistic, for the usurpation of individual responsibility, preventing people from doing what they want, or otherwise interfering in consumer decision making, expressly for the purpose of promoting consumer welfare (Buchanan, 2008). Policies that smack of choice editing, whether from the food industry or at the government food policy level, have an impact on consumer autonomy, and suggest that 'others' are better placed than consumers in determining what those consumers need (Manning *et al.*, 2006). An example of this paternalism is the Food Ethics Council (2014) proposing that the overall baseline for the nutritional quality of food should be raised through regulation and choice editing, and that the consumer should 'trust' regulators and the food supply chain to make choices for them.

Firms too have a responsibility to the consumer. Amaeshi *et al.* (2007) argue that being a responsible corporation is challenging within a free market paradigm because these firms are expected to take responsibility for their global supply chains, and to assure the practices of all the individuals and organisations involved within their scope of influence. Further, they suggest the potential for irresponsible supplier practices, especially in terms of the potential harm to branded products, puts pressure on businesses to protect their brands by assessing and controlling the practices of their suppliers. Multinational corporations (MNCs), therefore, have an incentive to be proactive while governments may be unable to provide acceptable assurances for a variety of reasons (e.g. state capture, limited jurisdiction, weak regulatory mechanisms) (see Benabou and Tirole, 2010) and in any case they often look to business to self-regulate.

Assurance of food security and food integrity (which is not clearly defined in the literature, but includes food safety) requires the integrated engagement of supply chain actors and regulators at all stage of food policy, food production, distribution and this must be supported by effective information exchange. Therefore any assessment of food security and the wider vulnerability of sections of society, especially with respect to value/economy food chains, must consider the ethical dimension of food production, and whether consumers purchasing economy products can trust the supply chain.

Conclusions

This chapter has examined the food choices facing the socio-economically disadvantaged of the UK, an example of a developed economy. The impact on food prices of the 2007–2008 financial crisis has served to sharpen the vulnerability of this section of British society as they choose poor quality food because the price of more nutritious food becomes out of reach. This group of the general population tend to inhabit an urban landscape of poor access to nutrient-rich foods at a price they can afford. The growing national health problems associated with the consumption of energy-dense foods is escalating as is the cost to health services in a country where such services are free at the point of delivery. The lack of awareness, or general acceptance, among the socio-economically disadvantaged of a more high risk lifestyle means that they are less accessible to policy instruments designed to change food consumption behaviour. Clearly, from a public health policy perspective, access to, and the take up of, higher nutrition foods by disadvantaged neighbourhoods needs to be considered a policy priority for government.

The existence of value or economy food products presents both a nutritional risk to the vulnerable, an increased health cost to government, and an ethical and legal risk to those organizations who supply such energy-dense products. The vulnerable (i.e., low-income groups) are not completely absolved from being responsible for what they eat, just because they are vulnerable. Free market thinking demands that consumers be free to choose to consume products while understanding that over-excess can cause health problems. Government by virtue of being elected do have a responsibility to the citizenry for food security and public health and education, as do the corporations that formulate, process, distribute and sell these energy-dense foods. Pharmaceutical and tobacco companies have to consider and publish the long-term effects of the drugs and tobacco products they market, and given the potential long-term harm of poor diets, food manufacturers and retailers should also be required to develop protocols on the health effects of the products they sell and identify their mitigation strategies, as well as consider how their customers make informed choices. It is encouraging to see the Tesco supermarket's planned introduction of the 'healthy little differences tracker' that measures the nutritional content of their customers' shopping baskets, which will provide information to their consumers of the results of their food choices (Tesco and Society, 2014).

For MNCs the people they serve can be remote, characterless and compartmentalised as a demographic market segment. The classification of demographic groups and the food products they can access and afford can lead to a loss of empathy with the challenges these groups face. It is crucial that MNCs' strategy deliver value to customers in whatever form that takes. Many food products are sold at retail level as loss-leaders, often below the cost of production in order to gain customer footfall and retain customer loyalty. However the term 'value' has taken on new meaning in the food supply chain. Value products are often seen as low-cost food choices, where the quality of the product is minimised to meet cost targets to such a point that the micronutrient value is potentially compromised.

Low-income households are vulnerable (potentially storing up future health problems) when purchasing these value products because manufacturers are generally using higher levels of sugar and salt as low cost preservatives, or as flavour enhancers with reduced quality ingredients. Businesses should consider this factor as part of their corporate social responsibility (CSR) strategy, especially as the costs of diet-related health care goes on rising in developed economies such as the US and the UK. As Benabou and Tirole (2010) highlight corporations often have lower costs of transaction than governments due to their market orientation and lower levels of bureaucracy so there are economic drivers that influence governments to avoid regulation, and use policy initiatives implemented through food retailers instead. This chapter demonstrates the interdependence of private and public actors and their joint responsibility for addressing food and health related outcomes. There are conflicts of interest for MNCs between maintaining shareholder value and delivering benefits to all food consumers. The responsibility of how to deliver these valuable benefits to all consumers sits with the executives that run companies and their supply base. The ability to access nutritious food has policy implications for urban planning, wage levels, welfare controls and education and health care provision, at both local and national levels.

Governments cannot delegate to the market total responsibility for the quality of food supplied. Globalisation has provided many benefits to consumers, in terms of low cost food, but in the process new challenges need to be overcome, in terms of providing food that is safe and of a nutritious quality, and ensuring access to that food by the socio-economically disadvantaged. However the challenge becomes more acute, as global populations become more urbanised and supply chains more complex. Competition continues to drive down the cost of food at the point of sale, yet still seeking to retain retail margin. Set against these tough competitive conditions, the economics of food supply seem to have given rise to supply networks that are less transparent, accountable, and seemingly less ethical and more open to criminal activity. This has wider implications for governments in terms of the extent to which they should leave food and health policy implementation to a free market approach; the need for future cities and towns that provide low income communities access to affordable nutrient rich food; and the need to enable a sense of coherence and cohesion within families and communities.

MNCs also need to reflect on their interaction with the socio-economically disadvantaged populations they serve, and the potential impact on brand value if their buying policies and retail practices continues to rest on profiting from the sale of low nutritional value foods. This reflection must also include finding ways of rooting out food substitution and food fraud by unscrupulous individuals and firms within the food supply chain seeking to meet certain price criteria (or maximise profits), and on MNCs pressuring suppliers to further reduce prices. However delivery of affordable, nutritious food is underpinned by an understanding of what it means to be food vulnerable in a developed country. This understanding must encompass a process of removing stigma and reducing marginalisation and creating a greater sense of empathy for what it is to be financially vulnerable especially where this is due to a lack of education, income and opportunity. Retail organisations and policy makers that understand this challenge and can develop policies and practices that enhance individual autonomy in low income communities will benefit not only shareholders but the greater community.

References

Amaeshi, K., Osuji, O.K. and Nnodim, P. (2007), *Corporate control and accountability in supply chains of multinational corporations: clarifications and managerial implications*, No. 46–2007, International Centre for Corporate Social Responsibility, Nottingham University Business School, Nottingham, UK.

Appelhans, B.M., Milliron, B., Woolf, K., Johnson, T.J., Pagoto, S.L., Schneider, K.L., Whited, C.M. and Ventrelle, J.C. (2012), Socioeconomic status, energy cost, and nutrient content of supermarket food purchases, *American Journal of Preventive Medicine*, 42(4): 398–402.

Benabou, R. and Tirole, J. (2010), Individual and corporate social responsibility, *Economica*, 77(305): 1–19.

Bordor, J.N., Rose, D., Farley, T.A., Swalm., C. and Scott, S.K. (2007), Neighbourhood fruit and vegetable availability and consumption: the role of small food stores in an urban environment, *Public Health Nutrition*, 11(4): 413–20.

Bowman, S. A., Gortmaker, S. L., Ebbeling, C. B., Pereira, M.A. and Ludwig, D. S. (2004), Effects of fast-food consumption on energy intake and diet quality among children in a national household survey, *Pediatrics*, 113(1): 112–18.

Buchanan, D.R. (2008), Autonomy, paternalism and justice: ethical priorities in public health, *American Journal of Public Health*, 98(1): 15–21.

CDC. (2014), *A look inside food deserts*. Available at: www.cdc.gov/features/fooddeserts/ (accessed on 4 April 2014)

Cederberg, M., Hartsmar, N. and Lingarde, S. (2009), *Thematic report: social disadvantage, educational policies that address social inequality*, (EPASI), 2: 3–18.

Celnik, D., Gillespie, L. and Lean, M.E.J. (2012), Time-scarcity, ready-meals, ill-health and the obesity epidemic, *Trends in Food Science and Technology*, 27(1): 4–11.

Cheng, H. (2012), Cheap capitalism: a sociological study of food crime in China, *British Journal of Criminology*, 52(2): 254–73.

Combat Poverty (2014), *Glossary*. Available at: www.combatpoverty.ie/povertyinireland/ glossary.htm (accessed on 4 April 2014).

Cooper, S. and Nelson, M. (2003), Economy' line foods from four supermarkets and brand name equivalents: a comparison of their nutrient contents and costs, *Journal of Human Nutrition and Dietetics*, 16(5): 339–47.

Cowburn, G. and Stockley, L. (2005), Consumer understanding and use of nutrition labelling: a systematic review, *Public Health Nutrition*, 8(1): 21–8.

Czinkota, M., Kaufmann, H.R. and Basile, G. (2014), The relationship between legitimacy, reputation, sustainability and branding for companies and their supply chains, *Industrial Marketing Management*, 43(1): 91–101.

Defra. (2006), *Food security and the UK: an evidence and analysis paper*. Food Chain Analysis Group, December 2006. Available at: http://ipcc-wg2.gov/njlite_download2.php?id=8916 (accessed on 10 May 2013)

Drewnowski, A. (2010), The cost of US foods relative to their nutritive value. *American Journal of Clinical Nutrition*, 92(5): 1181–1188.

Drewnowski, A. and Darmon, N. (2005), Food choices and diet costs: an economic analysis. *Journal of Nutrition*, 135(4): 900–4.

Elia, M. and Stratton, R.J. (2009), *Calculating the cost of disease related malnutrition in the UK in 2007. In combating malnutrition: recommendations for action*. A report from the Advisory Group on Malnutrition led by BAPEN. [M Elia and CA Russell, editors]. Redditch, UK: BAPEN.

EPRS (2014), *European Parliamentary Research Service, briefing document 'Fighting fraud'*, 130679REV1 Issued 16 January 2014.

European Parliament, The (EP). (2013), *The European Parliament draft report on the food crisis, fraud in the food chain and the control thereof (2013/2091(INI))* produced by the Committee on the Environment, Public Health and Food. PR\1005774EN.doc.

Faculty of Public Health (FPH). (2005), *Food poverty and health*, May 2005. Available at: www.fph.org.uk/uploads/bs_food_poverty.pdf (accessed 4 April 2014).

Food Ethics Council (2014), Available at: www.foodethicscouncil.org (accessed 4 April 2014).

Forget, G. and Lebel, J. (2001). An ecosystem approach to human health. *International Journal of Occupational and Environmental Health*, 7(2): S1-S38.

Frauenfelder, M. (2005), *Most rotten cheese". The world's worst: a guide to the most disgusting, hideous, inept, and dangerous people, places, and things on Earth*. San Francisco, CA: Chronicle Books.

Freijer, K., Tan, S.S, Koopmanschap, M.A., Meijers, J.M.M, Halfens, R.J.G. and Nuijten, M.J.C. (2013), The economic costs of disease related malnutrition, *Clinical Nutrition*, 32(1) 136–41.

FSP. (2011), *Food Statistics Pocketbook 2011*, Food Statistics Branch, Defra.

FSP. (2013), *Food Statistics Pocketbook 2013*, Food Statistics Branch, Defra.

Goodin, R.E. (1985), *Protecting the vulnerable: a reanalysis of our social responsibilities*. Chicago, IL: University of Chicago Press.

Jetter, K.M. and Cassady, D.L. (2006), The availability and cost of healthier food alternatives, *American Journal of Preventive Medicine*, 30(1): 38–44.

Johnson, S.R., Burt J.A. and Morgan, K.J. (1981), The food stamp program: participation, food cost and diet quality for low-income households (USA), *Food Technology*, 35(10): 55–70.

Kottow, M. (2007), *Ética de protección: una propuesta de protección bioética*. Bogotá, Colombia: Universidad Nacional de Colombia.

Larson, N. I., Story, M. I. and Nelson, M. C. (2009), Neighborhood environments: disparities in access to healthy foods in the US, *American Journal of Preventive Medicine*, 36(1): 74–81.

Lebel, J. (2003), *Health: an ecosystem approach*. Ottawa, Canada: International Development Research Centre.

Maniates, M. (2010), *Editing Out Unsustainable Behavior*, in *Worldwatch Institute's State of the World 2010: Transforming Cultures, From Consumerism to Sustainability*, Available at: http://blogs.worldwatch.org/transformingcultures/wp-content/uploads/2009/11/SOW 2012-PreviewVersion.pdf (accessed on 2 January 2015).

Manning, L. and Baines, R.N. (2004), Globalisation. A study of the poultry meat supply chain, *British Food Journal*, 106(10/11): 819–36.

Manning L., Baines R.N. and Chadd S.A. (2006), Ethical modelling of the food supply chain, *British Food Journal*, 108(5): 358–70.

Monsivais, P., Mclain, J. and Drewnowski, A. (2010), The rising disparity in the price of healthful foods: 2004–2008, *Food Policy*, 35: 514–20.

Newman, C.L., Howlett, E. and Burton, S. (2014), Impact of fast food concentration for preschool-aged childhood obesity, *Journal of Business Research*, 67(8): 1573–1580.

Olsen, N.V., Menichelli, E, Sorheim, O. and Naes, T. (2012), Likelihood of buying healthy convenience food: An at-home testing procedure for ready-to-heat meals, *Food Quality and Preference*, 24(1): 171–8.

Packard, C.J., Cavanagh, J., McLean, J.S., McConnachie, A., Messow, C.M., Batty, G.D., Burns, H., Deans, K.A., Sattar, N., Shiels, P.G., Velupillai, Y.N., Tannahill, C. and Millar, K. (2012), Interaction of personality traits with social deprivation in determining mental wellbeing and health behaviours. *Journal of Public Health* (May 2), 34(4): 615–24.

Poleshuck E.L. and Green C.R. (2008), Socioeconomic disadvantage and pain, *Pain*, 136(3): 235–8.

Posselt, H. (2000), *Socio-economic disadvantage across urban, rural and remote areas. Paper delivered at the 10th Biennial Conference of the Australian Population Association. Melbourne 28th November to 1st December 2000*. Melbourne, Australia.

Puhl, R.M. and Heuer, C.A. (2010), Obesity stigma: important considerations for public health, *American Journal of Public Health*, 100(6): 1013–1028.

Reid, M. (2011), Behind the 'Glasgow effect', *Bulletin of the World Health Organization*, 89(10): 701–76.

Russell, D.W. and Russell, C.A. (2010), Here or there? Consumer reactions to corporate social responsibility initiatives: egocentric tendencies and their moderators, *Marketing Letters*, 21(1): 65–81.

Seligman, H.K., Jacobs, E.A., Lopez, A., Tschann, J. and Fernandez, A. (2011), Food insecurity and glycemic control among low-income patients with Type 2 Diabetes, *Diabetes Care*, 35(2): 233–38.

Sustainable Development Commission (SDC). (2006), Sustainable Consumption Roundtable Report. *Looking back, Looking forward: Lessons in choice editing for sustainability. 19 case studies into drivers and barriers to mainstreaming more sustainable products*. Available at: www.sd-commission.org.uk/data/files/publications/Looking_back_SCR.pdf (accessed on 4 April 2014).

Swinburn, B.A. (2008), Obesity prevention: the role of policies, laws and regulations, *Australia and New Zealand Health Policy*, 5: 12. doi:10.1186/1743–8462-5-12.

Tesco and Society Report. (2014), Available at: http://tescoplc.com (accessed on 10 January 2015).

Thornton, L.E., Bentley, R.J. and Kavanagh, A.M. (2011), Individual and area-level socioeconomic associations with fast food purchasing, *Journal of Epidemiological Community Health*, 65(10): 873–80.

Toader, E., Damir, D. and Toader, T. (2013), Vulnerabilities in the medical care, *Procedia – Social and Behavioral Sciences*, 92: 936–40.

Traub, L. G. and Odland, D. D. (1979), *Convenience Food and Home-Prepared Foods: Comparative Costs, Yield and Quality*. Washington, DC: US Department of Agriculture.

Trench, P.C., Narrod, C., Roy, D. and Tiongco, M. (2011), *Responding to health risks along the value chain*. Available at: www.ifpri.org/sites/default/files/publications/oc69ch11.pdf (accessed on 10 January 2014).

United Nations Food and Agriculture Organisation (FAO). (2013), *The state of food and agriculture report, thirty-eighth session*, 15–22 June 2013, Rome. Available at: www.fao.org/worldfoodsituation/foodpricesindex.en (accessed 10 May 2013).

United Nations Food and Agriculture Organisation (FAO). (2014), Available at: *World Food Situation: FAO Food Price Index* (accessed 4 April 2014).

Walsh, D., Bendel, N., Jones, R. and Hanlon, P. (2010), It's not "just deprivation": Why do equally deprived UK cities experience different health outcomes? *Public health*, 124(9): 487–95.

Williams, E.D., Magliano, D.J., Zimmet, P.Z., Kavanagh, A.M., Stevenson, C.E., Oldenburg, B.F. and Shaw J.E. (2012), 'Area-level socioeconomic status and incidence of abnormal glucose metabolism. The Australian diabetes, obesity and lifestyle (AusDiab) study", *Diabetes Care*, 35(7): 1455–61.

Winston, M.E. (1999), Indivisibility and interdependence of human rights. Text of public lecture, as presented at the Nebraska Union, University of Nebraska–Lincoln, Lincoln, Nebraska, USA September 3, 1999.

6 Explaining corporate social performance through multi-level analysis*

Orr Karassin and Aviad Bar-Haim

* Note: A preliminary paper based on this research was presented at the 2nd International Symposium on Corporate Responsibility & Sustainable Development. Guangdong University of Foreign Studies, Guangzhou, China. April 9th, 2013 – April 12th, 2013.

** The authors would like to acknowledge grants by the Friedrich Ebert Stiftung-Israel branch and the Open University Research Fund, which made possible the research leading to this chapter.

Introduction

For over two decades, self-regulation initiatives have been heralded as necessary supplements and potential replacements for government regulation of firms (Fiorino, 2006; Gouldson and Murphy, 1998; Tietenberg, 1998). One increasingly popular form of self-regulation is corporate social responsibility (CSR). CSR has developed as a means of addressing the demands on business from a range of actors, including governments, consumers, pressure groups and investors (Pearce and Barbier, 2000). Performance in CSR involves 'context-specific organizational actions and policies that take into account stakeholders' expectations and the triple bottom line of economic, social, and environmental performance' (Aguinis, 2011: 855; also Elkington, 2001; Rupp, 2011; Rupp et al., 2010).

An enduring question that has engaged generations of CSR scholars from diverse disciplinary backgrounds is what brings about economically, socially and environmentally responsible (or irresponsible) behaviour in firms (Aguinis and Glavas, 2012; Crilly et al., 2008; Matten and Moon, 2008; Vogel, 2005). A derivative and practical question is, then, how to promote responsible behaviour and strengthen internal and external mechanisms supporting CSR. Answering both questions engages conceptual and analytical challenges of defining what constitutes as corporate social performance (CSP) and establishing the numerous inner and external factors affecting firm behaviour.

The basic motivation of this chapter is to present and test a research model that provides a relatively comprehensive analytical portrayal of the internal and external environments and mechanisms that potentially affect CSP in firms. In so doing we aim to address what has been dubbed as the 'first knowledge gap' in CSR research, namely multilevel empirical study of CSR, integrating several levels of analysis (Aguinis and Glavas, 2012: 953). Such multilevel analysis addresses at once external institutional factors alongside internal organizational and individual factors, in an attempt to assess the relationships of these with CSP

Inevitably, the model presented and discussed in further detail in the following section is informed by diverse research fields: regulatory and social license studies inform the upper institutional level, which addresses regulators and stakeholders pressures; organizational behaviour and organizational studies inform the following organizational level dealing with organizational culture, industrial profile and organizational characteristics, leadership and managerial attitudes; similarly, another stream of organizational behaviour studies inform the subsequent individual level addressing organizational commitment, job satisfaction and organizational citizenship behaviour; finally the CSP level relies heavily on sustainability and CSP indicator studies.

This chapter presents initial findings from the application and testing of the proposed model in the context of the Israeli industrial sector. This is the first (known) empirical study of CSR in Israel, though previous normative studies and assessments of CSR in Israel have been conducted (e.g., Abraham-Weiss and Weiner, 2010; Harari, 2011).

Lessons from literature: internal and external factors affecting CSP

Attempts to assess CSP have usually focused on a single or, at most, on two levels and only very rarely on three levels of analysis (Aguinis and Glavas, 2012). Regulatory studies that have informed the institutional level confirm that both regulatory pressures and demands from stakeholders affect social and environmental performance of firms. Even so, to what extent either provides explanations of actual policies and programmes remains unascertained (Gunnigham et al., 2004; Koehler, 2007).

Research conducted under the theoretical premise that firms are amoral profit calculators has provided ample evidence that environmental compliance as well as beyond-compliance behaviour occurs when sufficiently costly and deterrent enforcement is employed (Faure et al., 2009; Henriques and Sadorsky, 1996; Kagan and Scholz, 1984; Meegeren, 2001). Nevertheless, elevated sanctions have not necessarily been documented as bringing about an equivalent improvement in environmental performance (Stafford, 2002).

In some cases softer forms of regulation such as regulation by permits and negotiated agreements have been found as no less effective than coercive enforcement (Reijnders, 2003). Moreover, societal sanctions employed as part of the 'social license' involving public pressure, negative media attention and expectations of resulting damage to reputation (May, 2005; van Erp, 2011) have also been found as significant explanatory variables of compliance and beyond compliance (Gunnigham et al., 2004; Kagan et al., 2003; Maxwell et al., 2000; Thornton et al., 2009).

An alternative theoretical view of the firm as capable of complying with regulatory requirements and societal demands based on normative, and ethical motivations, has suggested that interactions with stakeholders can bring about improved CSR (Gunningham *et al.*, 2003; Pies at al., 2009; Scherer and Palazzo, 2011; Tyler *et al.*, 2008; Tyler, 2012; Vandenbergh, 2003). Yet most studies have remained on the conceptual level (e.g. Prakash and Potoski, 2006; Vachon and Klassen, 2006), with fewer attempting empirical validation (e.g., Zhang *et al.*, 2008).

While most regulatory studies focused on institutional level factors have addressed regulatory or stakeholder pressures exclusively, few have integrated these with organizational level effects (examples of studies that have integrated two to three levels are Borck and Coglianese, 2011; Henriques and Sadorsky, 1996; Liu *et al.*, 2010). At the same time, organizational research has focused primarily on corporate characteristics impacting CSR, yet not always choosing characteristics comprehensively (see e.g., Nuttaneeya *et al.*, 2012 who investigate the correlation between CSR, stock yield and net profit in Australian industrial enterprises). The large sample of 523 American companies in the study of Lindgreen *et al.* (2009) is exceptional in relating to multiple corporate profile traits such as main markets, types of products, year of establishment, organizational and workforce structure and more.

A cultural, rather than corporate profile, understanding of firms has addressed the types of organizational norms that promote or hinder CSR (Ketola, 2008). Waldman *et al.* (2006) lead a broad effort to identify organizational cultural typologies that enhance or impede managerial tendency to promote CSR. This study did not, however, address the causal relationship to CSR variables. Murillo and Lozano (2006) address the need to assess CSR in cultural contexts, however, do not apply widely accepted cultural types to their case study analysis. Übius and Alas (2009) made a more formal attempt to address the relationships between the widely used organizational cultural typology of Cameron and Quinn (1999) and CSP, and found several positive correlations. Other works are that of Sarker (2013) on the impact of cultural codes on CSR in Australian mines, or Jaakson *et al.* (2009), on the effect of organizational culture on service organizations in Estonia.

Leadership has also attracted interest as a possible significant mediator in predicting CSR (Angus-Leppan *et al.*, 2010; Egri and Herman, 2000; Waldman and Siegel, 2008). Even so, the relationship between leadership and CSR has similarly not been subject to comprehensive empirical research (see literature review in Strand, 2011, and the indirect impact of leadership in Groves and Larocca, 2011).

A central theme in addressing the individual level of CSR, or what has been referred to as the 'micro foundations' of CSR, has been an investigation of the relationships between workers' attitudes at the workplace and CSR (Aguinis and Glavas, 2012). Three well established workplace attitudes have been explored in this regard: job satisfaction (JS), organizational commitment (OC) and organizational citizenship behaviour (OCB). The central hypothesis advanced by much of this research strand has been that CSR (and most usually perceived

CSR) may be an antecedent to JS, OC or OCB (Chun *et al.*, 2013; Ellemers *et al.*, 2011; Ali *et al.* 2010; Turker, 2009; Valentine and Fleischman, 2008). Organizational behaviour studies have almost entirely neglected the alternative causal relationship, namely that JS, OC and OCB may contribute to achieving CSP. Examples include the work of Abdullah and Rashid (2012) that address CSR programmes as predictors of OCB. In a similar vein, Vlachos *et al.* (2013) judge the effect of CSR efforts on job satisfaction and charismatic leadership. Yet again, in Tziner (2013), CSR is the independent variable and work attitudes are the dependent variables.

A multilevel model of CSP

It is clear from the literature analysis that aiming to closely model the antecedents to CSP requires the consideration of four levels of analysis. Addressing these is necessary for the full depiction of the inner and external forces and mechanisms shaping firm achievement of CSP. These four levels are depicted in Figure 6.1: the institutional, organizational, individual levels are postulated as antecedents to the final performance level.

The upper, institutional, layer addresses the institutional environment, in which corporations operate and are required to employ different CSR practices, pursuant to regulatory or social pressures. It depicts the external pressures that are placed on the firm to comply and achieve both compliance and beyond-compliance practices. These pressures derive from two main sources: regulators holding formal authority over the firm; and various stakeholders that obtain power over the firm. Both stakeholder and regulators are diverse groups in nature, and may include in reality a multitude of actors and groups, acting at the local, national and supra-national levels. Stakeholders are likely to include the firm's customers, employees, suppliers, financial institutions such as banks and insurers, the surrounding community and NGOs (Clarkson, 1995; Donaldson and Preston, 1995;).

The model commences by relating to the power of both groups of actors. Power has been described as the salient trait determining the degree to which organizations pay attention to different stakeholders (Mitchell *et al.*, 1997; Parent and Deephouse, 2007). Power is assessed subjectively by managements' perception of the degree of influence or the ability of the external actors to impact the ongoing activities or future of the firm. It is the actor's perceived influence and authority that is assessed, as this determines the response of firms to the actor's interests and demands.

Demands or conditions set by actors may be economic, compliance (legal) or beyond-compliance (ethical and philanthropic) in nature (Carroll, 1979). For example, regulators may present compliance demands for acquiring licenses, implementing measures for reducing risks or self- monitoring. Potential demands by stakeholders are varied and may very well contradict each other. It is then the role of the firm's management to balance these conflicting claims (Donaldson and Preston, 1995; Evan and Freeman, 1993;).

The pressures (marked in the Figure 6.1 as implied or latent in structural equations models' terms) placed by both stakeholders and regulators in the model are a function of power weighted by demands. An actor may be considered powerful by the firm (e.g., customers) but may pose very little, if any, concrete CSR demands on it. The opposite may also be true. Actors placing most pressures on firms could be those with a high degree of power and numerous substantial CSR demands.

The organizational level includes four groups of variables: company profile, organizational culture, the role of management in CSR and workplace leadership (as perceived by firm employees). Organizational culture is probably the most complex phenomenon of these, with many definitions and measures. Common to these is the understanding of organizational culture as the behaviour of people within an organization and the meaning that people attach to those behaviours. Culture includes the vision, values, norms, symbols, language, assumptions, beliefs, practices and habits of the organization (see, e.g., Needle, 2010; Schein, 2006;). Another central tenant of understanding organizational culture is the idea that organizations often have very differing cultures as well as subcultures and these may at times co-exist or conflict (Deal and Kennedy, 2000; Kotter and Heskett, 1992; Schein, 1992).

The individual level depicts the attitudes of workers and managers in the investigated industrial facilities. This level is explored through three parameters: organizational commitment (OC), job satisfaction (JS) and organizational citizenship behaviour (OCB).

Following the conceptual paper by Collier and Estaban (2007) we hypothesize that where employees' values and visions are aligned with those of the organization CSR goals this alignment will translate into effective CSP. Drawing on the relationship between goals theory (Locke, 1997: 2004) and CSR, it is possible that where the previously mentioned work behaviours and attitudes derive from a specific set of CSR goals, CSP will indeed be enhanced.

In operationalizing OC we rely on what has for some 30 years been the leading approach to OC as developed by Meyer and Allen (1984, 1997). This approach is multidimensional and relates to OC as a derivative of three scales: affective, normative and continuance. The continuance dimension assesses the extent to which employees feel committed to their organization by virtue of the costs that might be associated with leaving. Affective commitment, also known as emotional commitment, is characterized by positive feelings of identification with, attachment to, and involvement in, the work organization. Finally, normative commitment is defined as a feeling of obligation to continue working for the organization (Meyer *et al.*, 1990; Meyer and Allen, 1997). These attitudes may stem from an obligation internalized by an individual before or after joining an organization, or reflect an internalized social norm that one should be loyal to one's organization.

JS can be understood as the degree to which an individual is content with his or her job; whether he or she likes the job or not (Spector, 1997). JS is in all likelihood the most widely investigated theme in organizational behaviour. It is also the most enigmatic (e.g. Judge *et al.*, 2001). What is relatively in consensus is that JS is important to corporations, whether as a contributor to performance or self-standing. We rely on a multi-scale analytical construction of JS as measured by five dimensions of satisfaction. These are satisfaction with: peers and colleagues, workplace ambience, the job itself, salary and a general satisfaction with the workplace and work (Smith *et al.*, 1969).

OCB refers to discretionary individual behaviour that is not directly or explicitly recognized by the formal reward system (Organ, 1988; Organ, 1997). It, much like JS, has been a widely studied topic in organizational behaviour research during the previous two decades (see Podsakoff and MacKenzie literature review, 1997). In Organ's and following works, OCB was constructed as a five-factor model consisting of altruism, courtesy, conscientiousness, civic virtue and sportsmanship (for definitions of these, see Law *et al.*, 2005; Organ, 1997; Organ *et al.*, 2006,). Yet empirical research indicated that managers often have difficulty recognizing some of these fine distinctions, and tend to lump the different factors of OCB into a single 'helping behaviour' dimension (MacKenzie *et al.*, 1991, 1993; Podsakoff and MacKenzie, 1994). In a meta-analysis of the OCB literature, LePine *et al.* (2002) found that these five dimensions are very highly correlated and do not have much differentiation among antecedents, indicating some overlap in the dimensions. Following this line of criticism, we adopt a single dimension of OCB as 'helping behaviour'.

At the 'ground' level of the model are the CSP variables, or dependent variables of the model. The inherent complexity of measuring CSR is twofold. First, CSR is an essentially contested concept, with many varying definitions that suggest differing theoretical understandings (Daglsrud, 2008). To compound the difficulty, although some progress has been made on addressing CSR measurement at the organizational level (Clarkson, 1995; Sze kely & Knirsch, 2005), there is still no generally established method nor rigorous metric for such measurement (Wolfe and Aupperle, 1991; Carroll, 1999; Gjølberg, 2009). CSP, in contrast, is a way of making CSR applicable and putting it into practice (Maron, 2006). In contrast to CSR, CSP, although difficult to measure, can be transformed into measurable variables. Different approaches to such operationalization exist, but what they have in common is that CSP is constructed as a multi-dimensional scale covering a wide range of dimensions (van Beurden and Gössling, 2008).

The model described in this chapter incorporates uniquely formed indices measuring CSP through six dimensions: economic, environmental, labour, social, product and corporate governance. These indices are based on a selection of indicators generated through a panel study of 60 experts representing various stakeholder groups.

The outcome of the panel process is a set of indicators (see Appendix I) that incorporates the main dimensions of corporate sustainability. These indicators are similar to those included in the 'Global Reporting Initiative', what is in all probability the most widely used worldwide standard for voluntary sustainability reporting (Brown *et al.*, 2009; Marimona, 2012). To add to this we examine voluntary programmes and activities executed by the firms. These programmes are defined as non-compulsory, voluntary activities, not mandated by the regulator and most usually philanthropic in nature.

We test the direct relationships (included in the model, see Figure 6.1, as full line arrows) between each of the upper levels of the model and the performance

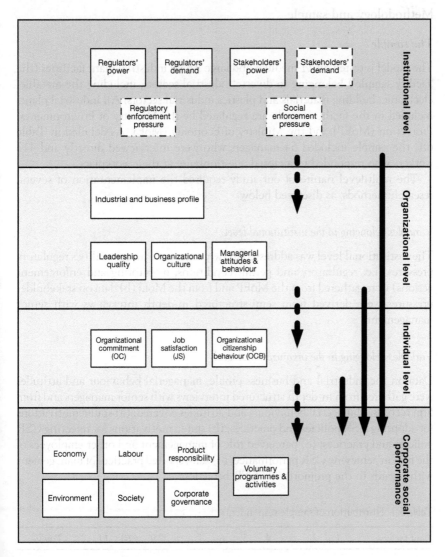

Legend:

1. Directly measured variable ———
2. Latent variable (not directly measured) — ·· —
3. Not measured in this study – – – –

Figure 6.1 A multilevel model of CSP

level. This creates a complex non-recursive path model that aims to elucidate and evaluate the main factors affecting CSP. Non-direct effects (included in the model as striped arrows) have yet to be tested, but would in the future address the mechanisms and inner relations between levels that bring about those results.

Methodology and sample

The sample

The model is tested on 11 medium and large Israeli industrial plant facilities (the 'facility sample') belonging to diverse industrial sectors, including the metallic, electronic, building materials and plastics industrial sectors. All industrial plants included in the facility sample are regulated by the Ministry of Environmental Protection (MoEP) and the Ministry of Economy (MoE). As detailed in Table 6.1, the sample included 54 managers who were interviewed directly and 412 workers who responded to a closed questionnaire at their workplace.

The multilevel nature of our study required the implementation of several research methods, as discussed below.

Variables belonging to the institutional level

The institutional level was addressed in two ways: (a) data on facility's regulatory pressures (i.e. regulatory and permit conditions, monitoring and enforcement actions) were gathered from the MoEP and from the MoE; (b) data on stakeholder pressures were derived from semi-structured in-depth interviews with senior management.

Variables belonging to the organizational level

Data on the industrial and business profile, managerial behaviour and attitudes were gathered from in-depth structured interviews with senior managers and from firm records. Managerial behaviours and attitudes covered: (a) stated motivations for adopting CSR policies and practices; (b) stated motivations for rejecting CSR policies and practices; (c) perceived role of management and other employees of the firm in achieving CSR performance; (d) self-reported practices of management with regards to the promotion of CSR behaviour.

Table 6.1 Distribution of sample respondents

Plant facility	1	2	3	4	5	6	7	8	9	10	11	Total
# Managers interviewed	5	3	5	5	6	5	5	5	5	5	5	54
# Workers responded to questionnaire	70	29	34	37	26	34	33	35	43	28	43	412

Data on other variables included in this level, leadership quality and organizational culture were derived from the workers' questionnaires. The leadership scale was based on the Multifactor Leadership Questionnaire (MLQ) developed by Avolio and Bass (1999) and amended by Ling *et al.* (2008).[1] As in other leadership questionnaires, workers were asked to refer to their direct managers and not necessarily to the senior management of the facility. The data did not reconstruct the original dimensions of the MLQ, in particular, transformational and rewarding leadership styles. Therefore, we constructed a new one-dimensional scale of leadership quality, with good reliability (Cronbach α = 0.80).

The organizational culture scales used items from the Assessment Instrument (OCAI) questionnaire, developed by Cameron and Quinn (1999), and the Organizational Cultural Inventory (OCI) questionnaire, developed by Cooke and Lafferty (1989).

Variables belonging to the individual level

Data for all three organizational behaviours included in the individual level were measured by a Likert-type questionnaire that incorporated items from widely-used instruments, for example, the OC questionnaire developed by Allen and Meyer (1990), in its Hebrew version by Bar-Haim (2007); OCB was initially measured through items from the questionnaire developed by Podsakoff *et al.* (1990), and is considered to have been validated after measurement issues were identified in the original questionnaire by Organ (1988, 1997). Yet, like MacKenzi *et al.* (1991, 1993) and Podsakoff and MacKenzie (1994) we could not extract the original dimensions of OCB from the data and adopted a single scale of OCB 'helping behaviour' with good reliability of (Cronbach α = 0.74). To assess JS we employed the job description index (JDI), as recently updated by Bowling Green State University, Ohio (BGSU, 2009).

Variables belonging to the performance level

Data for performance variables were collected at the plant level through a facility performance questionnaire and corroborated, where possible, by external information obtained from regulators. The performance questionnaire included a detailed set of 24 items divided into six categories: economy (EC), environmental protection (EN), labour relations (LA), social involvement (SO), product responsibility (PR) and corporate governance (CG). See: Appendix I for the 24 CSP indicators in this study.

Also included in the performance are 'voluntary (philanthropic) programmes'. Data for this variable was obtained from the answers of the managers' sample open-ended question regarding voluntary programmes undertaken by the facility.

Analysis of relationships between voluntary programmes, as well as the CSP indicators, by the preceding layers of the model was done mainly by Categorical Regression (CATREG). CATREG extends the standard approach of linear regression by simultaneously scaling nominal, ordinal and numerical variables.

The procedure quantifies categorical variables, so that the quantifications reflect characteristics of the original categories (van der Kooij et al., 2006). Where there was only one predictor, we estimated the relationships from a zero-order Pearson correlation r for both variance proportion and beta effect. Where multivariate techniques or single Pearson correlation could not be used, for reasons such as sample size or collinearity, or non-linearity, we employed non-parametric Spearman's rho ρ, rank order correlation analysis.

Predicting voluntary (philanthropic) programmes

Operationalization

Based on reports by 54 managers we were able to group the firms in our sample into three types:

a   Firms with labour and human-resource development voluntary programmes and activities.
b   Firms with environmental and labour-related voluntary programmes and activities.
c   Firms with multiple voluntary programmes on environmental, labour and social issues.

Nine out of 11 firms in the sample reported on beyond-compliance activities. One firm was found to have only type (a) labour programmes. One firm was found to have type (b) environmental and labour programmes, and the remaining seven firms were found to belong to type (c), having multiple environmental, labour and social programmes.

The focus of many of the beyond-compliance environmental programmes was on activities with a clear economic rational. Voluntary initiatives were reportedly aimed at the improvement of resource and energy efficiency, through reduction of raw material use, reuse and recycling. More costly programmes, with a narrower rate of return, were reported by only two facilities (the implementation of green building standards in a new industrial facilities and solar photovoltaic (PV) roof installation). One facility reported on the adoption of beyond-compliance practices, with regards to the clean air regulations (i.e. early adoption of the duties in the Clean Air Act 2008). Such voluntary programmes aimed at the improvement of resource and energy efficiency fit well into the 'business case' for CSR. These would be characterized as rational preferences motivated primarily from an economic/financial perspective. Interviewed managers often stated that although activities are important for social reasons, they were justified in implementing most environmental programmes by economic efficiency considerations. Such an approach has been characterized by Vogel (2005: 20–1) as 'doing good to do well' or 'responsibility–profitability connection'. It can also be characterized as a narrow view of the business case, as such initiatives may produce direct and clear links to firm financial performance or immediate cost savings (Carroll and Shabana, 2010).

Social programmes were quite diverse in nature but usually included the philanthropic activities aimed at the 'adoption' of a social welfare organization or education facility. These initiatives included at times minor monetary donations, but mainly were characterized by the provision of in-kind resources (such as computers), and donating employees volunteer hours to the adopted organization.

Labour programmes reported as beyond compliance, referred mainly to the integration of special needs or minority populations in the workforce and the provision of on-the-job and classroom training to these groups. Improving general workforce surroundings and employment conditions, such as bonuses and welfare activities, were not mentioned by managers within this framework.

The institutional level: stakeholder pressures

We attempted to predict voluntary programmes and activities by the pressures forced by a single group or all stakeholders groups from within the institutional level (customers, workers, suppliers, community organizations and financial organizations). However, regression analyses yielded no significant effects or prediction power of the stakeholder pressures on voluntary programmes. This finding contrasts the prevailing view that stakeholders do influence CSR (e.g., Corcoran and Shackman, 2007; Ditlev-Simonsen and Wenstop, 2013; O'riordan and Fairbrass, 2014;). Yet, in emerging economies, previous research has similarly shown that stakeholder engagement in CSR implementation is low or virtually lacking. In these countries, CSR initiatives may be driven not by outside stakeholders but rather by the internal action of firm managers and employees (Weyzig, 2006).

The institutional level: regulatory demands

A second attempt to predict voluntary programmes was done through assessing the correlations between beyond-compliance and the regulatory demands made by the regulators included in the study (see Table 6.2). As mentioned earlier, the labour and workplace health and safety regulator (the MoE) and the environmental regulator (the MoEP) were included in the study. The demands made by these regulators, through licensing requirements, inspections, administrative and criminal proceedings are assessed separately as predictors of the adoption and execution of voluntary programmes.

High correlations are found between various regulatory demands and beyond-compliance programmes and activities. Environmental inspections and licensing requirements are both found to have high correlations with regulatory demands while health and safety inspections and environmental enforcement actions (administrative and criminal proceedings) are found to have moderate positive correlations. Health and safety administrative proceedings are found to have moderate negative correlations. This finding was unexpected, and would require additional investigation to offer a plausible explanation.

Table 6.2 Voluntary programs and regulatory demands (environment and economy
        regulators)*

Voluntary programs	Spearman ρ
Environmental licensing demands	.800
Environmental administrative and criminal proceedings	. 407
Environmental Inspections	. 855
Health and safety administrative proceedings	−.557
Work, health and safety, accident related Inspections	.654

* Significant (p<0.05)

While the general outcome of the correlation analysis indicates a moderately high relationship between regulatory demands and the adoption of voluntary programmes, the explanation for this is not definite. In essence, the regulatory demands surveyed are all strictly compliance oriented. Also, officials of the regulatory agencies interviewed indicated that at present both the MoEP and MoE do not have extensive programmes actively promoting voluntary initiatives among regulated firms. Moreover, even where specific initiatives exist (such as greenhouse gas reporting by industry or inclusive employment) they usually do not have clear incentives attached to joining them. Also, they are not directed at community volunteering, which is found to be the core of voluntary initiatives taken by firms. Indeed, this finding is especially perplexing in light of the weak or null correlations found between regulatory demands and the rest of the CSP indicators used in the study (see below).

In consideration of the above it may be suggested that the relationship between regulator pressure and the adoption of voluntary programmes can be partially explained by the mediating effect of corporate motivation of presenting itself to the regulators as worthy corporate citizens. This stipulation requires further research and validation.

The organizational level: leadership quality and organizational culture

Voluntary programmes and activities are found to be strongly predicted by the quality of leadership (negative relationship) and the organizational culture strength (positive relationship). The model succeeds in capturing more than 70 per cent of the variance in the dependent variable (voluntary programmes), as illustrated in Table 6.3.

However, leadership quality acts as a negative predictor. This indicates that high-quality leadership decreases the odds of voluntary programmes and activities while strong organizational culture encourages them.

We expected our finding regarding the reversed relationship between leadership and the adoption of voluntary programmes to give rise to controversy, as previous research has emphasized leadership as a major vehicle for improving commitment to CSR (Aguilera et al., 2007; Groves and Larocca, 2011; Hemingway and Maclagan, 2004; Hemingway, 2005; Vogel, 2005; Waldman

Table 6.3 Predicting voluntary programs through organizational culture and leadership

Model summary

Multiple R	R-square	Adjusted R-square	Apparent prediction error
.876	.767	.729	.233

ANOVA

	Sum of squares	df	Mean Square	F	Sig.
Regression	33,729	6	5.622	20.252	.000
Residual	10,271	37	.278		
Total	44,000	43			

Coefficients

	Beta	df	F	Sig.	Importance	Zero-order
Leadership	−.904	3	13.867	.000	.612	−.519
Organizational culture	.803	3	38.534	.000	.388	.370

et al., 2006). We recall the measurement change of the leadership factor due to some statistical constraints (see above). However, the strong negative relationship between leadership quality and beyond-compliance programmes and activities is valid, and we can only suggest a preliminary explanation. It is possible that firms enjoying stronger perceived leadership are more conservative and stable in nature. Strong leaders may not need to incorporate soft and voluntary initiatives into daily activities of the firm. They may feel that they do not need CSR initiatives as a means of improving either employee motivation or managerial effectiveness. It is possible they perceive and act upon traditionalist leadership as capable of achieving these goals without 'reinforcement' from special activities and programmes.

The organizational level: managerial attitudes and behaviours

Among the different managers' attitudes and behaviours, we found that self-reported practices of management with regards to the promotion of CSR behaviour are a significant predictor of voluntary programmes and activities. Self-reported practices of management included information collection on corporate CSP and the setting and achievement of CSP goals in addition to economic performance goals. This component alone succeeded in capturing over 70 per cent of the variance in the dependent variable. At the same time, the correlations with additional attitudes that were addressed were not confirmed, as illustrated in Table 6.4. For example, various declared motivations for adopting CSR, were not found as significantly related to CSP. These included: (a) reduction of regulatory burden; (b) improvement of financial efficiency; (c) enhancement of corporate image; (d) attractiveness of firm to employees; (d) strengthening of ethical commitment to community.

This finding confirms quite a straight-forward hypothesis. Namely, that a manager who (a) does not focus solely on economic and industrial performance, (b) uses various strategies to advance social and environmental goals and (c) places emphasis on receiving credible information on social and environmental

Table 6.4 Predicting beyond-compliance through managerial attitudes and behaviours

Model summary

Multiple R	R-square		Adjusted R-square	Apparent prediction error
.679	.461		.249	.539

ANOVA

	Sum of squares	df	Mean square	F	Sig.
Regression	18.421	11	1.675	2.173	.048
Residual	21.579	28	.771		
Total	40.000	39			

Coefficients

	Beta	df	F	Sig.	Importance	Zero-order
Motivations for adopting CSR	−.266	3	.516	.675	.073	−.126
Motivations for rejecting CSR	−.238	2	.517	.602	−.014	.027
Managers' self-reported behaviour regarding CSR	.622	4	8.011	.000	.627	.464
Perceived roles of actors and actions in CSR	.477	2	1.009	.377	.314	.303

performance is more likely to succeed in advancing CSR voluntary programmes and activities in the firm. This exemplifies that declared motivations, are not a good predictor of actual results and indeed active practical involvement, collecting information goal-setting and programme advancement, serve as much closer and clearer predictors of performance.

The individual level: organizational commitment

We measured three types of organizational commitment (affective, normative and continuance-utilitarian). Among these different forms, the only type of organizational commitment (OC) that was found to have a significant negative correlation with CSR voluntary programmes is continuance or utilitarian OC, as illustrated in Table 6.5. This finding is surprising, as it could be assumed that normative or affective (emotional) OC would be more likely predictors of CSR voluntary programmes, especially when employee involvement is required to sustain these. Yet, the utilitarian form of OC, having to do with commitment to the organization associated with costs of leaving and job security, is found to explain more than 60 per cent of the variance in the dependent variable. This finding, contrary to our expectation and what is known in the literature, deserves additional

Table 6.5 Predicting beyond-compliance by organizational commitment

Model summary				
Multiple R	R-square		Adjusted R-square	Apparent prediction error
.851	.724		.661	.276

ANOVA					
	Sum of squares	df	Mean square	F	Sig.
Regression	31.862	8	3.983	11.484	.000
Residual	12.138	35	.347		
Total	44.000	43			

Coefficients						
	Beta	df	F	Sig.	Importance	Zero-order
Affective OC	1.160	2	2.032	.146	−.022	−.013
Normative OC	−1.174	3	1.762	.172	.735	−.453
Continuance (utilitarian) OC	−.633	3	11.682	.000	.285	−.326

exploration and confirmation (see: Gill et al., 2011; Herscovitch and Meyer, 2002; Wasti, 2005;)

The individual level: job satisfaction

Job satisfaction (JS), in general, and with pay in particular, are strong predictors and exhibit positive relationships with voluntary programmes and activities, as illustrated in Table 6.6. JS from workplace ambience has significant negative effect though. The negative relationship is puzzling and would require further exploration in order to verify this finding and provide an explanation.

This finding may be interpreted as seemingly inconsistent with the previous finding that stakeholder power in general and employees' power, amongst this, did not exhibit a direct effect on voluntary programmes. A possible explanation is that positive attitudes (job satisfaction) of workers as internal agents working within the organization have greater force in shaping organizational practices than the (perceived) power of workers as external stakeholders. While the institutional-level model views workers as exterior agents forcing or lifting pressure over the

Table 6.6 Predicting voluntary programs through job satisfaction (JS)

Model summary

Multiple R	R-square		Adjusted R-square	Apparent prediction error
1.000	1.000		1.000	.000

ANOVA

	Sum of squares	df	Mean square	F	Sig.
Regression	44.000	12	3.667	690619.310	.000
Residual	.000	31	.000		
Total	44.000	43			

Coefficients

	Beta	df	F	Sig.	Import-ance	Zero-order
JS-with people	−.549	1	1.437	.24	.083	−.152
JS-workplace ambience	−1.046	3	20.715	.000	.712	−.681
JS-work itself	−.393	2	2.089	.141	.055	−.139
JS-pay	.461	3	4.877	.007	.102	.222
JS-general	.654	3	5.987	.002	.046	.071

firm, the individual level sees employees as agents within the organization, working cohesively within the firm and shaping the firm through their daily attitudes and practices. Working as internal rather than external agents, employee attitudes have direct impacts over organizational performance, when a positive satisfaction is prevalent rather than power and pressure relationships characteristic of demands from stakeholders.

The individual level: organizational citizenship behaviour

Since OCB is defined as discretionary individual behaviour that is not directly or explicitly recognized by the formal reward system, it seems only natural that such behaviour would serve as an antecedent of voluntary activities at the firm level. However, OCB has been found to have no significant correlation with voluntary programmes. The fact that no such association is found is against expectations, and requires additional exploration in search of an explanation.

Predicting CSP

Industrial and business profile

The data accumulated by the study on the industrial profile included such characteristics as industrial sector, ownership structure (publicly traded or not), exporting orientation, density of competition, number of employees, geographical location, additional production facilities, proximity to residential areas, human resource characteristics (such as workforce composition, division between production and administrative workers), age, coverage of collective employment agreements and union membership, as well as major changes occurring in the preceding five years.

Not all characteristics are presented in the following Table 6.7. The omitted characteristics are those which were found to have no sufficient variation and therefore no significant correlations could be determined. Keeping in mind the limitations of sample size and the consequent constraints on performing multivariate analyses, the data presented in Table 6.7 shows that correlations between industrial and business profile and CSP is not substantial. Scattered correlations were found between the specific performance indicators of energy efficiency and landfilling dangerous materials – however, these correlations show no clear or theoretically significant pattern.

It is worthwhile noting that firms with little or no competition from overseas have a greater tendency to include human rights clauses in their contracts and to address these issues in company codes of conduct. This finding could be interpreted as contrary to some assertions made in literature that have suggested companies working in competitive environments, with higher import penetration are likely to have superior CSP (Fernández-Kranz and Santaló, 2010). Moreover, multinational enterprises (MNEs) would be more attentive to human rights and social issues, if they are subjected to the scrutiny of their global supply and demand

Table 6.7 Industrial profile characteristics and CSP*

	Firms age	Location		Competitors		Major changes in last five years		
		Southern	Industrial zone	Little local competition	Little foreign competition	Opened new facilities	Closed facilities	Growth
Local expenditure and investment in R&D			0.43	0.46				
Existence of EMS and environmental safety officer			-0.60		-0.52			
Frequency of reporting data to the regulator	-0.44							
Percentage of recycled water	0.71							
Not exceeding air quality standards			-0.43		-0.41			-0.42
Energy efficiency measures	-0.83	0.73	0.88	0.73		-0.73		
Dangerous materials landfilled	0.56	-0.74	-0.89	-0.89		0.74	–	0.44
Dangerous materials reused				0.63				
Dangerous materials neutralized on site					-0.47	-0.55		
Labor practices		-0.42			-0.46		-0.42	
Difference in average hourly pay-men woman		-0.60						
Human rights contract and company code clauses	-0.56			0.42	0.76		-0.61	0.43
Product responsibility checks and risks	-0.83			0.47		-0.52		0.57
Product safety complaints received					0.43			
Corporate governance- anti- corruption and transparency measures							0.48	

Legend: Spearman rank order correlations ρ. Marked correlations are significant at $P < 0.05$.

chains and public pressures (see Gamerschlag *et al.*, 2011; Lim and Phillips, 2008; Preuss and Brown, 2012).

Yet, we find that it is companies working in localized settings or having little competition from global markets (rather than MNEs) that are more receptive to human rights and social issues. We offer two possible explanations for this phenomenon. The first is that low levels of competition and exposure to global markets may indeed mean companies are allowed more leeway in addressing general social concerns in addition to their bottom line. As less competition would generally entail larger profit margins and higher stability, this finding may be interpreted as consistent with much of the CSR – financial performance literature that has asserted a positive relationship between financial performance and CSP (Griffin and Mahon, 1997; Margolis and Walsh, 2003; van Beurden and Gössling, 2008). However, since we did not find a direct relationship between profitability (as an independent organizational profile variable) and improved CSP, this explanation is qualified. A second possible explanation for this finding could be that local companies depend on their locally built reputation and legitimacy provided by local stakeholders, far more than MNEs (Tochman *et al.*, 2012). The search for local legitimacy may direct such local firms to improve their human rights policy and to administer tools for its implementation.

Individual, organizational and institutional variables

Fifteen indicators or scales (combining two or more indicators) are used to depict CSP at the firm level. A tabular summary of the relationship between these indictors and the components of our multilevel model are depicted in Table 6.8. JS is the strongest predictor of CSP for all indicators closely followed by OC, both having high and significant correlations with CSP. OCB was found to have no significant impact on CSP indicators. These findings for the individual level are consistent with the findings in the previous section, regarding the impact of these variables on voluntary programmes.

JS and OC are classic strong determinants of the nature of the workforce. Based on literature, we also know that organizational culture is a strong antecedent to JS and OC (Lock and Crawford, 1999). Although more complicated path models should be examined in the future, at this stage, the summary in Table 6.8 demonstrates that organizational culture and leadership are also of particular importance and are relatively strong predictors of CSP in and of themselves. Nonetheless, attitudes and behaviours of management have only moderate to low prediction power, with regards to performance.

Table 6.8 further demonstrates that stakeholders generally have a low to null impact on CSP. This finding, possibly more than others, reflects the localized nature of our study and the preliminary stage of development of CSR, both in corporate culture and in the conciseness of the general public in Israel. We suggest that stakeholders hold little influence over performance since their demands (which could not be independently corroborated, as is the case with regulators) are generally weak and non-substantive. That is to say, stakeholders have neither

Table 6.8 Summary of relationships between model's upper levels and CSP

Indicators (Spearman ρ rank order correlations)								
Model Level	Individual			Organizational		Institutional		
Performance Indicator	Org. Commit	JS	OCB	Leader-ship & Org. culture	Managerial attitudes & behaviour	Stakeholders pressure	Regul. power	Regul. demand
Local expenditure avesnd intment in R&D (Indicators A2+A4)	H	H	N	H	L	M	N	N
Existence of EMS and environmental safety officer (Indicators B6+B7)	H	H	M	M	N	N	M	L
Frequency of reporting data to the regulator (Indicator B8)	H	H	N	H	N	N	N	N
Percentage of recycled water (Indicator B9)	M	H	N	M	M	N	N	M
Not exceeding air quality standards (Indicator B10)	H	H	N	M	N	N	N	N
Energy efficiency measures (Indicator B11)	M	H	N	M	L	N	N	N
Dangerous materials landfilled (Indicator B12)	H	H	N	H	M	M	N	M

Dangerous materials reused (Indicator B12)	H	H	N	H	H	M	N
Dangerous materials neutralized on site (Indicator B12)	H	H	M	H	L	N	N
Labor practices (Indicators C13+C15+C16)	H	H	N	L	N	N	N
Difference in average hourly pay-men woman (Indicator C17)	H	H	H	H	N	N	M
Human rights contract and company code clauses (Indicators D19 + D20)	H	H	N	H	M	N	N
Product responsibility checks and risks (Indicator E21)	H	H	N	H	N	N	N
Product safety complaints received (Indicator E22)	H	H	L	H	N	N	M
Corporate Governance Scale (Indicator F23+F24)	H	H	M	H	N	M	N

Legend:
1. Indicator numbers following the name of the performance indicator relate to the indicators as they appear in Appendix I.
2. Correlations are determined as high (H) when $\rho > \pm 0.7$; medium (M) $\rho > \pm 0.4$–0.6; low (L) $\rho < \pm 0.4$, only when significant. Non-significant correlations are assigned N.

extensive nor consistent demands relating to the various themes of CSR, although they may have specific singular demands. As to financial institutions (banks and insurance companies), the lack of concrete demands was stressed by numerous interviewees. Other stakeholders, such as customers, suppliers and employees were also, occasionally, mentioned by some interviewees as having no tangible demands in terms of CSR.

Finally, regulators' demands show a low level of correlation with CSP. We suggest that this finding, yet again, is highly dependent on the localized nature of the model application. Regulators tend not to encourage or motivate beyond-compliance behaviour among firms, and when coupled with relatively high compliance demands by regulators, generated mixed results in this area. Most CSP indicators show low to null correlation with regulatory demands. Nonetheless, five indicators show moderate correlations with regulatory demands. It is worthwhile noting that these stronger correlations are not exclusive to indicators oriented towards compliance, and appear with indicators oriented towards beyond-compliance behaviour as well. At the same time, the impact of regulatory power (the perceived power of regulators by managers) is null. If both of these factors (regulatory power and demands) are assessed together to generate regulatory pressure, the impact of regulators on CSP must be determined as weak.

The direct relationships of the upper levels of the model with CSP are graphically portrayed in Figure 6.2.

Summary

Multilevel analysis is regarded as crucial to forming a fuller, wider and more empirically valid understanding of the evolution of CSP in the business sector (Aguinis and Galavas, 2012). Despite its importance, to date few attempts have been made to elucidate and validate a comprehensive model that includes both inner and external potential factors affecting CSP. In this chapter, we present such an integrated model, relating the performance level to the upper institutional, organizational and individual levels. This is, to the best of our knowledge, the first analytical attempt to integrate a four level analysis of CSR.

As the application of the model is preliminary, the findings require several qualifications. Additionally, we suggest future attempts to apply the model may necessitate some expansions and improvements. The sample size for the institutional and performance levels reduced the possibilities of performing multivariate analyses, and mandated at this stage of the research project the reliance on bivariate analyses such as Pearson correlations and Spearman rank order correlations. Within the institutional level, we were unable to independently establish the individual demands of stakeholders, and were required to rely on perceived stakeholder power only. Finally, because of the preliminary nature of the study we have yet to conduct path analyses (structural equation models [SEM]) to address the full dynamics of our model.

Taking these qualifications into bear, we find that the individual level shows the most significant relationships with CSP. Particularly, we establish that elevated

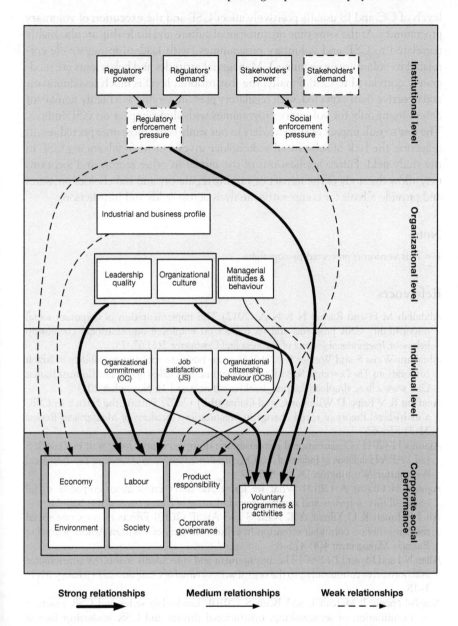

Figure 6.2 Summary of relationships found in model

levels of OC and JS usually positively affect CSP and the execution of voluntary programmes. At the same time organizational culture and leadership are also highly correlated to CSP and voluntary programmes (with leadership negatively cor-related to voluntary programmes). Managerial attitudes and behaviours are mod-erately correlated to CSP. Finally, the institutional level is much less dominant and effective than expected, with regulatory pressure serving as a highly significant determinant only for voluntary programmes with slight impact on CSP indices. The low to null impact of stakeholders in our study is the most unexpected result, reflecting the lack of substantial stakeholder involvement in advancing CSP in the study field. Future applications of the model in other sectors and locations may allow the study of the impact of varying regulatory and stakeholder pressures and provide a basis for comparative analysis across fields and jurisdictions.

Note

1   This version is protected by copyright.

References

Abdullah M H and Rashid N R N A (2012) The implementation of corporate social responsibility CSR programs and its impact on employee organizational citizenship behavior *International Journal of Business and Commerce* 2(1) 67–75

Abraham-Weiss S and Weiner R (2010) It is our business: social responsibility of Israeli corporations *The Corporate Social Responsibility Institute College of Law and Business* Ramat Gan www.clb.ac.il/uploads/online_booklet.pdf accessed 16 November 2014

Aguilera R V Rupp D Williams C and Ganapathi J (2007) Putting the S back in CSR: a multi-level theory of social change in organizations *Academy of Management Review* 32(3) 836–63

Aguinis H (2011) Organizational responsibility: doing good and doing well in Zedeck S (ed.) APA *Handbook of Industrial and Organizational Psychology* American Psychological Association Washington DC pp 855–79

Aguinis H Glavas A (2012) What we know and don't know about corporate social responsibility: a review and research agenda *Journal of Management* 38(4) 932–68

Ali I Rehman K U Yilmaz A K Nazir S and Ali JF (2010) Effects of corporate social responsibility on consumer retention in cellular industry of Pakistan *African Journal of Business Management* 4(4) 475–85

Allen N J and Meyer J P (1990) The measurement and antecedents of affective continuance and normative commitment to the organization *Journal of Occupational Psychology* 63(1) 1–18

Angus-Leppan T Metcalf L and Benn S (2010). Leadership styles and CSR practice: an examination of sensemaking, institutional drivers and CSR leadership *Journal of Business Ethics* 93(2) 189–213

Avolio B J and Bass B M (1999) Re-examining the components of transformational and transactional leadership using the Multifactor Leadership Questionnaire *Journal of Occupational and Organizational Psychology* 72(4) 441–62

Bar-Haim A (2007) Rethinking organizational commitment in relation to perceived organizational power and perceived employment alternatives *International Journal of Cross Cultural Management* 7(2) 203–17

BGSU (2009) Job description index www.bgsu.edu/arts-and-sciences/psychology/services/ job-descriptive-index.html accessed 20 November 2014

Borck J C and Coglianese C (2011) Beyond compliance: explaining business participation in voluntary environmental programs in Parker C and Lehmann-Nielsen V (eds) *Explaining Compliance Business Responses to Regulation* Cheltenham UK Edward Elgar pp 139–69

Cameron K S and Quinn R E (1999) *Diagnosing and Changing Organizational Culture* Reading UK Addison-Wesley

Carroll A B (1999) Corporate social responsibility: evolution of a definitional construct. *Business and Society* 38(3) 268–95

Carroll A B and Shabana K M (2010) The business case for corporate social responsibility: a review of concepts *International Journal of Management Reviews* 12(1) 85–105

Carroll A E (1979) A three dimensional conceptual model of corporate social performance *Academy of Management Review* 4(4) 497–505

Chun J S Shin J Choi N J and Kim M S (2013) How does corporate ethics contribute to firm financial performance the mediating role of collective organizational commitment and organizational citizenship behavior *Journal of Management* 39(4) 853–77

Clarkson M E (1995) A stakeholder framework for analyzing and evaluating corporate social performance *The Academy of Management Review* 20(1) 92–117

Collier J and Esteban R (2007) Corporate social responsibility and employee commitment *Business Ethics: A European Review* 16(1) 19–33

Cooke R A and Lafferty J C (1989) *Organizational Culture Inventory* Plymouth MI Human Synergistics

Corcoran D J and Shackman J D (2007) A theoretical and empirical analysis of the strategic value of beyond-compliance occupational health and safety programs *Journal of Business Strategies* 24(1) 49–68

Crilly DSchneider S C and Zollo M (2008) Psychological antecedents to socially responsive behavior *European Management Review* 5(3) 175–90

Deal T E and Kennedy A A (2000) *Corporate Cultures: The Rites and Rituals of Corporate Life* London Perseus Books

Ditlev-Simonsen C and Wenstøp F (2013) How stakeholders view stakeholders as CSR motivators *Social Responsibility Journal* 9(1) 137–47

Donaldson T and L E Preston (1995) The stakeholder theory of the corporation: concepts evidence and implications *Academy of Management Review* 20(1) 65–91

Egri C P and Herman S (2000) Leadership in the north American environmental sector: values leadership styles and contexts of environmental leaders and their organizations *Academy of Management Journal* 43(4) 571–604

Elkington J (2001) Enter the triple bottom line in Henriques A and Richardson J (eds) *The Triple Bottom Line does it all add up? Assessing the Sustainability of Business and CSR* London Earthscan pp 1–16

Ellemers N Kingma L Van de Burgt J and Barreto M (2011) Corporate social responsibility as a source of organizational commitment and satisfaction *Journal of Organizational Moral Psychology* 1(2) 97–124

Evan W F and Freeman R E (1993) A stakeholder theory of modern corporation: kantian capitalism in Beauchamp T and Bowie N (eds) *Ethical Theory and Business* Englewood Cliffs NJ Prentice Hall pp 75–84

Faure M G Ogus A I and Philipsen N J (2009) Curbing consumer financial losses: the economics of regulatory enforcement *Law and Policy* 31(2) 161–91

Fernández-Kranz D and Santaló J (2010) When necessity becomes a virtue: the effect of product market competition on corporate social responsibility *Journal of Economics and Management Strategy* 19(2) 453–487

Fiorino D J (2006) *The New Environmental Regulation* Cambridge MA Institute of Technology Press

Gamerschlag R Möller K and Verbeeten F (2011) Determinants of voluntary CSR disclosure: empirical evidence from Germany *Review of Managerial Science* 5(2–3) 233–62

Gill H Meyer J P Lee K Shin K and Yoon C (2011) Affective and continuance commitment and their relations with deviant workplace behaviors in Korea *Asia Pacific Journal of Management* 28(3) 595–607

Gjølberg M (2009) Measuring the immeasurable? Constructing an index of CSR practices and CSP in 20 countries *Scandinavian Journal of Management* 25(1) 10–22

Gouldson A and Murphy J (1998) Integrating environment and economy through ecological modernisation: an assessment of the impact of environmental policy on industrial innovation OCEES Research Paper No 16 Oxford Centre for the Environment Ethics and Society Mansfield College University of Oxford

Griffin J J and Mahon J F (1997) The corporate social performance and corporate financial performance debate *Business and Society* 36(1) 5–31

Groves K S and Larocca M A (2011) Responsible leadership outcomes via stakeholder CSR values: testing a values-centered model of transformational leadership *Journal of Business Ethics* 98 37–55

Gunningham N Kagan R A and Thornton D (2003) *Shades of Green Business Regulation and the Environment* Stanford CA Stanford University Press

Gunningham N Kagan R A and Thornton D (2004) Social license and environmental protection: why businesses go beyond-compliance *Law and Social Inquiry* 29(2) 307–41

Harari M (2011) The missing billions: aggressive tax planning and social responsibility of Israeli Corporations *The Corporate Social Responsibility Institute College of Law and Business Ramat Gan*. www.clb.ac.il/uploads/TAAGIDIM.pdf accessed 16 November 2014.

Hemingway C A (2005) Personal values as a catalyst for corporate social entrepreneurship *Journal of Business Ethics* 60(3) 233–49

Hemingway C A and Maclagan P W (2004) Managers' personal values as drivers of corporate social responsibility *Journal of Business Ethics* 50(1): 33–44

Henriques I and Sadorsky P (1996) The determinants of an environmentally responsive firm: an empirical approach *Journal of Environmental Economics and Management* 30(3) 381–95

Herscovitch L and Meyer J P (2002) Commitment to organizational change: extension of a three-component model *Journal of Applied Psychology* 87(3) 474–87

Jaakson K Vadi M and Tamm K (2009) Organizational culture and CSR: An exploratory study of estonian service organizations *Social Responsibility Journal* 5(1) 6–18

Judge T A Bono J E Thoresen C J and Patton G K (2001) The job satisfaction-job performance relationship: a qualitative and quantitative review *Psychological Bulletin* 127(3) 376–407

Kagan R A and Scholtz J (1984) The 'criminology of the corporation' and regulatory enforcement strategies in Hawkins K and Thomas J (eds) *Enforcing Regulation* Kluwer Boston Nijhoff Publishing pp 67–95

Kagan R A Gunningham N and Thornton D (2003) Explaining corporate environmental performance: how does regulation matter? *Law and Society Review* 37(1) 51–90

Ketola T (2008) A holistic corporate responsibility model: integrating values discourses and actions *Journal of Business Ethics* 80(3) 419–35

Koehler D A (2007) The effectiveness of voluntary environmental programs—a policy at a crossroads? *The Policy Studies Journal* 35(4) 689–722

Kotter J P Heskett J L (1992) *Corporate Culture and Performance* New York The Free Press

Law S K Wong C and Chen X Z (2005) The construct of organizational citizenship behavior: Should we analyze after we have conceptualized? In D L Turnipseed Ed *Handbook of organizational citizenship behavior* pp 47–65 New York Nova Science Publishers

LePine J A Erez A and Johnson D E (2002) The nature and dimensionality of organizational citizenship behavior: A critical review and meta-analysis *Journal of Applied Psychology* 87(1) 52–65

Lim S J Phillips J (2008) Embedding CSR values: the global footwear industry's evolving governance structure *Journal of Business Ethics* 81(1) 143–56

Lindgreen A Swaen V Johnston W (2009) Corporate social responsibility: an empirical investigation of US organizations *Journal of Business Ethics* 85(S2) 303–23

Ling Y Simsek Z Lubatkin M H and Veiga J F (2008) Transformational leadership's role in promoting corporate entrepreneurship: examining the CEO-TMT interface *Academy of Management Journal* 51(3) 557–76

Liu X Liu B Shishime T Yu Q Bi J and Fujitsuka T (2010) An empirical study on the driving mechanism of proactive corporate environmental management in China *Journal of Environmental Management* 9(1) 1707–17

Lock P and Crawford J (1999) The relationship between commitment and organisational culture subculture leadership style and job satisfaction in organisational change and development *Leadership and Organisational Development Journal* 20(7) 365–73

Locke E A (1997) The motivation to work: what we know in Maehr M L and Pintrich P R (eds) *Advances in Motivation and Achievement* (Vol 10) Greenwich CT JAI Press pp 375–412

Locke E A (2004) What should we do about motivation theory? Six recommendations for the twenty first century *Academy of Management Review* 29(3) 388–403

MacKenzie S B Podsakoff P M and Fetter R (1991) Organizational citizenship behavior and objective productivity as determinants of managerial evaluations of salespersons' performance *Organizational Behavior and Human Decision Processes* 50(1) 123–50

MacKenzie S B Podskoff P M and Fetter R (1993) The impact of organizational citizenship behavior on evaluations of salesperson performance *Journal of Marketing* 57(1) 70

Margolis J D and Walsh J P (2003) Misery loves companies social initiatives by business *Administrative Science Quarterly* 48 268–305

Marimona F Alonso-Almeidab M Rodríguezc M Alejandroc C A K (2012) The worldwide diffusion of the global reporting initiative: what is the point? *Journal of Cleaner Production* 33 132–44

Maron I Y (2006) Toward a unified theory of the CSP-CFP link *Journal of Business Ethics* 67(2) 191–200

Matten D and Moon J (2008) Implicit and explicit CSR: a conceptual framework for comparative understanding of corporate social responsibility *Academy of Management Review* 33(2) 404–24

Maxwell J W Lyon T P Hackett S C (2000) Self-regulation and social welfare: the political economy of corporate environmentalism *Journal of Law and Economics* 43(2) 583–619

May P (2005) Compliance motivations: perspectives of farmers home builders and marine facilities *Law and Policy* 27(2) 317–47

Meegeren P (2001) Blue bags or refuse tourism: social acceptance of closed policymaking *Society and Natural Resources* 14(1) 77–86

Meyer J P Allen N J and Gellatly I R (1990) Affective and continuance commitment to the organization: Evaluation of measures and analysis of concurrent and time lagged relations *Journal of Applied Psychology* 75(6) 710–20

Meyer J P Allen N J (1984) Testing the 'side-bet theory' of organizational commitment: some methodological considerations *Journal of Applied Psychology* 69(3) 372–78

Meyer J P and Allen N J (1997) *Commitment in the Workplace: Theory Research and Application* Thousand Oaks CA Sage Publications

Mitchell, R K Agle B R and Wood D J (1997) Toward a theory of stakeholder identification and salience: Defining the principle of who and what really counts. *Academy of Management Review* 22(4) 853–86.

Murillo D and Lozano J M (2006) SMEs and CSR: an approach to CSR in their own words *Journal of Business Ethics* 67(3) 227–40

Needle D (2010) *Business in Context: An Introduction to Business and Its Environment* (5th edn) Andover UK South Western Educational Publishing

Nuttaneeya A T Wayne O'Donohue and Hecker R (2012) Capabilities proactive CSR and financial performance in SMEs: empirical evidence from an Australian manufacturing industry sector *Journal of Business Ethics* 109(4) 483–500

Organ D W (1988) *Organizational Citizenship Behavior: The Good Soldier Syndrome* Lexington MA Lexington Books

Organ D W (1997) Organizational citizenship behavior: it's construct cleanup time *Human Performance* 10(2) 85–97

Organ D W Podsakoff P M and MacKenzie S P (2006) *Organizational Citizenship Behavior: Its Nature Antecedents and Consequences* London Sage Publications

O'Riordan L and Fairbrass J (2014) Managing CSR stakeholder engagement: A new conceptual framework *Journal of Business Ethics* 125(1) 121–45

Parent M M and Deephouse D L (2007) A case study of stakeholder identification and prioritization by managers *Journal of Business Ethics* 75(1) 1–23

Pearce D and Barbier E B (2000) *Blueprint for a Sustainable Economy* London Earthscan

Pies I Hielscher S and Beckmann M (2009) Moral commitments and the societal role of business: an ordonomic approach to corporate citizenship *Business Ethics Quarterly* 19(3) 375–401

Podsakoff P M and MacKenzie S B (1994) Organizational citizenship behavior and sales unit effectiveness *Journal of Marketing Research* 31 351–63

Podsakoff P M and MacKenzie S P (1997) Impact of organizational citizenship behavior on organizational performance: a review and suggestion for future research *Human Performance* 10(2) 133–51

Podsakoff P M MacKenzie S B Moorman R H and Fetter R (1990) Transformational leader behaviors and their effects on followers' trust in leader satisfaction and organizational citizenship behaviors *The Leadership Quarterly* 1(2) 107–42

Prakash A and Potoski M (2006) Racing to the bottom? Trade environmental governance and ISO 14001 *American Journal of Political Science* 50(2) 350–64

Preuss L and Brown D (2012) Business policies on human rights: an analysis of their content and prevalence among FTSE 100 firms *Journal of Business Ethics* 109(3) 289–99

Reijnders L (2003) Policies influencing cleaner production: the role of prices and regulation, *Journal of Cleaner Production* 11(3) 333–38

Rupp D E (2011) An employee-centered model of organizational justice and social responsibility *Organizational Psychology Review* 1(1) 72–94

Rupp D E Williams C A and Aguilera R V (2010) Increasing corporate social responsibility through stakeholder value internalization and the catalyzing effect of new governance:

an application of organizational justice self-determination and social influence theories in Schminke M (ed.) *Managerial Ethics: Managing the Psychology of Morality* New York Routledge pp 69–88

Sarker T K (2013) Voluntary codes of conduct and their implementation in the Australian mining and petroleum industries: is there a business case for CSR? *Asian Journal of Business Ethics* 2(2) 205–24

Schein E H (1992) *Organizational Culture and Leadership: A Dynamic View* San Francisco CA Jossey-Bass p 9

Schein E H (2006) *Organizational Culture and Leadership* (3rd edn) San Francisco CA Jossey-Bass

Scherer A G and Palazzo G (2011) The new political role of business in a globalized world a review of a new perspective on CSR and its implications for the firm governance and democracy *Journal of Management Studies* 48(4) 899–931

Smith P C Kendall L M and Hulin C L (1969) *The Measurement of Satisfaction in Work and Retirement* Chicago IL Rand McNally

Spector P E (1997) *Job satisfaction: Application assessment causes and consequences* Thousand Oaks CA Sage

Stafford S (2002) The effect of punishment on firm compliance with hazardous waste regulations *Journal of Environmental Economics and Management* 44(2) 290–308

Strand R (2011) Exploring the role of leadership in corporate social responsibility: a review *Journal of Leadership Accountability and Ethics* 8(4) 84–96

Szekely F and Knirsch M (2005) Responsible leadership and corporate social responsibility: metrics for sustainable performance *European Management Journal* 23(5) 628–47

Thornton D Kagan R A Gunningham N (2009) When social norms and pressures are not enough: environmental performance in the trucking industry *Law and Society Review* 43(2) 405–36

Tietenberg T (1998) Disclosure strategies for pollution control *Environmental and Resource Economics* 113(4) 587–602

Tochman C J Eden L and Miller S R (2012) Multinationals and corporate social responsibility in host countries: does distance matter? *Journal of International Business Studies* 43(1) 84–106

Turker D (2009) How corporate social responsibility influences organizational commitment *Journal of Business Ethics* 89(2) 189–204

Tyler T R (2012) The Psychology of self-regulation: normative motivations for compliance in Parker C and Lehmann-Nielsen V (eds) *Explaining Compliance Business Responses to Regulation* Cheltenham UK Edward Elgar pp 78–99

Tyler T R Dienhart J and Thomas T (2008) The ethical commitment to compliance: building value based cultures that encourage ethical conduct and commitment to compliance *California Management Review* 50(2) 31–51

Tziner A (2013) Corporative social responsibility CSR activities in the workplace: a comment on Aguinis and Glavas 2013 *Revista De Psicología Del Trabajo y De Las Organizaciones* 29(2) 91

Übius U and Alas R (2009) Organizational culture types as predictors of corporate social responsibility *Engineering Economics* 16(1) 90–9

Vachon S and Klassen R D (2006) Extending green practices across the supply chain *International Journal of Operations and Production Management* 26(7) 795–821

Valentine S and Fleischman G (2008) Ethics programs perceived corporate social responsibility and job satisfaction *Journal of Business Ethics* 77(2) 159 van Beurden P and Gössling T (2008) The worth of values – a literature review on the relation between corporate social and financial performance *Journal of Business Ethics* 82(2) 407–24

van der Kooija A J Meulmana J J Heiserb W J (2006) Local minima in categorical multiple regression *Computational Statistics and Data Analysis* 50(2) 446–62

van Erp J (2011) Naming and shaming in regulatory enforcement In Parker C and Lehmann-Nielsen V (eds) *Explaining Compliance Business Responses to Regulation* Cheltenham UK Edward Elgar pp 322–43

Vandenbergh M P (2003) Beyond elegance: a testable typology of social norms in corporate environmental compliance *Stanford Environmental Law Journal* 22(1) 55–144

Vlachos P A Panagopoulos N G and Rapp A A (2013) Feeling good by doing good: employee CSR-induced attributions job satisfaction and the role of charismatic leadership *Journal of Business Ethics* 118(3) 577–88

Vogel D (2005) *The Market for Virtue The Potential and Limits of Corporate Social Responsibility* Washington DC Brookings Institute Press

Waldman D A D and Siegel D (2008) Defining the socially responsible leader *Leadership Quarterly* 19(1) 117–31

Waldman D A Sully D L Washburn N House R J Adetoun B Barrasa A and Grachev M (2006) Cultural and leadership predictors of corporate social responsibility values of top management: a globe study of 15 countries *Journal of International Business Studies* 37(6) 823–37

Wasti S A (2005) Commitment profiles: combinations of organizational commitment forms and job outcomes *Journal of Vocational Behavior* 67(2) 290–308

Weyzig F (2006) Local and global dimensions of corporate social responsibility in Mexico *Journal of Corporate Citizenship* 2006(24) 69–81

Wolfe R and Aupperle K (1991) Introduction to corporate social performance: methods for evaluating an elusive construct *Research in Corporate Social Performance and Policy* 12 265–68

Zhang B Bi J Yuan Z Ge J Liu B and Bu M (2008) Why do firms engage in environmental management? An empirical study in China *Journal of Cleaner Production* 16(10) 1036–45

Part 4

Effecting sustainable partnerships

7 A theory of public–private sustainable development partnerships

Duane Windsor

Introduction

This chapter seeks to advance conceptual development of a theory of public–private sustainable development partnerships. The justification for this theory is that 'Sustainable development requires concerted collaborative actions at all levels from macro to micro and across all sectors' (Austin, 2007: 49). Four central research questions have been identified (Austin, 2007: 49). (1) What are the motivations for collaboration? (2) How do partnerships evolve over time? (3) How do partnerships create value for participants? (4) What are the key performance determinants (see Greve, 2010)? A considerable amount of literature has been published on various aspects of these research questions. This chapter addresses the four questions through the application of a proposed theory of public–private sustainable development partnerships to three examples: the Chad-Cameroon Petroleum Development and Pipeline Project in Africa; the Merck Mectizan® Donation Program (MDP) operating in Africa, Latin America and Yemen; and the global anti-corruption role of Transparency International (TI).

The extant conceptualization tends, however, to be fragmented rather than integrated. The literature on multi-stakeholder partnerships (Pinkse and Kolk, 2012; Roloff, 2008a, 2008b; Svendsen and Laberge, 2005) directs attention to issues of accountability, legitimacy (Herlin, 2013) and performance (Bäckstrand, 2006; Murray et al., 2010). This literature tends to fragment into partnerships between businesses and non-governmental organizations (NGOs) (O'Connor and Shumate, 2014; Vock et al., 2014), or between governments and NGOs (Millar, 2013), or between businesses and governments (Ward, 2014). The literature also tends to highlight specific problems such as conflict minerals (Lehr, 2010; Kolk and Lenfant, 2012); and emphasize NGOs as key actors (Dahan et al., 2010; Doh, 2003; Kourula and Laasonen, 2010).

To formulate a theory of public–private sustainable development partnerships involves, to reiterate Austin (2007), understanding logic and practice of collective action across all levels from global to local and simultaneously across all sectors (Selsky and Parker, 2005, 2010). This chapter thus addresses the question of how public and private interests and international and national institutions might interact cooperatively to help foster long-term environmental conservation and socio-economic development in developing countries. The theory will discuss the roles of four kinds of organizations: profit-oriented enterprises; governments (national and sub-national), international institutions (UN Global Club, WTO, etc.) and civil society organizations (NGOs, non-profits, foundations, social enterprises, etc.). The theory is thus at a minimum based on a four-sector framework. Notions of public and private interests and of public and social choice may cut across these organizational forms. Partnerships will likely vary considerably by country and industry and social issue. Definition of boundaries and interaction relationships will vary accordingly. The most macro level involves truly global regimes (Fransen ad Kolk, 2007; Waddell, 2003). The most micro level may be a local community or a specific environmental preserve (IUCN, 2012). At all levels, there should be a fully four-sector involvement (Goggins and Rochlin, 2000; Le Ber and Branzei, 2010).

An emerging body of literature has argued for a strong version of political corporate social responsibility (CSR) in both developed and developing countries (Palazzo and Schere,r 2008; Scherer and Palazzo, 2007, 2011; Scherer *et al.*, 2013; Scherer *et al.*, 2014). Across both types of countries, a firm should support democratic principles. In developing countries, firms may have also increasing responsibility for helping provide public goods as well as democratization as governments prove relatively incapable of doing so. Weisbrod (1975) treats non-profit organizations as suppliers of public goods to heterogeneous populations in conditions under which governments undersupply those public goods (Kingma, 1994). Heterogeneity means considerable variation in demand across people and locations. NGOs might be considered analogously as supplying public interest goods. This chapter explores the options for fostering partnerships (complementary approaches) as distinct from substitution approaches. There is thus an overarching theory within which the political CSR argument should be placed. This theory should take account of formal and informal bargaining among the four kinds of organizations that will be engaged in sustainable development partnerships. There is a wide array of international institutions and other forms of international policy regimes that in fragmented fashion try to address development issues.

The chapter is structured as follows. This introduction explains the aims and approach of the chapter. The main features of the proposed theory follow in the next section. A theory of public–private sustainable development partnerships will initially be fairly abstract in outline and content. This initial abstraction is unavoidable in getting at the key elements of how partnerships might be formed and operated. The rest of the chapter provides in sequence three specific examples used to help illustrate the theory in operation. The examples combine various elements of the four-sector framework. Each example is the topic of a section. The methodology of the chapter is to outline a theory, or conceptual framework, developed logically from a reading of literature and to show the variations occurring in the three specific examples. The theory is positive and prescriptive in character. 'Positive' means that the theory is developed in conjunction with the empirical examples cited; 'prescriptive' means that the theory is to be applied in practice to the greatest extent feasible in specific conditions. The purpose of the theory is to strengthen understanding of how public–private partnerships can advance sustainable development goals. Those goals are normative in orientation, in the sense that sustainable development aims at improvement of both the natural environment and human welfare. The conclusions section focuses on the implications and limitations of the proposedtheory for managers, scholars, and others.

The first example is the consortium formed by the World Bank and ExxonMobil, and the latter's business partners, to develop an oil pipeline from Chad through Cameroon. The example involves cross-sector conflict (anti-corruption controls and NGO resistance) as well as cross-sector cooperation. All four sectors were involved. The businesses and Chad wanted to execute the project, but the businesses would not act without World Bank risk mitigation. NGOs attempted to block the project at the level of the World Bank and then closely monitored the project until its effective failure in 2008 through World Bank withdrawal. A four-sector framework can operate without direct and willing cooperation. How well the project performed for the economic and social development of Chad and Cameroon is still being debated.

The second example is the long established and still operating Merck Mectizan® Donation Program (MDP) for free distribution of an anti-river blindness medication with WHO, governmental, local community and foundation participation. In this instance, a profit-oriented corporation Merck was the initiating entity; and WHO and governments tended to resist initially. In the longer-term a multi-partner structure has developed for distribution of the medication, including expansion from river blindness to elephantiasis. The program has become a model for other health initiatives in tropical developing countries.

The third example is how the anti-corruption principle of the UN Global Compact (UNGC) and the UN Convention against Corruption (UNCAC) operates through parallel implementation by governments, NGOs (particularly Transparency International) and enterprises. Parallel action is an alternative to direct partnership efforts, which are now developing. While there is now a global anti-corruption regime formally expressed in inter-governmental accords, corruption remains persistent and pervasive. In this setting, Transparency International (TI), an NGO, has been a key actor for mobilizing anti-corruption reform efforts within countries.

Four-sector theory of sustainable development partnerships

The foundation of the theory is the positive argument that sustainable development can be addressed successfully only by collective action of all four sectors at all levels from global to local. (More sectors might be added in future research if deemed relevant.) The roles of the sectors can, however, vary considerably as the three examples will illustrate. This chapter does not undertake to demonstrate that sustainable development is feasible; rather the focus is on a public–private theory of sustainable development partnerships that are necessary rather than automatically sufficient.

The very concept of sustainable development, which has a strongly normative orientation, is arguably a problem. A widely quoted definition of sustainable development is that adopted in the Brundtland Report on *Our Common Future* (Brundtland, 1987: 43) for the United Nations (Borowy, 2014):

> Sustainable development is development that meets the needs of the present without compromising the ability of future generations to meet their own needs. It contains within it two key concepts:
>
> - the concept of 'needs', in particular the essential needs of the world's poor, to which overriding priority should be given; and
> - the idea of 'limitations' imposed by the state of technology and social organization on the environment's ability to meet present and future needs.

The Brundtland Report definition contains conflicting goals of environmental protection versus economic and social development to alleviate poverty (Hueting, 1990; Jacob, 1994); and these conflicting goals lack reconciliation in a context of continuing population growth in the developing countries. The report makes needs of the poor 'essential' and thus a normative imperative. In reality, de-growth may be needed rather than sustainable growth (Martínez-Alier et al., 2010). The solutions must be worked out by the sustainable development partnerships at all levels of action.

The Limits of Growth study completed for the Club of Rome in 1972 forecasted that within 100 years, if growth trends remained unchecked, the limits to physical growth on earth would be reached (see Kaldor, 1986). The third edition of the study argues that a sustainable society is technically and economically feasible through (1) slowing growth in consumption and population and (2) at the same time greatly increasing efficiency of material and energy use (Meadow et al., 2004).

The world population in August 2014 exceeded 7.185 billion people.[1] Birth rate exceeds death rate. The 2014 revised projection of the UN Population Division expects for the year 2050 a low (optimistic) level of nearly 8 billion people, a medium (most likely) level of about 9.2 billion and a high (pessimistic) level of about 10.5 billion.[2] The revision increases somewhat the low projection and decreases somewhat the medium and high projections, based on revision in estimated fertility rates. Basically, developed areas are maintaining population and developing areas are increasing population. Whether a Malthusian overpopulation catastrophe scenario, a 1798 formulation dependent on diminishing returns to agricultural production, may occur or not (Aikanathan et al., 2014; Findeis and Pervez, 2014), population growth and increased consumption per capita place pressure on limited resources; and global climate change is occurring and arguably accelerating.

Green consumerism – defined as consumer responsibility to maintain economic growth for alleviation of world poverty and to bear the burden for sustainability costs – is arguably not likely to be the solution to sustainable development (Akenji, 2014). The fundamental requirement is structural change, which must be driven by organizations and institutions. Encouraging green consumption is important, but the effects of green products, eco-labels, consumer awareness campaigns, etc., will be incremental and cumulative rather than dramatic and rapid (Akenji, 2014).

A normative argument favouring environmental protection would be that a lack of truly 'sustainable development' might be catastrophic in that development would outstrip sustainability. A tipping point, or threshold, is a point at which a system (of any kind, but here in particular human-environmental systems) shifts radically and possibly irreversibly into a different state condition (Brook *et al.*, 2013). While conceding that there can be catastrophic ecological tipping points at local and regional scales, Brook *et al.*, (2013) argues that planetary scale tipping points in the terrestrial biosphere are unconfirmed claims. Those authors point out that there is spatial heterogeneity in human drivers and human responses and also lack of strong interconnectivity across continents. There is thus an important distinction between tipping points, or thresholds, at the global and regional or local levels. There may or may not be a global tipping point at which the planet biosphere fails; such a global threshold is an issue for certain kinds of regimes and organizations and governance of such regimes including international institutions may be an especially difficult problem. Little is yet known about governance at such large scales (see Galaz *et al.*, 2014). Those authors analyse three cases of global network responses to global change-induced 'tipping points' for ocean acidification, fisheries collapse and infectious disease outbreaks (illustrated by the recent Ebola crisis in West Africa). Their cases suggest that research is needed into information processing and early warning, multi-level and multi-network responses, diversity in response capacity and the balance between efficiency and legitimacy. Generally, cross-sector cooperation will be more immediately useful at local and regional scales (Findeis and Pervez, 2014).

The four-sector theory conceptualized here is presumably most compatible with a market economy setting, but the varieties of market-like economies can be pretty broad in range. A reasonably democratic government is also most desirable, as the Chad pipeline example shows; but the Merck example suggests that democratic government is not automatically necessary in the health sector. The essential distinctions are between a market economy and a non-market economy, on the one hand, and between a clear legal framework and government operation outside of a legal framework. The distinctions can be combined in a two-by-two matrix for classifying kinds of economies (Rose, 1992 provided this approach). A command economy, featured in the former USSR and similar Communist states and away from which China is evolving, is a legal but non-market approach in which the state constitutionally owns (or in China strongly influences) the means of production and earlier practiced central planning. Within a command economy, there is typically operating an illegal black market in part to help in meeting central planning requirements, violation of which could be treated as a crime (Rose, 1992). Rose suggests that, as conditions move within a non-market context to operation outside the law (through collapse of the state), there arises a parasitical economy in which illegitimate force is used to seize resources. For purposes of this chapter, as conditions within a market economy move to operation outside the law there arises a shadow economy, or informal economy, in which unregulated market exchanges occur (Neuwirth, 2011; Schneider and Enste, 2002). An underground economy has the connotation of tax evasion through non-reporting (Cebula and Feige, 2012).

The combination of legal framework and market economy can occur in a number of variations across a reasonably broad range. The essentially non-regulated laissez faire capitalist economy with a small government does not exist much in the real world. The main variants are three-sector regulatory capitalism, indicative guidance, social market economy and the proposed model of a civil economy. Three-sector regulatory capitalism, as in the United States and the United Kingdom, involves varying mixes of business, government and voluntary (civil society) sectors (Weisbrod, 1975). Japan and France have practiced indicative guidance (*dirigisme* in France) to help avoid market failure through relatively voluntary coordination of private and public activities. Much of Western Europe – Austria, Belgium, Germany, the Netherlands, Scandinavia, and Switzerland – adheres to a social market economy (*Soziale Marktwirtschaft*) model, or European social model, for a coordinated market economy, which combines the market economy with social policy in various approaches (Ebner, 2006; Leterme 2014).

While given a number of interpretations, the proposed concept of civil economy tends to suggest increased emphasis on the common good in economic and political behaviour (Bruyn, 2000), and thus often a desired trend (Lazonick, 2003) towards some combination of co-operatives (Arcas *et al.*, 2014; Bernardi and Miani, 2014), smaller businesses (Manfra, 2002), and social enterprises (Santos, 2012) in place of today's large, often global corporations.

One theory of social entrepreneurship is that the phenomenon involves motives to pursue sustainable solutions to problems, neglected by both businesses (i.e., commercial entrepreneurs) and governments (i.e., public goods providers), with positive externalities for society (Santos, 2012). There is a trade-off between value creation (emphasized by social entrepreneurs) and value capture (emphasized by commercial entrepreneurs) (Santos, 2012). A theory should explain conditions for neglect and how to address the trade-off between value creation and value capture.

The four-sector theory of public–private sustainable development partnerships is compatible with any of these approaches to combining a clear legal framework with a market economy (Hall and Soskice, 2001). A theory of the modern capitalist economy (how it functions) is not thereby a theory of economic and social development; a functioning market economy is the result of development, not the cause of development (Lazonick, 2003). Organizations and institutions are the foundations for the entrepreneurial and technical innovations that drive economic and social development (Lazonick, 2003). 'To reap the advantages of a "market economy", a society must first put in place the organizations and institutions that generate the innovative capabilities that underpin economic development and that make possible the emergence of well functioning markets in capital, labour and products' (Lazonick, 2003: 9). The situation in developing countries is more complex due to typically greater levels of corruption, greater governmental incapacity, severe economic and social development needs due to poverty and increasing destruction of natural resources.

Chad-Cameroon Petroleum Development and Pipeline Project

A four-sector approach in which conflict rather than cooperation occurs was reflected in the Chad–Cameroon Petroleum Development and Pipeline Project. That project, promoted by the World Bank, in an effort to help develop Chad (one of the world's poorest countries), failed in its sustainable development and anti-corruption goals in 2008 with withdrawal of the World Bank from further efforts to direct revenues to the country's population (Clausen and Attaran, 2011) in the face of pervasive government corruption. In January 2006, Chad unilaterally changed the pipeline governing law in its favour. However, oil has continued to flow; and the commercial venture partners involved in developing the pipeline have remained at work in Chad. This example illustrates the likely importance of four-sector cooperation but also that projects can occur under conflict conditions. The Chad government and the World Bank (acting in support of a business consortium) had opposing interests; and NGOs opposed the project from the outset. The project had important environmental, health and revenue redistribution dimensions.

In January 1999, following several years of negotiation with the World Bank, the government of Chad enacted a Petroleum Revenue Management Law (PRML) to permit construction and operation of a pipeline to transport oil more than 1,000 kilometers (650 miles) from southern Chad through Cameroon to an Atlantic Ocean port for ocean shipping. Chad, poor and landlocked in the centre of northern (sub-Saharan) Africa, with a shrinking Lake Chad in the southwest, has one resource – oil located in southern Chad – for economic development. Chad has faced invasions from Libya, military coups, and refugee problems from Darfur (western Sudan).[3]

The production field in Chad and pipeline through Cameroon involved a joint venture of ExxonMobil, Petronas of Malaysia and ChevronTexaco, which required some funding support from the World Bank in order to proceed (Esty, 2001). The pipeline was buried to minimize environmental and social impacts. It crosses deserts and forests, goes under rivers and passes through areas of indigenous populations including forest Pygmies and habitats for black rhinos.

The project development included extensive environmental and social assessments, emphasized public–private partnerships, attempted to manage oil revenues for poverty reduction and addressed occupational and public health issues (Utzinger et al., 2005).

Given the pervasive corruption in Chad and Cameroon, the World Bank imposed special controls and monitoring devices to try to safeguard revenues for economic development benefiting the population (Gould and Winters, 2007; Norland, 2003). The PRML framework was intended to operate generally as follows (Gould 2012). Revenues owing to Chad would go to a bank escrow account in London subject to World Bank control. Those revenues would be released to Chad so as to help avoid boom–bust cycles in the international oil price tending to generate inflation during boom and government budget cuts during bust fostering distributional conflict within Chad. Debt service payments would be deducted first; and then 10 per cent of the net revenues (after deduction) would go to a Future Generations Fund held for redistribution after Chad oil production ceased. From the other 90 per cent of the net revenues, 80 per cent of that amount would go to priority development sectors such as health, education, rural development and environmental protection; 5 per cent would go to develop the oil-producing region in the south (at Doba, a Christian area in a predominantly Muslim country), and 15 per cent would go to the government as discretionary funds. A *Collège*, comprised of five government representatives (two members of parliament, the head of the central bank, the director of the treasury and a Supreme Court justice) theoretically independent of the president and four non-governmental representatives (one each from Chadian NGOs, unions, human rights organizations and religious groups), was appointed to oversee governmental spending.

In 2000, the World Bank extended two relatively small loans. The first loan of US$17.5 million went to both the *Collège* and certain government ministries to improve budgeting and auditing capacity and upgrade financial management software. The second loan of US$23.7 million was to support environmental management capacity and to create a pilot development fund for the Doha region. The business consortium provided US$3.7 billion in capital in combination with further World Bank loans. The World Bank's participation was 3 per cent, and served as 'risk mitigation' for the business consortium's reputation.

The project has been under close scrutiny from various independent monitoring groups, civil society organizations and human rights groups (Utzinger *et al.*, 2004). The initial role of the NGOs was to mobilize pressure against the project, seeking initially to persuade the World Bank to reject the arrangements. The expressed position of the NGOs was that the project would harm the environment and the health and livelihood of the populations in Chad and Cameroon. The Chad government was hardly democratic. The decision problem for the World Bank was whether the population's welfare could be improved, with oil the only resource to that purpose. Amnesty International (2005) subsequently issued a report highly critical of the World Bank and the joint venture in terms of conduct and impacts on Chad and Cameroon. There have been difficulties in the project development and operation, reflected in reports concerning Pygmy communities in Cameroon and health effects of the pipeline project.

A grassroots consultation by the Forest Peoples Project with the Bagyeli Pygmy communities in Cameroon and discussions with other key stakeholders and agencies, including NGOs, concluded that there were significant information gaps and poor communication with resulting confusion concerning the Indigenous Peoples Plan (IPP) and the Compensation Plan (CP). The study also found daily discrimination against the Bagyeli from Bantu farmers and local governments (Nelson *et al.*, 2001).

Like many sub-Saharan African countries, Chad and Cameroon had and still has a variety of tropical diseases and other health issues antedating the pipeline project. Malaria has remained a serious health problem along the pipeline corridor (Songue *et al.*, 2013). The aims of the pipeline project included efforts to improve health and social conditions in the two countries. It has not been clear how well these aims have been achieved. An evaluation study (Utzinger *et al.*, 2005) proposed a longitudinal demographic surveillance system including regular household surveys to assess community and regional health status. The project reportedly helped implement community health outreach programming (CHOP) through innovative public–private partnerships including the business consortium, government agencies, international organizations and civil society organizations (Utzinger *et al.*, 2004). External monitoring groups have criticized the lack of a regional health plan, a cumulative impact assessment and provision of clean water and sanitation outside the narrowly defined project area (the Doha production field and the pipeline corridor). There has been continuing concern over insufficient attention to HIV infection, AIDS and tuberculosis and serious local shortages of well-qualified health personnel (Utzinger *et al.*, 2004). As Utzinger *et al.*, (2004) point out, the scope and limits of corporate sector responsibility for addressing these broad health issues in the two countries as distinct from the narrowly defined project area is unresolved in theory (see Windsor, 2009).

The World Bank was trying to demonstrate that the so-called resource curse or Dutch disease – that countries heavily dependent on natural resource exports perform poorly on development measures – was not inevitable. (The term Dutch disease refers to the 1959 discovery of a natural gas field, which arguably led to a decline in the Netherlands' manufacturing sector.) The pipeline project design was intended to demonstrate that good governance and economic policies are mitigating variables lying between natural resource exports and development performance (Pegg, 2006). Although then the largest private sector investment in sub-Saharan Africa, critics predicted that poverty alleviation would not result (Pegg, 2006). Oil began flowing through the pipeline in 2004 (Pegg, 2009). During 2005 and 2006, increasing domestic and international problems led the government of Chad into disputes with the World Bank and the business consortium. In September 2009, the World Bank formally ended its role (Pegg, 2009). It is less likely that the resource curse in some general sense was operating like a natural law, but rather that the oil revenues simply went into established corrupt institutions which were not altered by the World Bank's control scheme (Pegg, 2009). In late 2005, the Chad government simply informed the World Bank that it intended to alter the PRML so as to obtain more oil revenue to be used for non-development purposes. It is reasonable to presume that the president's political survival was at stake if he did not divert more of the oil revenue to patronage and other purposes. In October 2005, the president called for immediate release of the Future Generations Fund to the government. The World Bank backed down, apparently under pressure from France and the United States (Pegg, 2009), concerned in part over threats to the government's stability and need for oil – in addition to the possibility of increased Chinese presence in oil operations in Africa (Massey and May, 2006).

The outcome is thus arguably dependent on the specific conditions in Chad, including being located south of Libya and west of Darfur. The Chad government renegotiated the taxation scheme with Chevron and Petronas to obtain reportedly an additional US$450 million (Pegg, 2009). The implicit threat was that the Chinese were waiting in the wings. In March 2007, the *Collège* stopped reporting on budget allocations (Pegg, 2009). Rising oil prices simply put more revenues into the Chad budget, reportedly used for large public works projects featuring contracts going to the president's political supporters as patronage (Pegg, 2009).

Mectizan® Distribution Program (MDP)

'There is a special duty when you are selling medicine as opposed to pantyhose or hubcaps' (Caplan, 2011).[4] This special duty was accepted by Merck, which pioneered a model program for free distribution of a medication to developing countries.

The original and classic instance (Collins, 2004; Coyne and Berk, 2002) of private–public partnership collaboration (Sturchio and Colatrella, 2002; Thylefors *et al.*, 2008) to provide a basic health care service is the still operating Mectizan® (ivermectin) Distribution Program (MDP) to palliate initially river blindness (onochocerciasis) and then also elephantiasis (lymphatic filariasis). MDP is the oldest disease-specific drug donation program in the pharmaceutical industry.[5] The Merck river blindness program became an important and effective CSR initiative and subsequently attracted outside support (Hanson and Weiss, 1991; Vagelos and Galambos, 2003, 2006). The medication is reportedly very safe and effective, as well as low cost to manufacture (distribution cost being a separate matter).

At first, Merck – the discoverer of the medication – had to fund free distribution and manage that distribution itself. Basically government agencies and the World Health Organization (WHO) were either without available funds or reluctant. Today, there are donor organizations such as the Carter Center,[6] Bill and Melinda Gates Foundation,[7] the Clinton Foundation[8] and The Global Fund To Fight AIDS, Tuberculosis and Malaria.[9],[10] The WHO has long been actively engaged. The African Programme for Onchocerciasis Control (APOC) set up in 1995 by WHO and the World Bank to expand the earlier Onchocerciasis Control Programme in West Africa (OCP) relies on active community participation to handle distribution of ivermectin treatment.[11]

In 1975, a researcher at Merck Research Laboratories suggested that an antibiotic developed against parasites in animals might palliate river blindness in humans. (People take a low-cost tablet annually.) Onchocerciasis is trans-mitted to human populations by black flies breeding near rivers and streams that spread small parasitic worms by their bite. Part of the collaboration effort aims at eliminating black fly infestation.

Since the cost to develop and test the drug for human treatment would be costly and the population to be served was too poor to purchase the drug, there was unlikely to be a financial return on the investment (Omura and Crump, 2004; Waters *et al.*, 2004). The management decided to proceed with development and then free distribution at the company's expense, given the initial reluctance of UN and governmental agencies to participate.

After several years of clinical trials, Merck decided in October 1987 to fund free distribution through the Mectizan Donation Program (MDP). The decision, made by the board of directors, rested on the commitment of Merck chairman (1986–1994) and CEO (1985–1994) P. Roy Vagelos, MD (Ciulla, 1999; Nichols, 1994). Before joining Merck in 1975, becoming head of the research labs (1975–85), Vagelos had been a researcher at the National Heart Institute and an academic at the School of Medicine of Washington University, St. Louis.

The value orientation of the company tilted strongly in the direction of a positive decision. George W. Merck, a long-term CEO, had stated: 'We try never to forget that medicine is for the people. It is not for the profits. The profits follow, and if we have remembered that, they have never failed to appear'. Merck CEO Roy Vagelos announced the company's commitment to donate Mectizan to treat river blindness for as long as needed; the Mectizan Donation Program (MDP) and the Mectizan Expert Committee was formed and a secretariat established at the Task Force for Global Health to provide medical, technical and administrative oversight of Mectizan donation.

In 1991, Merck, the MDP, WHO and NGO partners established a Non-Governmental Development Organization (NGDO) Coordination Group for Onchocerciasis Control. The partnership worked with ministries of health and provision of funding. In 1993, the program was expanded to six countries in Latin America. In 2007, Colombia became the first country able to stop treatment with Mectizan and enter a three-year post-treatment surveillance phase; in 2011, Colombia applied for WHO certification of the elimination of onchocerciasis transmission. In 2009, Togo finished mass treatment for lymphatic filariasis; Yemen followed suit in 2011. In 2010, Ecuador became the second country to enter post-treatment surveillance.[12]

By 2011, there had been more than one billion onchocerciasis treatments; and annually there were 140 treatments for onchocerciasis and 130 million treatments for lymphatic filariasis.[13] By 2004, Merck was providing river blindness treatment to more than 40 million people annually in Africa, Latin America and Yemen.[14] In 1998, Merck extended use of Mectizan against elephantiasis (lymphatic filariasis) in countries where it co-exists with river blindness. In these countries, Mectizan is co-administered with albendazole, donated by GlaxoSmithKline.[15] By 2003, Merck was treating more than 20 million individuals annually for elephantiasis. There have been more than one billion treatments to more than 117,000 communities in 28 countries in Africa, six countries in Latin America and in Yemen. Reportedly, disease transmission has been interrupted with no new cases identified in several countries or regions.[16]

Ultimately, 'The donation and distribution of Mectizan and albendazole involves a large, global public-private partnership of UN agencies, bilateral donors, multilateral development agencies, governmental and nongovernmental organizations, local communities, and the private sector'.[17] And the Merck–Glaxo partnership stimulated similar actions by other pharmaceutical companies: 'The remarkable partnership between the two companies encouraged other companies to donate drugs for "neglected tropical diseases" resulting in a wide network of partners working toward a common goal of enabling access to medicines and, ultimately, to reducing poverty in countries afflicted with these diseases'.[18]

Promoting the global anti-corruption regime

A key contributor to the anti-corruption movement is the NGO Transparency International (TI), headquartered in Berlin, Germany.[19] Peter Eigen, a lawyer by training and former World Bank official with service in East Africa, founded the NGO in 1993. At present, TI has more than 100 country chapters, subject to accreditation processes; it also appoints individual members. Chapters and individual members can withdraw or be removed, expelled, or suspended.

A global anti-corruption regime is formally in place, as evidenced by the fact that corruption is officially illegal in virtually all countries (whatever the actual unofficial practices) and prohibited by UN and various regional anti-corruption conventions. Corruption, governmental and commercial, is nevertheless a widespread phenomenon (Dreher et al., 2007), which has proven difficult to extirpate (Brewster, 2014). Corruption of and within the public sector includes bribery (offer of payment), extortion (demand for payment by explicit or implied threat) and facilitation (or facilitating) payments (i.e. 'grease') made to minor officials for expediting officially approved actions. These practices are typically illegal in the country where occurring. The OECD in 2009 issued a recommendation against facilitating payments (Searcey, 2009) – which while legal under the US Foreign Corrupt Practices Act (FCPA) of 1977 are illegal under the UK Bribery Act 2010 and commonly under national legislation. Depending on one's view, much of political lobbying and campaign donations might be regarded as effectively legalized corruption in the public sector. Kaufmann and Vicente, (2011) make such a distinction (between legal corruption and illegal corruption).

The case against corruption is that it undermines democracy, protects inefficient government and serves as a form of unofficial tax on economic growth (Aidt et al., 2008). Foreign direct investment (FDI) works against corruption, but corruption deters FDI (Al-Sadig, 2009; Egger and Winner, 2006). The chief difficulty impeding enforcement is the reality that many government officials are corrupt and businesses have incentives to pay bribery, extortion or facilitation for market entry (Berg et al., 2012; Damania et al., 2004; Weissmann et al., 2014).

The largest and most significant case against a non-U.S. firm was the U.S. and German investigations of the German firm Siemens AG (Baron, 2008; Schubert and Miller, 2008). Siemens allegedly engaged in systematic bribery around the world (Baron, 2008). Corrupt payments occurred through some 2,700 consultant agreements in various countries. A new management cooperated with the authorities and instituted internal changes. In December 2006, Michael J. Hershman, president and CEO of The Fairfax Group, and a co-founder with Peter Eigen of TI in 1993, was appointed as the independent compliance advisor to the board of directors of Siemens.[20] The resulting penalties amounted to about $1.6 billion in addition to over $1 billion spent internally on investigations and reforms. During 2001–2007, an estimated $1.4 billion in corrupt payments occurred, about $800 million (or 57 percent) in telecommunications (Berg *et al.*, 2012), all concealed by false records. Until February 1999, bribes were deductible expenses under the German tax code, as in about 14 EU countries in total. The spokesman for the association of federal criminal investigators in Germany was quoted as stating: 'Bribery was Siemens's business model. Siemens had institutionalized corruption' (Schubert and Miller, 2008).

The most significant recent revelation about a U.S. firm concerned Walmart in Mexico and Central America. Mexico enacted new anti-corruption legislation in the wake of the revelations. News reports revealed Walmart had closed an internal investigation and failed to report to U.S. law enforcement officials alleged bribery by executives of its Mexico and Central America subsidiary in connection with obtaining governmentally issued construction permits for new locations (Foroohar, 2012; Wunker, 2012). From 1991, Walmart, reportedly the largest private employer in Mexico, opened more than 2,100 locations in Mexico, about 20 per cent of all its stores worldwide. Walmart allegedly had received multiple reports of corruption violations in various other countries during 2006 (Foroohar, 2012), with India apparently being a particular problem.

Sub-Saharan Africa is commonly perceived as a very corrupt region, including a number of very corrupt countries (Hanson, 2009). Like the Chad–Cameroon Pipeline Project, the Lesotho Highlands Water Project (LHWP) was another very important development project in sub-Saharan Africa. The LHWP was a combined water supply and hydropower project of the governments of Lesotho and South Africa. Whereas in the Chad–Cameroon project, pervasive governmental corruption was a concern for the World Bank and the operating consortium of foreign companies, in the LHWP the problem was that a particular well-placed government official received bribes from the various foreign companies involved in the project. The High Court of Lesotho found that the CEO of the Lesotho Highlands Development Agency (LHDA) had accepted at least $2 million in bribes from agents for some 12 multinational enterprises from various countries over a decade (Canada, France, Germany, Italy, South Africa, Switzerland and Sweden, and the United Kingdom). Swiss authorities granted access to banking account information in 1999 (see Darroch, 2004; Earle and Turton, 2005).

The Prague Declaration on Governance and Anti-Corruption, issued on 21 March 2012, represents the work of the first World Forum on Governance, convened in Prague, the Czech Republic, in November 2011. The forum included participants from governments, business, investors, media and non-governmental advocacy groups. The Prague Declaration provides a 10-principle action plan for implementation of anti-corruption efforts (Mann *et al.*, 2012), and include: (1) anti-bribery policy; (2) financial disclosure rules for politicians and government officials; (3) prosecution for official corruption; (4) open government; (5) corporate zero tolerance for and disclosure concerning corruption; (6) investor responsibilities; (7) transparent campaign and party finance; (8) lobbying rules; (9) protection for whistle-blowers; and (10) protections for NGOs and media.[21]

What is required for successful anti-corruption reform is collective action by business, governmental, international and civil society organizations (Eigen, 2013; Pieth, 2014; World Bank Institute, 2008). The Extractive Industries Transparency Initiative (EITI)[22] and the Wolfsberg private banking group's Wolfsberg Anti-Money Laundering Principles for Private Banking[23] are instances of business-based efforts (Maggetti, 2014). EITI focuses on disclosure of payments in the energy and mining sectors (Aaronson, 2011).[24] The World Bank Institute identifies anti-corruption declarations, principle-based initiatives, integrity pacts and certifying business coalitions (Pieth, 2014).

The UN Global Compact (UNGC) includes an anti-corruption principle (Principle 10) stating: 'Businesses should work against corruption in all its forms, including extortion and bribery'. The anti-corruption principle is grounded in the UN Convention against Corruption (UNCAC) (adopted 2003, entered into force 14 December 2005). UNCAC calls for prevention, criminalization, international cooperation and asset recovery mechanisms by the signatory countries. A Conference of the States Parties reviews implementation and facilitates activities.[25]

The UN Global Compact (UNGC), launched 26 July 2000, by the UN secretary-general, is the world's largest corporate citizenship and sustainability initiative. UNGC now reports more than 12,000 participants, including over 8,000 businesses in 145 countries. UNGC also includes governments, labour organizations and civil society organizations, with the UN working as convener and facilitator (Ruggie, 2002). Businesses should file periodic Communications on Progress (COP) and can be dismissed from membership for failure to do so.[26] UNGC operates a system of local networks, whose representatives meet in the Annual Local Networks Forum coordinated and chaired by the Global Compact Office. The forum works to assemble experiences, best practices and recommendations to improve effectiveness of local networks.[27] These networks are concerned with all 10 UNGC principles, including environmental, human rights and labor as well as corruption issues.

The history of the movement toward the UNCAC began with the FCPA of 1977 and a Swedish anti-bribery statute of 1978. The first regional accord was the Inter-American Convention against Corruption (OAS Convention) of 1996; followed by the OECD Convention on the Bribery of Foreign Public Officials in International Business Transactions (OECD Convention) of 1997. There are a number of other regional accords, including within the European Union (EU) and the Council of Europe (COE).[28]

In this setting, Transparency International (TI), an NGO, has been a key actor for mobilizing anti-corruption reform efforts within countries. TI articulates its mission and vision statements, incorporating its core values, as follows[29]:

Our mission

Our Mission is to stop corruption and promote transparency, accountability and integrity at all levels and across all sectors of society. Our Core Values are: transparency, accountability, integrity, solidarity, courage, justice and democracy.

Our vision

Our Vision is a world in which government, politics, business, civil society and the daily lives of people are free of corruption.

Among the key initiatives undertaken by TI over the years are[30]: publishing the annual Corruption Perceptions Index (CPI) inaugurated in 1995; organizing from 1995 the biennial global International Anti-Corruption Conference (IACC); recommending to the OECD denial of tax deductibility of foreign bribes – adopted in 1996; publishing the TI Source Book from 1996; publishing the Bribe Payers Index (BPI) inaugurated in 1999; helping to facilitate creation of the Wolfsberg principles in 2000; and publishing from 2001 the comprehensive Global Corruption Report. From 1996, the World Bank has made anti-corruption performance a condition for its assistance. In 2004, TI helped develop the Partnering Against Corruption Initiative (PACI) of the World Economic Forum (WEF), which now includes CEOs from more than 125 major companies.[31]

The most recent five-year strategy, adopted in 2011, identified six priorities through 2015[32]: increased empowerment of people and partners; increased anti-corruption implementation by institutions, businesses, and the international financial system; more effective law enforcement; increased integrity in public and business life; strengthened networking; and enhanced individual and collective performance at all levels.

Conclusions

This chapter conceptualizes a four-sector theory of sustainable development partnerships as positive and prescriptive. Positively, the theory draws on the extant literature and three examples to identify important elements of a necessary but not sufficient cross-sector cooperative approach to sustainable development at all levels from global to local. The three examples are the Chad–Cameroon Petroleum Development and Pipeline Project, the Merck Mectizan® Donation Program (MDP) and the role of Transparency International (TI) in promoting effective enforcement of the formal global anti-corruption regime. In Chad, the World Bank undertook a unique experiment to direct revenues to the poor and away from the corrupt government. The Chad–Cameroon project illustrates the failure of the World Bank experiment in corruption control, but that failure arguably reflects more the particular situation in Chad than the design and operation of the anti-corruption program. Thus the failure in Chad should not be viewed automatically as an obvious indictment of the control program. The role of NGOs in the Chad project was to oppose the World Bank support and then to monitor the project closely. That role did not contribute to the withdrawal of the World Bank, an action precipitated by the Chad government. The Merck MDP program illustrates a positive instance of cross-sector cooperation initiated by a corporation. The TI example illustrates the key role that NGOs can play in promoting global regimes and local implementation, in the anti-corruption sphere. Corruption, as illustrated in Chad, is pervasive and persistent.

The chapter addresses four central research questions through application of a proposed theory of public–private sustainable development partnerships to the three examples. The four research questions concern motivation, evolution, value creation and key performance determinants. The three examples provide some key learning lessons.

The first lesson concerns the role of four-sector cooperation in relationship to motivation. The motivation for governments, civil society organizations and international institutions to cooperate with business is simply that business is essential for some sustainable development partnerships. Businesses have several possible motivations for cross-sector partnership participation (Tercek and Adams, 2013; Warhurst, 2005). One motive is moral: some executives wish to help with sustainable development issues. Another motive is concern for legitimacy, external and internal, which can occur through corporate social responsibility (CSR) actions including joining the voluntary UN Global Compact. Concern for legitimacy (Palazzo and Scherer, 2006; Scherer *et al.*, 2013) typically reflects direct stakeholder pressure, especially by NGOs. A study of 288 firms in China suggests that firms emphasize philanthropy in seeking legitimacy from outsider stakeholders and emphasize sustainability in seeking legitimacy from insider stakeholders (Zheng *et al.*, 2014). The business participants in the Chad-Cameroon pipeline project were interested in a profitable opportunity but needed World Bank support as well as government cooperation before undertaking a risky venture. Merck's motivation for the Merck Mectizan® Donation Program (MDP) was quite different: Merck led the way motivated by some sense of social responsibility and a capability to address a social health need. Their initiative may have been a financial burden in the short term, but ultimately Merck's approach attracted foundation, government and WHO support and participation. Businesses join TI anti-corruption efforts in part because bribery is illegal and extortion is a tax on profitability.

The second lesson concerns the need for patience over time in recognition of the important role of evolution. Four-sector cooperation while necessary is neither sufficient nor inherently always the best strategy, which is dependent on circumstances. The Chad project illustrates this problem. NGOs have opposed the Chad project. While the World Bank ultimately withdrew and its experiment in anti-corruption control failed in Chad, that failure did not reflect NGO opposition but rather the government's shift in policy toward greater direct control of oil project revenues. Clearly government motivation can and does unfold. The problem would not have arisen if the government remained committed to the World Bank approach; the NGOs opposed the project because they did not think that the government would be so committed. This set of circumstances does not mean that the pipeline project has not contributed value to Chad and Cameroon. Strategy and performance may also be evolutionary. Merck proceeded independently to implement its MDP against resistance. Initially, WHO and aid agencies were reluctant to support and fund the Merck program. That situation ultimately evolved to multiple-sector cooperation. Other cooperating parties joined later in the evolution of the Merck program. The Merck MDP has resulted, ultimately, in a new model of cooperation for pharmaceutical companies. TI works country by country, as well as through information dissemination and international coordination meetings, to help implement enforcement of what is officially prohibited. Transparency International (TI) country chapters may encounter governmental resistance or indifferent, and each chapter must develop a specific cooperation strategy appropriate for country circumstances.

The third and fourth lessons, combined here for discussion, concern the need for case-by-case assessment of value creation and key performance determinants. The reason for a combined discussion is that performance drives value creation; and the determinants of this relationship vary by case. Value has been created in two of the cases examined in this chapter. Despite withdrawal of the World Bank, the Chad–Cameroon pipeline is operating and producing economic wealth for the two countries and the foreign companies involved, and thus can be said to be performing. The debate over the economic benefits of the project to the population is thus far from over. The issue for the World Bank is the distribution of that wealth within Chad and the failure of the anti-corruption program. The Merck Mectizan® Donation Program (MDP) has definitely had a marked effect in reducing a crippling disease in tropical countries. The performance and value creation are well demonstrated. Over the long run, Merck remains a very profitable firm and the cost of MDP has fallen in relationship to rising profitability. Several countries have entered post-treatment surveillance status. The effect of Transparency International (TI) on corruption is more difficult to assess. There is a formal global consensus against corruption, which TI has helped to bring into existence. The reduction of actual corruption requires careful country-by-country investigation. Increased transparency and anti-corruption reform measures may be yielding gradual reductions in country, but measurement precision is difficult. One can reasonably suggest that no effort at controlling corruption might result in even worse conditions in various countries.

The basic limitations of the methodology in this chapter are that the approach depends on developing a reasonable articulation of a proposed four-sector theory of sustainable development partners on the basis of a reading of relevant literature and interpretation of three empirical examples. The chapter does not provide a fully developed theory, but focuses on conceptualization of the essential elements. The chapter provides a first-cut at the proposed theory. The justification is that sustainable development, whether feasible or not, is clearly important. The chapter is not a systematic review of a quite large and diverse literature. Three examples might be criticized as too few, and dependent on the author's selection bias. The criticisms have merit; and the chapter should be assessed as to limitations accordingly. However, the current situation is that the extant literature is highly fragmented, tending to focus on specific combinations and specific issues. Empirical experience is similarly scattered across such specific combinations and specific issues. The three examples explicated in this chapter are selected to help illustrate variations likely to occur within the rubric of an overarching theory of public-private sustainable development partnerships. Organizations should assess strategic choices accordingly.

Notes

1 US Census Bureau, U.S. and World Population Clock, http://www.census.gov/pop clock/ [13 August 2014].
2 http://esa.un.org/unpd/ppp/Figures-Output/Population/PPP_Total-Population.htm [13 August 2014]. See United Nations (2014), *Probabilistic population projections based on the world population prospects: the 2012 revision.* Population Division, DESA. ST/ESA/SER.A/353. Available from: http://esa.un.org/unpd/ppp/ [20 November 2014].
3 Chad has a population of some 11.5 million of many different tribal groups of mixed African and Arabic origins speaking a range of languages (Campbell 2013b). The Saharan north is Muslim; the tropical south is Christian; the Sahelian central region is mixed (Gould & Winters 2012, p. 318). Libya is to the north and Sudan to the east. Cameroon, lying between Chad and the Atlantic Ocean, has more than 200 racial and tribal groups including some pygmies in the southern forest area (Campbell 2013a).
4 Arthur Caplan is director of the Center for Bioethics at the University of Pennsylvania.
5 http://www.merck.com/about/featured-stories/mectizan1.html [20 November 2014].
6 http://www.cartercenter.org/health/river_blindness/program_staff.html [20 November 2014].
7 http://www.gatesfoundation.org/ [20 November 2014].
8 https://www.clintonfoundation.org/ [20 November 2014].
9 http://www.theglobalfund.org/en/ [20 November 2014].
10 In addition to AIDS, malaria, tuberculosis, devastating health problems in tropical countries also include guinea worm, schistomsomias (bilharziasis), and trachoma.
11 www.who.int/apoc/en [20 November 2014].
12 http://www.mectizan.org/achievements [20 November 2014].
13 http://www.mectizan.org/achievements [20 November 2014].
14 In many countries outside the US, Merck operates as Merck Sharp & Dohme (MSD).
15 http://www.mectizan.org/partners/merck [20 November 2014].
16 http://www.mectizan.org/about/history [20 November 2014].
17 http://www.mectizan.org/about/history [20 November 2014].
18 http://www.mectizan.org/about/history [20 November 2014].
19 http://www.transparency.org/ [20 November 2014].
20 http://www.fairfaxco.us/bio_hershman.php [20 November 2014].
21 See Council of Europe, Committee of Ministers, Resolution (97) 24, 'On the Twenty Guiding Principles for the Fight Against Corruption', 6 November 1997. Available from: http://www.coe.int/t/dghl/monitoring/greco/documents/Resolution(97)24_EN.pdf [20 November 2014].

22 https://eiti.org/ [20 November 2014]. In 2005, Peter Eigen, founder of Transparency International (TI), joined the Extractive Industry Transparency Initiative (EITI) as chair of its new International Advisory Group.

23 http://www.wolfsberg-principles.com/pdf/standards/Wolfsberg-Private-Banking-Prinicples-May-2012.pdf [20 November 2014].

24 https://eiti.org/eiti/history [20 November 2014].

25 http://www.unodc.org/unodc/en/treaties/CAC/index.html [20 November 2014].

26 http://www.unglobalcompact.org/ParticipantsAndStakeholders/index.html [20 November 2014].

27 http://www.unglobalcompact.org/NetworksAroundTheWorld/index.html [20 November 2014].

28 A list of international anti-corruption conventions, with links to full texts, is available through a Transparency International website http://archive.transparency.org/global_priorities/international_conventions [20 November 2014].

29 http://www.transparency.org/whoweare/organisation/mission_vision_and_values [20 November 2014].

30 http://www.transparency.org/whoweare/history [20 November 2014].

31 http://www.weforum.org/issues/partnering-against-corruption-initiative [20 November 2014].

32 http://www.transparency.org/whoweare/organisation/strategy_2015/0/ [20 November 2014].

References

Aaronson, SA 2011, 'Limited partnership: business, government, civil society, and the public in the Extractive Industries Transparency Initiative (EITI)', *Public Administration and Development*, vol. 31, no. 1, pp. 50–63.

Aidt, T, Dutta, J and Sena, V 2008, 'Governance regimes, corruption and growth: theory and evidence', *Journal of Comparative Economics*, vol. 36, no. 2, pp. 195–220.

Aikanathan, S, Sasekumar, A, Chenayah, S, Basiron, Y and Sundram, K 2014, 'Modelling oil palm's sustainable management and practices: a framework based on economic principles', *Journal of Oil Palm, Environment and Health: An official publication of the Malaysian Palm Oil Council (MPOC)*, vol. 5, pp. 1–7. Available from: www.jopeh.com.my/index.php/jopecommon/article/view/79/109 [accessed 19 November 2014].

Akenji, L 2014, 'Consumer scapegoatism and limits to green consumerism', *Journal of Cleaner Production*, vol. 63, no. 15, pp. 13–23.

Al-Sadig, A 2009, 'The effects of corruption on FDI inflows', *Cato Journal*, vol. 29, no. 2, pp. 267–94.

Amnesty International UK 2005, *Contracting out of human rights: the Chad-Cameroon pipeline project*. Amnesty International UK, London, September 6. Available from: www.amnesty.org/en/library/info/POL34/012/2005 [accessed 19 November 2014].

Arcas-Lario, N, Martín-Ugedo, JF, and Minguez-Vera, A 2014, 'Farmers' satisfaction with fresh fruit and vegetable marketing Spanish cooperatives: an explanation from agency theory', *International Food and Agribusiness Management Review*, vol. 17, no. 2, 127–46. Available from: www.ifama.org/files/IFAMR/Vol%2017/Issue%201/17i1.pdf#page=135 [accessed 19 November 2014].

Austin, JE 2007, 'Sustainability through partnering: conceptualizing partnerships between businesses and NGOs', in Glasbergen, P Biermann, F and Mol, APJ (eds), *Partnerships, governance and sustainable development: reflections on theory and practice*, eds P Glasbergen, F Biermann and APJ Mol, Cheltenham, UK: Edward Elgar, pp. 49–67.

Bäckstrand, K 2006, 'Multi-stakeholder partnerships for sustainable development: rethinking legitimacy, accountability and effectiveness', *European Environment*, vol. 16, no. 5, pp. 290–306.

Baron, DP 2008, 'Siemens: anatomy of bribery', *Stanford Graduate School of Business, Case P-68*, 20 October.

Berg, SV, Jiang, L and Lin, C 2012, 'Regulation and corporate corruption: new evidence from the telecom sector', *Journal of Comparative Economics*, vol. 40, no. 1, 22–43.

Bernardi, A and Miani, M 2014, 'The long march of Chinese co-operatives: towards market economy, participation and sustainable development', *Asia Pacific Business Review*, vol. 20, no. 3, pp. 330–55.

Borowy, I 2014, *Defining sustainable development for our common future: a history of the World Commission on Environment and Development*. London: Routledge.

Brewster, R 2014, 'The domestic and international enforcement of the OECD Anti-Bribery Convention', *Chicago Journal of International Law*, vol. 15, no. 1, pp. 84–109.

Brook, BW, Ellis, EC, Perring, MP, Mackay, AW, and Blomqvist, L 2013, 'Does the terrestrial biosphere have planetary tipping points?' *Trends in Ecology and Evolution*, vol. 28, no. 7, pp. 396–401.

Brundtland, G et al. 1987, *Our common future: report of the 1987 World Commission on Environment and Development*, Oxford: Oxford University Press.

Bruyn, ST 2000, *A civil economy: transforming the marketplace in the twenty-first century.*, Ann Arbor: University of Michigan Press.

Campbell, CJ 2013a, 'Cameroon', in *Campbell's atlas of oil and gas depletion*, New York: Springer, 2nd edn, pp. 31–3.

Campbell, CJ 2013b, 'Chad', in *Campbell's atlas of oil and gas depletion*, New York: Springer, 2nd edn, pp. 33–5.

Caplan, A 2011 (February 10). Cited in 'Profits and social responsibility: chastened drug makers step up efforts to bring affordable medicines to poor countries'. Available from: http://knowledge.wharton.upenn.edu/article.cfm?articleid=2710 [accessed 19 November 2014].

Cebula, RJ and Feige, EL 2012, 'America's unreported economy: measuring the size, growth and determinants of income tax evasion in the U.S.', *Crime, Law and Social Change*, vol. 57, no. 2, pp. 265–85.

Ciulla, JB 1999, 'The importance of leadership in shaping business values', *Long Range Planning*, vol. 32, no. 2, pp. 166–72.

Clausen, F and Attaran, A 2011, 'The Chad-Cameroon Pipeline Project – assessing the World Bank's failed experiment to direct oil revenues towards the poor', *The Law and Development Review*, vol. 4, no. 1, pp. 30–65.

Collins, K 2004, 'Profitable gifts: a history of the Merck Mectizan donation program and its implications for international health', *Perspectives in Biology and Medicine*, vol. 47, no. 1, pp. 100–09.

Coyne, PE and Berk, DW 2002, 'The Mectizan® (ivermectin) donation program for riverblindness as a paradigm for pharmaceutical industry donation programs. Africa Region', World Bank, May. Available from: http://apps.who.int/medicinedocs/documents/s17517en/s17517en.pdf [accessed 20 November 2014].

Dahan, NM, Doh, J and Teegen, H 2010, 'Role of nongovernmental organizations in the business-government-society interface: introductory essay by guest editors', *Business & Society*, vol. 49, no. 4, pp. 567–69.

Damania, R, Fredricksson, PG and Mani, M 2004, 'The persistence of corruption and regulatory compliance failures: theory and evidence', *Public Choice*, vol. 121, no. 3, pp. 363–90.

Darroch, F 2004 (August 8), 'The Lesotho Highlands Water Project: bribery on a massive scale'. Available from: www.worldhunger.org/articles/04/africa/darroch.htm [accessed 20 November 2014].

Doh, JP 2003, 'Nongovernmental organizations, corporate strategy, and public policy: NGOs as agents of change', in *Globalization and NGOs*, JP Doh and H Teegen (eds), Westport, CT: Praeger, pp. 1–18.

Dreher, A, Kotsogiannis, C and McCorriston, S 2007, 'Corruption around the world: evidence from a structural model', *Journal of Comparative Economics*, vol. 35, no. 3, pp. 443–66.

Earle, A and Turton, A 2005, 'Corruption on the Lesotho Highlands Water Project – a case study', African Water Issues Research Unit (AWIRU), University of Pretoria. Stockholm, Sweden: World Water Week. Available from: www.swedishwaterhouse. se/swh/resources/20051010171048Earle_Turton_Presentation_Corr_case_study.pdf [accessed 20 November 2014].

Ebner, A 2006, 'The intellectual foundations of the social market economy: theory, policy, and implications for European integration', *Journal of Economic Studies*, vol. 33, no. 3, pp. 206–23.

Egger, P and Winner, H 2006, 'How corruption influences foreign direct investment: a panel data study', *Economic Development and Cultural Change*, vol. 54, no. 2, pp. 459–86.

Eigen, P 2013, 'International corruption: organized civil society for better global governance', *Social Research: An International Quarterly*, vol. 80, no. 4, pp. 1287–1308.

Esty, BC 2001, 'The Chad-Cameroon Petroleum Development and Pipeline Project (A and B)', Harvard Business School cases, 9–202–010 and 9–202–012.

Findeis, JL and Pervez, S 2014, 'Population and the environment', in *Handbook of regional science*, MM Fischer and P Nijkamp (eds), Berlin and Heidelberg: Springer, pp. 1085–1103.

Foroohar, R 2012, 'Walmart's discounted ethics: its Mexican bribery scandal shows the perils of bowing to local "custom"', *TIME*, vol. 179, no. 18, May 7, p. 19.

Fransen, LW and Kolk, A 2007, 'Global rule-setting for business: a critical analysis of multi-stakeholder standards', *Organization*, vol. 14, no. 5, pp. 667–84.

Galaz, V, Österblom, H, Bodin, O and Crona, B 2014, 'Global networks and global change-induced tipping points', *International Environmental Agreements: Politics, Law and Economics*, online (in press). Available from: http://link.springer.com/article/10.1007/s10784–014–9253–6# [accessed 20 November 2014].

Googins, BK and Rochlin, SA 2000, 'Creating the partnership society: understanding the rhetoric and reality of cross-sectoral partnerships', *Business and Society Review*, vol. 105, no. 1, pp. 127–44.

Gould, JA and Winters, MS 2007, 'An obsolescing bargain in Chad: shifts in leverage between the government and the World Bank', *Business and Politics*, vol. 9, no. 2, Article 4. Available from: www.bepress.com/bap/vol9/iss2/art4 [accessed 20 November 2014].

Gould, JA and Winters, MS 2012, 'Petroleum blues: the political economy of resources and conflict in Chad', in *High-value natural resources and peacebuilding*, P Lujala and SA Rustad (eds), London: Earthscan, pp. 313–36. Available from: www.eli.org/sites/default/files/313–36_gould_and_winters.pdf [accessed 20 November 2014].

Greve, C 2010, 'Public-private partnerships in business and government', in *The Oxford handbook of business and government*, D Coen, W Grant and G Wilson (eds), Oxford: Oxford University Press, pp. 585–99.

Hall, PA and Soskice, D (eds) 2001, *Varieties of capitalism: the institutional foundations of comparative advantage*, Oxford: Oxford University Press.

Hanson, K and Weiss, S 1991, 'Merck & Co., Inc.: Addressing Third-World Needs (A, B, C, D)', Harvard Business School cases 991–021–22–23–24.

Hanson, S 2009 (August 6), 'Corruption in Sub-Saharan Africa', Council on Foreign Relations, New York and Washington, DC. Available from: www.cfr.org/africa-sub-saharan/corruption-sub-saharan-africa/p19984 [accessed 23 November 2014].

Herlin, H 2013, 'Better safe than sorry: nonprofit organizational legitimacy and cross-sector partnerships', *Business & Society*, doi:10.1177/0007650312472609, first published on January 15, 2013. Available from: http://bas.sagepub.com/content/early/2013/01/11/0007650312472609.abstract [accessed 20 November 2014].

Hueting, R 1990, 'The Brundtland report: a matter of conflicting goals', *Ecological Economics*, vol. 2, no. 2, pp. 109–17.

International Union for Conservation of Nature (IUCN), Forest Preservation Programme 2012, *Collaboration and multi-stakeholder dialogue: a review of the literature*, Version 1.1, March, Gland, Switzerland. Available from: http://cmsdata.iucn.org/downloads/collaboration_and_multi_stakeholder_dialogue.pdf [accessed 20 November 2014].

Jacob, M 1994, 'Toward a methodological critique of sustainable development', *The Journal of Developing Areas*, vol. 28, no. 2, pp. 237–52.

Kaldor, N 1986, 'Limits on growth', *Oxford Economic Papers, New Series*, vol. 38, no. 2, pp. 187–98.

Kaufmann, D and Vicente, PC 2011, 'Legal corruption', *Economics and Politics*, vol. 23, no. 2, 195–219.

Kingma, BR 1994, 'Public good theories of the non-profit sector: Weisbrod revisited', *Voluntas: International Journal of Voluntary and Nonprofit Organizations*, vol. 8, no. 2, pp. 135–48.

Kolk, A and Lenfant, F 2012, 'Business–NGO collaboration in a conflict setting: partnership activities in the Democratic Republic of Congo', *Business & Society*, vol. 51, no. 3, pp. 478–511.

Kourula, A and Laasonen, S 2010, 'Nongovernmental organizations in business and society, management, and international business research: review and implications from 1998 to 2007', *Business & Society*, vol. 49, no. 1, pp. 35–67.

Lazonick, W 2003, 'The theory of the market economy and the social foundations of innovative enterprise', *doi: 10.1177/0143831X03024001598 Economic and Industrial Democracy*, vol. 24, no. 1, 9–44.

Le Ber, M.J and Branzei, O 2010, '(Re)forming strategic cross-sector partnerships: relational processes of social innovation', *Business & Society*, vol. 49, no. 1, pp. 140–72.

Lehr, A 2010, 'Old and new governance approaches to conflict minerals: all are better than one', *Harvard International Law Journal*, vol. 52, November, pp. 148–70.

Leterme, Y 2014, 'The social market economy in a globalised world', post 25 February from OECD Deputy Secretary-General Yves Leterme, based on a speech he gave on 17 February to the 5. Frankfurter Ludwig-Erhard-Dialog at Frankfurt's Goethe University. Available from: http://oecdinsights.org/2014/02/25/the-social-market-economy-in-a-globalised-world/ [accessed 20 November 2014].

Maggetti, M 2014, 'Promoting corporate responsibility in private banking: necessary and sufficient conditions for joining the Wolfsberg Initiative Against Money Laundering', *Business & Society*, vol. 53, no. 6, pp. 787–819.

Manfra, P 2002, 'Entrepreneurship, firm size and the structure of the Italian economy', *Journal of Entrepreneurial Finance*, vol. 7, no. 3, pp. 99–111.

Mann, TE, Davis, SM, Minow, N and Ornstein, N 2012 (March 21), 'Prague Declaration on Governance and Anti-Corruption'. Available from: www.brookings.edu/research/reports/2012/03/21-prague-declaration-mann [accessed 20 November 2014].

Martínez-Alier, J, Pascual, U, Franck-Dominique, V and Zaccai, E 2010, 'Sustainable degrowth: mapping the context, criticisms and future prospects of an emergent paradigm', *Ecological Economics*, vol. 69, pp. 1741–47.

Massey, S and May, R 2005, 'Dallas to Doba: oil and Chad, external controls and internal Politics', *Journal of Contemporary African Studies*, vol. 23, no. 2, pp. 253–76.

Meadows, D, Randers, J and Meadows, D 2004, *Limits to growth: the 30-year update*, Chelsea Green, White River Junction (third study in series).

Millar, H 2013, 'Comparing accountability relationships between governments and non-state actors in Canadian and European international development policy', Canadian Public Administration, vol. 56, no. 2, pp. 252–69.

Murray, A, Haynes, K and Hudson, LJ 2010, 'Collaborating to achieve corporate social responsibility and sustainability?: possibilities and problems', *Sustainability Accounting, Management and Policy Journal*, vol. 1, no. 2, pp. 161–77.

Nelson, J, Kenrick, J and Jackson, D 2001 (May), 'Report on a consultation with Bagyeli Pygmy communities impacted by the Chad-Cameroon oil-pipeline project', Forest Peoples Project, Moreton-in-Marsh, UK. Available from: www.forestpeoples.org/sites/fpp/files/publication/2010/07/ccpbagyeliconsultmay01eng.pdf [accessed 20 November 2014].

Neuwirth, R 2011, 'Street markets and shantytowns forge the world's urban future: shantytowns, favelas and jhopadpattis turn out to be places of surprising innovation', *Scientific American*, vol. 305, September, pp. 56–63.

Nichols, NA 1994, 'Medicine, management, and mergers: an interview with Merck's P. Roy Vagelos', *Harvard Business Review*, vol. 72, no. 6, pp. 104–14.

Norland, DR 2003, 'Innovations of the Chad/Cameroon Pipeline Project: thinking outside the box', *Mediterranean Quarterly*, vol. 14, no. 3, pp. 46–59.

O'Connor, A and Shumate, M 2014, 'Differences among NGOs in the business–NGO cooperative network', *Business & Society*, vol. 53, no. 1, pp. 105–33.

Omura, S and Crump, A 2004, 'Timeline: the life and times of Ivermectin – a success story. *Nature Reviews Microbiology*, vol. 2, pp. 984–89.

Palazzo, G and Scherer, AG 2006, 'Corporate legitimacy as deliberation: a communicative framework', *Journal of Business Ethics*, vol. 66, no. 1, pp. 71–88.

Palazzo, G and Scherer, AG 2008, 'Corporate social responsibility, democracy, and the politicization of the corporation', *Academy of Management Review*, vol. 33, no. 3, pp. 773–5.

Pegg, S 2006, 'Can policy intervention beat the resource curse? Evidence from the Chad–Cameroon pipeline project', *African Affairs* (London), vol. 105, no. 418, pp. 1–25.

Pegg, S 2009, 'Briefing: chronicle of a death foretold: the collapse of the Chad-Cameroon Pipeline Project', *African Affairs* (London), vol. 108, no. 431, pp. 311–20.

Pieth, M 2014, 'Collective action and corruption', in *Preventing corporate corruption: The anti-bribery compliance model*, S Manacorda, F Centonze and G Forti (eds), Dordrecht, The Netherlands: Springer, pp. 93–108.

Pinkse, J and Kolk, A 2012, 'Addressing the climate change – sustainable development nexus: the role of multistakeholder partnerships', *Business & Society*, vol. 51, no. 1, pp. 176–210.

Roloff, J 2008a, 'A life cycle model of multi-stakeholder networks', *Business Ethics: A European Review*, vol. 17, no. 3, pp. 311–25.

Roloff, J 2008b, 'Learning from multi-stakeholder networks: issue-focused stakeholder management', *Journal of Business Ethics*, vol. 82, no. 1, pp. 233–50.

Rose, R 1992, 'Toward a civil economy', *Journal of Democracy*, vol. 3, no. 2, pp. 13–26.

Ruggie, JG 2002, 'The theory and practice of learning networks: corporate social responsibility and global compact', *Journal of Corporate Citizenship*, vol. 5, pp. 27–36.

Santos, FM 2012, 'A positive theory of social entrepreneurship', *Journal of Business Ethics*, vol. 111, pp. 335–51.

Scherer, AG and Palazzo, G 2007, 'Toward a political conception of corporate responsibility: business and society seen from a Habermasian perspective', *Academy of Management Review*, vol. 32, no. 4, pp. 1096–1120.

Scherer, AG and Palazzo, G 2011, 'The new political role of business in a globalized world: a review of a new perspective on CSR and its implications for the firm, governance, and democracy', *Journal of Management Studies*, vol. 48, no. 4, pp. 899–931.

Scherer, AG, Baumann-Pauly, D and Schneider, A 2013, 'Democratizing corporate governance – compensating for the democratic deficit of corporate political activity and corporate citizenship', *Business & Society*, vol. 52, no. 3, pp. 473–514.

Scherer, AG, Palazzo, G and Matten, D 2014, 'The business firm as a political actor: a new theory of the firm for a globalized world', *Business & Society*, vol. 53, no. 2, pp. 143–56.

Scherer, AG, Palazzo, G and Seidl, D 2013, 'Managing legitimacy in complex and heterogeneous environments: sustainable development in a globalized world', *Journal of Management Studies*, vol. 50, vol. 2, pp. 259–84.

Schneider, F and Enste, DH 2002, *The shadow economy: an international survey*, Cambridge: Cambridge University Press.

Schubert, S and Miller, TM 2008, 'At Siemens, bribery was just a line item', *New York Times*, 21 December. Available from: www.nytimes.com/2008/12/21/business/world business/21siemens.html?pagewanted=all [accessed 21 July 2012].

Searcey, D 2009, 'Small-scale bribes targeted by OECD', *Wall Street Journal*, 11 December. Available from: http://online.wsj.com/article/SB126041281940684861.html [accessed 21 July 2012].

Selsky, JW and Parker, B 2005, 'Cross-sector partnerships to address social issues: challenges to theory and practice', *Journal of Management*, vol. 31, no. 6, pp. 849–73.

Selsky, JW and Parker, B 2010, 'Platforms for cross-sector social partnerships – prospective sensemaking devices for social benefit', *Journal of Business Ethics*, vol. 94, no. 1, pp. 21–37.

Songue, E, Tagne, C, Mbouyap, P, Essomba, P and Moyou-Somo, R 2013, 'Epidemiology of malaria in three geo-ecological zones along the Chad-Cameroon Pipeline', *American Journal of Epidemiology and Infectious Disease*, vol. 1, no. 4, pp. 27–33.

Sturchio, JL and Colatrella, BD 2002, 'Successful public-private partnerships in global health: lessons from the MECTIZAN Donation Program', in *The economics of essential medicines*, (ed.) B Granville, London: Royal Institute of International Affairs, pp. 255–74.

Svendsen, AC and Laberge, M 2005, 'Convening stakeholder networks, a new way of thinking, being and engaging', *Journal of Corporate Citizenship*, vol. 19, pp. 91–104.

Tercek, MR and Adams, JS 2013, 'The business case for nature: sustainability efforts may be a matter of survival, both corporate and human', *The Conference Board Review*, vol. L, no. 2, pp. 38–47.

Thylefors, B, Alleman, MM and Twum-Danso, NAY 2008, 'Operational lessons from 20 years of the Mectizan Donation Program for the control of onchocerciasis', *Tropical Medicine and International Health*, vol. 13, no. 5, pp. 689–96.

Utzinger, J, Wyss, K, Moto, DD, Tanner, M and Singer, BH 2004, 'Community health outreach program of the Chad-Cameroon petroleum development and pipeline project', *Clinics in Occupational and Environmental Medicine*, vol. 4, no. 1, pp. 9–26.

Utzinger, J, Wyss, K, Moto, DD, Yémadji, N, Tanner, M and Singer, BH 2005, 'Assessing health impacts of the Chad–Cameroon petroleum development and pipeline project: challenges and a way forward', *Environmental Impact Assessment Review*, vol. 25, no. 1, pp. 63–93.

Vagelos, PR and Galambos, L 2003, *Medicine, science and Merck*, Cambridge: Cambridge University Press.

Vagelos, PR and Galambos, L 2006, *The moral corporation–Merck experiences*, New York: Cambridge University Press.

Vock, M, van Dolen, W and Kolk, A 2014, 'Micro-level interactions in business–nonprofit partnerships', *Business & Society*, vol. 53, no. 4, pp. 517–50.

Waddell, S 2003, 'Global action networks, a global invention helping business make globalisation work for all', *Journal of Corporate Citizenship*, vol. 12, no. 16, pp. 27–42.

Ward, JI 2014 (February 5), 'Coca-Cola's new formula for water stewardship: government partnership – Coca-Cola is helping to repair national watersheds that also happen to supply its own factories. Is that greenwashing or a sustainable model that other corporations should emulate?' Available from: www.theguardian.com/sustainable-business/coca-cola-usda-water-partnership-watersheds [accessed 20 November 2014].

Warhurst, A 2005, 'Future roles of business in society: the expanding boundaries of corporate responsibility and a compelling case for partnership', *Futures*, vol. 37, no. 2/3, pp. 151–68.

Waters, HR, Rehwinkel, JA and Burnham, G 2004, 'Economic evaluation of Mectizan distribution', *Tropical Medicine and International Health*, vol. 9, no. 4, pp. A16-A25.

Weisbrod, BA 1975, 'Toward a theory of the voluntary nonprofit sector in a three-sector economy', in *Altruism, morality, and economic theory*, E Phelps (ed.), New York: Russell Sage Foundation, pp. 171–95.

Weismann, MF, Buscaglia, CA and Peterson, J 2014, 'The Foreign Corrupt Practices Act: why it fails to deter bribery as a global market entry strategy', *Journal of Business Ethics*, vol. 123, no. 1, pp. 591–619.

Windsor, D 2009, 'Multinational corporations and basic health services', in *Doing well and good: the human face of the new capitalism*, J Friedland (ed.), Charlotte, NC: IAP – Information Age Publishing, pp. 197–214.

World Bank Institute 2008, 'Fighting corruption through collective action: a guide for business', *Version 1.0*. Available from: http://info.worldbank.org/etools/docs/antic/Whole_guide_Oct.pdf, [accessed 20 November 2014].

Wunker, S 2012 (April 25), 'Four lessons for Wal-Mart on corruption in emerging markets'. Available from: www.forbes.com/sites/stephenwunker/2012/04/25/four-lessons-for-wal-mart-on-corruption-in-emerging-markets/ [accessed 20 November 2014].

Zheng, Q, Luo, Y and Maksimov, V 2014, 'Achieving legitimacy through corporate social responsibility: the case of emerging economy firms', *Journal of World Business*, vol. 50, no. 3, pp. 389–403.

8 Meta-regulation for environmental monitoring and corporate sustainability reporting

Nadia B. Ahmad

Introduction

Corporations are using private sustainability reports to disclose economic, environmental, social and governance performance, but no clear regulations exist to mandate the structure and guidelines for these corporate sustainability initiatives. This chapter explores how sustainability reporting in concert with other disclosure mechanisms can be controlled by more precise metrics through the use of meta-regulation, which is a regulatory system aimed at encouraging self-regulation of firms. Corporate sustainability reports are similarly situated with corporate securities and financial statements in terms of their intended audience; shareholders, but unlike those reporting requirements sustainability reporting has typically suffered from a lack of standardization. While the Securities and Exchange Commission (SEC) offers guidance to companies in the development of financial reporting and imposes sanctions and fines for failure to comply with those guidelines, sustainability reporting is subject, by and large, to no particular standards. This lack of any cohesive regulatory framework minimizes the effectiveness of corporate environmental reporting.

The notable rise of corporate sustainability reporting (CSR) is indicative of a new wave of globalization that has a keen eye towards environmental best practices. As will be outlined in the chapter, the conceptual framework of CSR suffers from the lack of a clear regulatory regime. Evidence will be provided that suggests part of the success of CSR can be attributed to this lack of regulatory oversight; however, the failure to regulate simultaneously delegitimizes the substantial potential of CSR initiatives at the corporate as well as governmental level. This chapter provides an alternative to mandatory reporting and to that of no reporting; that is, meta-regulation as an emergent form of governance for CSR and as an increasingly valuable corporate tool.

For example, Colorado has mandated the public disclosure of chemical fluids used and released during hydraulic fracturing processes for oil and gas extraction. This measure is a step towards heightened corporate transparency. I will discuss ways to harmonize sustainability reporting with a legal and regulatory policy framework. Part II of this chapter provides a brief historical framework for the development of environmental reporting. Part III explores the evolution of corporate sustainability reporting and the way it is used by industry actors and other key stakeholders. Part IV delves into the concept of meta-regulation as a tool for enhancing the impact and effectiveness of CSR and Part V presents examples and examines the patterns of regulation and governance around hydraulic fracturing fluid reporting by Colorado oil and gas operators and other states of the United States.

Origins of environmental reporting

The primary early targets for environmental reporting were air pollution, water quality and wildlife conservation. The enactment of environmental laws in the United States ushered in a new era of awareness for sustainability. It could be argued that the trend for corporate sustainability grew from the legislative efforts at the state and federal level. For example, California enacted the first statewide pollution control act when then Governor Earl Warren signed California's County Air Pollution Control Act (CAPCA) in 1947.[1] The Clean Water Act (CWA) is the primary federal law in the United States governing water pollution. Passed in 1972, the act established the goals of eliminating releases of high amounts of toxic substances into water, eliminating additional water pollution by 1985 and ensuring that surface waters would meet standards necessary for recreation by 1983. The principal body of law in effect is based on the Federal Water Pollution Control Amendments of 1972 and was significantly expanded from the Federal Water Pollution Control Amendments of 1948. Major amendments were enacted in the Clean Water Act of 1977 and the Water Quality Act of 1987. The Clean Water Act does not directly address groundwater contamination, which is included in the Safe Drinking Water Act, Resource Conservation and Recovery Act and the Superfund Act.

The passage of the Endangered Species Act of 1973 (ESA) led to further layers of regulation on the impact of commercial activity on wildlife. The ESA was intended to be a means for conserving the ecosystems of endangered and threatened species and for the conservation of those species, and utilizing the authority of the federal government and its agencies for overseeing conservation initiatives. The scope of the ESA also considered water resource management issues that would arise related to conserving endangered species. The ESA defined the term 'commercial activity' as 'all activities of industry and trade, including, but not limited to, the buying or selling of commodities and activities conducted for the purpose of facilitating such buying and selling' (16 U.S.C. § 1532(2), 2000).

The recognition of the ecosystem's importance as a consideration in economic development was a major shift from previous centuries of human development and industrialization. In the United States, this paradigm shift signalled that human economic activities would have to be conducted with a degree of consideration for the natural world. The rule-making that lead up to the Environmental Impact Statements (EIS) mandate suggests a continuing policy of federal, state and local governments in coordination with public and private actors 'to use all practicable means and measures . . . in a manner calculated to foster and promote the general welfare' (Taylor, 1984: 33). The underlying EIS strategy was to develop a system by which the human and the natural worlds could co-exist and satisfy societal and economic needs for the current and future generations. This strategy mimicked the international call for sustainable development, as defined in *Our Common Future*, also known as the Brundtland Report, as 'development that meets the needs of the present without compromising the ability of future generations to meet their own needs' (WCED, 1987: 43). In fact, the United Nations Conference on the Human Environment in Stockholm, in 1972, 'represented a first taking stock of the global human impact on the environment, an attempt at forging a basic common outlook on how to address the challenge of preserving and enhancing the human environment' (Handl, 2012: 1). The Stockholm Declaration contained broad policy goals and concerned 'the need for a common outlook and for common principles to inspire and guide the peoples of the world in the preservation and enhancement of the human environment' (UNEP, 1972: 1). Post-Stockholm, 'global awareness of environmental issues increased dramatically, as did international environmental law-making proper' (Handl, 2012: 1).It could be argued that the increase in concern about environmental issues reflected in the passage of numerous environmental laws in the 1970s and early 1980s, and in particular the emphasis on understanding environmental activities reflected in the U.S. National Environmental Policy Act (1969) (NEPA), along with increased customer concerns about the environment led to sustainability reporting. Sustainability reporting addresses the impact of business practices on the environment. The establishment of federal, state and local laws to protect air, water, wildlife and natural ecosystems was inspired by a realization that commercial activity must harmonize with the ecological biosphere. Recognition among various stakeholders and constituencies that commercial activity at its very core can be destructive of natural wildlife habitats, deplete precious water resources and harm air quality gave rise to a desire to preserve and protect natural resources and motivated a host of environmental laws and regulations. While environmental laws were being enacted, the business community began to quantify and qualify how human development activities could impact ecosystem management and preservation. The next section shows how the formulation of sustainability reporting has become a business endeavour.

Sustainability reporting

Sustainable development encompasses two principles: (1) 'the concept of needs, in particular the essential needs of the world's poor, to which overriding priority should be given' and (2) 'the idea of limitations imposed by the state of technology and social organization on the environment's ability to meet present and future needs' (IISD). The United Nations Environment Programme (UNEP) expanded this definition of sustainable development to include 'the maintenance, rational use and enhancement of the natural resource base that underpins ecological resilience and economic growth' (UNEP, Decision 15/3, 1989).The Rio Declaration at the UN Conference on Environment and Development in 1992 and

Agenda 21, stressed the three elements of sustainable development – ecology, economy, and social justice: 'To conserve the basic needs of life, to enable all people to achieve economic prosperity, and to strive towards social justice' (Wellmer and Becker-Platen, 2002: 185).

Evolving public attitudes about sustainable development helped businesses recognize that a company's ultimate success or health cannot and should not be measured only by the financial bottom line, but also by social/ethical and environmental performance (Norman and MacDonald, 2004: 243). In other words, an increasing number of companies acknowledged that the bottom line should be comprehensively quantified by attention to people, planet and profits. The triple bottom line (3BL) is a way to understand the rise of CSR in business circles. The term '3BL' itself was coined by John Elkington to highlight the role environmental issues play in business (Elkington, 1999). Proponents of 3BL contend that 'the overall fulfillment of obligations to communities, employees, customers, and suppliers . . . should be measured, calculated, audited, and reported – just as the financial performance of public companies has been for more than a century' (Norman and MacDonald, 2004: 243). Of the two main approaches to sustainability, top-down and inside-out, 3BL is representative of the latter. Top down approaches focus on management, measurement and control, whereas inside-out strategies hammer on the significance of innovation and change (Henriques and Richardson, 2004). The 3BL approach should be utilized in corporate decision-making because environmental and social factors impact economic results.

A number of companies have begun to see that they need a green image to hold on to, or expand, their markets. Some of these companies have used sustainability or green reporting as part of this strategy but used data and information that was not uniform, was often hard to verify and could be characterized as 'green washing'. Other companies took the sustainability challenge more seriously and began changing practices and reporting on progress, although still using data that was hard to compare since there were no uniform reporting standards. By the mid-2000s many more companies were taking sustainability reporting more seriously, while the Global Reporting Initiative's reporting criteria began to influence reporting practice leading to some standardization of reporting. Companies were increasingly finding that sustainability work had real business value beyond just improved environmental performance, such as decreasing costs, anticipating problems, using resources more efficiently, allowing better management of the supply chain and reducing risk. While some green washing may remain, sustainability reporting today is more uniform, taken more seriously and valued by the companies themselves.

Consider the approach of the sustainability 'tipping point', where the concept of 'sustainability becomes a strategic business imperative – driven not by regulation, but rather by pressure from virtually the entire spectrum of corporate stakeholders' (Civins and Mendoza, 2008: 372). From the 1960s to the current period, three great waves of public pressure impacted the environmental agenda (Elkington, 2004): The roles and responsibilities of governments and the public sector have mutated in response to each of these three waves – and will continue to do so. Although each wave of activism has been followed by eased public concern, each successive wave has significantly expanded what policy-makers are expected to do about encouraging business to be more accountable for their social and environmental performance, while at the same time looking to business to be more imaginative in creating new sustainable product markets.

- Wave 1 brought an understanding that environmental impacts and natural resource demands have to be limited, resulting in an initial outpouring of environmental litigation. The business response was defensive, focusing on compliance, at best.
- Wave 2 brought a wider realization that new kinds of production technologies and new kinds of products are needed, culminating in the insight that development processes have to become sustainable – and a sense that business would often have to take the lead. The business response began to be more competitive.
- Wave 3 focuses on the growing recognition that sustainable development will require profound changes in the governance of corporations and in the whole process of globalization, putting a renewed focus on government and on civil society. Now, in addition to the compliance and competitive dimensions, the business response will need to focus on market creation (Elkington, 2004: 7).

The three pressure waves of the 3BL agenda have occurred on the domestic as well as international front. The United States was a pioneer, in some respects, and a resister, in other ways, in recognizing and implementing 3BL.

The United States started with litigation as the major driver of more sustainable conduct by industry and society. It then expanded beyond environmental regulation and litigation to leverage SEC reporting to drive more sustainable behaviour in private sector initiatives as companies became more receptive to sustainability issues. Due to environmental legislation, companies sought to implement and maintain compliance measures consistent with the corporate goal of increasing shareholder value by, in part, reducing the potential for regulatory penalties and injunctive relief (Civins and Mendoza, 2008). As a result of the enactment of the Superfund in 1980, corporations sought efforts for heightened corporate risk management and compliance, because the failure to comply with environmental statutes could lead to costly fines and subject a corporation to pricy litigation.

The courtroom has been used as a place to regulate the boardroom. The village of Kivalina, Alaska, sued several energy and utility companies for damages associated with increased erosion of the village's lands because of the loss of sea ice. In another suit, WildEarth Guardians alleged Xcel Energy, Inc. (Xcel) failed to monitor and limit air emissions at a coal-fired power plant in Denver. While Xcel did not admit to the allegations, a consent decree filed in federal court notes that Xcel has since taken affirmative steps to improving its monitoring of the emissions and intends to halt the burning of coal at this plant by 2018. The consent decree also indicates that Xcel will provide $447,700 to the non-profit Groundwork Denver for clean energy programs, including the installation of solar panels in the Globeville, Elyria or Swansea neighbourhoods. The company further offered energy-efficiency improvements to dozens of homes in the area and supported an open space project in Globeville.

The definition of environmental valuation is complex. Fines and lawsuits are not straightforward, because the true 'cost' of litigation and negative publicity is difficult to assess. Environmental valuation considers 'the environment as a commodity that can be broken down into different components and analysed just like any other commodity' (Richardson, 2004: 37). Sustainability accounting recognizes the role of greenhouse gas emissions, energy efficient technologies, water management, clean energy and biodiversity (Deloitte). It is sometimes referred to as environmental, social and governance (ESG) reporting. The SEC has a framework for regulating certain sustainability issues, including rules that mandate filings include 'discussions of trends, events, or uncertainties that will be reasonably likely to have a material effect on the company' (Civins and Mendoza, 2008: 372).

In its early phases during the 1970s and 1980s, sustainability reporting consisted of advertisements and annual report sections (Tepper Marlin and Tepper Marlin, 2003). The second phase of reporting really began with Ben & Jerry's, which in 1989 commissioned a 'social auditor' to work with the Ben & Jerry's staff on a report covering the activities of the company in 1988 (Marlin and Marlin 2003). The third phase of CSR reporting introduced not only third-party certification of the reports, but certification by bodies that are accredited to certify against social or environmental standards. Corporate sustainability programmes are becoming strategic business imperatives, driven by stakeholder pressures rather than by governmental directives. The guiding principles were that sustainable business practices were critical to long-term stakeholder value in an increasingly resource-constrained world and that sustainability factors represent both opportunities and risks for competitive companies. The Dow Jones Sustainability Indices (DJSI) are offered through a partnership between RobecoSAM and S&P Dow Jones Indices to track the stock performance of the world's leading companies on account of economic, environmental and social criteria. The purpose of the indices is to provide investors with benchmarks to integrate sustainability considerations in portfolios and offer an effective engagement platform for companies who are seeking to incorporate sustainable best practices in their business model.

One component of the sustainability indices is the ongoing monitoring of media and stakeholder commentaries and other publicly available information. This information is available from consumer organizations, NGOs, governments and international organizations. This data is used to identify companies' involvement and response to environmental, economic and social crisis situations that may have a damaging effect on a company's reputation and core business (DJSI). The question regarding sustainability initiatives is whether or not they do, indeed, create bona fide shareholder value, because the longer-term and intangible value are much more difficult to quantify for businesses. The shareholder value framework needs to be expanded to accommodate the value proposition of hard-to-measure initiatives, including sustainability projects. For now, a corporation that decides to develop a corporate sustainability program might consider, among other things, how to address the issues of what, when, where and how to report sustainability efforts and results.

The impetus for sustainability nationally paralleled the rise of sustainability on the global front. The US –while not a leader in sustainability – has been embracing the call for sustainable development, somewhat begrudgingly. In contrast, corporations have responded enthusiastically, with initiatives yielding more results than a regulatory or legal regime for sustainability because of their actual business success associated with sustainability.

Meta-regulation as an enforcement tool for sustainability

Corporate governance encompasses the established set of internal processes, customs, policies, laws and institutions affecting the way officers, directors and workers direct, administer or control a corporation. Corporate governance also regulates the relationships between the stakeholders and the overall corporate goals. Commentators suggest that the most successful forms of regulation emerge from a flexible rather than a legalistic method of implementation, because American techniques of regulation generate 'regulatory unreasonableness' (Bardach and Kagan, 1982). Historically, regulation consists of opposing binary approaches: no restrictions and command-and-control regulation (Coglianese, 2007). Coglianese and Mendelson (2010: 146–68) argue that the dichotomy between these two options 'fails to capture the full range of options that lie between the polar extremes of absolute discretion and total control'. Bridging this dichotomy – between a highly regulated environment (that marginalizes governance), and one where there is little formal regulation – is that of regulatory governance, a notion of decentralized control that incorporates 'pressures and policies deployed by a variety of actors, both governmental and non-governmental, to shape the behavior of firms and thereby address market failures and other public problems' (Coglianese and Mendelson, 2010: 146–68).

One approach to regulatory governance is meta-regulation, an emerging concept that describes the interaction between government regulation and self-regulation. It can be viewed as the state's oversight of self-regulatory arrangements (Hutter, 2001) and even the interactions among multifarious regulatory actors or levels of regulation as a process of 'regulating the regulators, whether they are public agencies, private corporate self-regulators or third party gatekeepers' (Parker, 2002: 15). On the institutional plane, meta-regulation is the regulation of one institution by another (Braithwaite, 1982). The essential elements of any regulatory instrument or approach are: target, regulator, command and consequences (Coglianese, 2007). The traditional view of regulation places the government in the regulator's role, but this role can also be assumed by non-governmental bodies or by industry trade associations (Coglianese, 2007).

A target will often be subjected to rules imposed by different governmental and non-governmental regulators, which may or may not coordinate their rules and rule-enforcement activity (Coglianese, 2007). The target is the entity to which the regulation applies and upon whom the consequences of non-compliance are imposed. The regulator is the entity that creates and enforces the rule or regulation (Coglianese, 2007). Command refers to what the regulator instructs the target to do or to refrain from doing. Consequences can require the attainment of specific outcomes and the adoption of specific means, or they can require the avoidance of general outcomes and the adoption of very general means. Consequences can vary in their size and certainty, and between negative consequences (such as fines or sanctions for noncompliance) and positive consequences (such as subsidies or regulatory exemptions for compliance) (Coglianese, 2007).

In other words, meta-regulation offers an internal mechanism for self-regulation through corporate targets. The role of the outside regulator in this scheme is to 'direct or shape targets to regulate themselves in any number of ways, from explicitly threatening future discretion-eliminating forms of regulation and sanctions, to providing rewards or recognition for firms that opt for self-control' (Coglianese and Nash, 2006: 3–30). In this regard, a government regulator could hone in on a problem and command the target to find a solution to that problem, and then the target, in turn, could create its own internal regulations (Parker, 2002) (Morgan, 2003). The primary regulator in such a case would be the government, but the target responds by developing what would otherwise be viewed as a self-regulatory system.

The goal behind the law is to encourage corporate consciences so that the corporation aims to do what it should do instead of only what it wants to do (Selznick, 2002). As a key feature of corporate governance, meta-regulation is 'the proliferation of different forms of regulation (whether tools of state law or non-law mechanisms) each regulating one another' (Parker, 2007: 207) (Heydebrand, 2003). With respect to governance, meta-regulation is seen 'as increasingly about "collaborations", "partnerships", "webs" or "networks" in which the state, state-promulgated law, and especially hierarchical command-and-control regulation, are not necessarily the dominant, and certainly not the only important, mechanism of regulation' (Parker, 2007) (Braithwaite, 2000). In its most sophisticated forms, meta-regulation is seen as 'continuous self-improvement, systemic dissemination of best practices, and mandatory incident reporting for institutional self-correction' (Archibald, 2008, 11) (Braithwaite et al., 2005). Meta-regulation is a mechanism that merges corporate governance and social responsibility into a regulatory synthesis (Gill, 2008). A combination of bright line rules and high-level principles provide both senior and junior level management guidance in developing meta-regulation (Ojo, 2011). For corporations that seek to highlight their corporate monitoring initiatives around sustainability, meta-regulation provides a governance mechanism for the development of voluntary corporate practices to support sustainability initiatives (Ojo, 2011).

Ann Marie Slaughter argues that a new world order has been created, consisting of disaggregated government agencies using information networks to coordinate cross-border policy issues for global governance (Slaughter, 2004). Joe W. Pitts, III suggests that this 'new world order' illustrates 'the relative, partial capacity of even powerful states and the need for greater coordination' (Pitts, 2009: 361–3) (Indus Canada, 2004). Christine Parker asserts that there are 'uncontestable public trust and democratic legitimacy issues involved with granting a greater role for corporations in global governance' (Parker, 2007: 207–37). Parker argues that meta-regulation can serve as a way of conceptualizing how law can be used to manage multiple threads of governance. Meta-regulatory law can recognize, incorporate or empower initiatives developed by non-state actors or partnerships of actors that can influence corporate governance processes (Parker, 2007) (Rees, 1988). Fostering a meta-regulatory approach to corporate sustainability initiatives would lead to enhanced corporate transparency. What may not have initially been construed as sustainability can be reconceptualized as such in the corporate framework. The next section explores the corporate framework of existing sustainability reporting in the context of oil and gas regulation.

Colorado's oil and gas drilling disclosure and monitoring requirements

Colorado is a battleground for energy development, particularly for rules governing hydraulic fracturing. The oil and gas companies have been pro-active in instituting a series of increased transparency initiatives to restore public confidence and quell environmental fears of the threats associated with hydraulic fracturing. Hydraulic fracturing is a process used in nine out of ten natural gas wells in the United States, where a mixture of millions of gallons of water, sand and chemicals are pumped underground to extract oil and gas deposits in shale rock. Industry officials are fretful of restrictions on corporate activities because of bans on hydraulic fracturing by the states of Vermont and New York (Bligh and Wendelbo, 2013). These outright restrictions on hydraulic fracturing are an underlying motivation for the development of industry-led sustainability programs. Most corporate actors are aware that if they fail to self-regulate their own activities, they will be subjected to more onerous and stringent requirements by the government nudged by environmental activists and community leaders. More broadly, corporate sustainability reporting (CSR) is part of the corporate formula to improve the oil and gas industry's public image and misperceptions regarding the occupational, health, and safety issues of oil and gas development.

The lack of baseline scientific studies on the impact of oil and gas drilling operations on human, animal and environmental safety means that sentiments against oil and gas drilling operations are based on a level of speculation. This lack of reliable data leaves open a lot of space for uninformed debate in shaping public perceptions on hydraulic fracturing. For example, Bamberger and Oswald's (2012) study' of the impact of gas drilling on human and animal health found a correlation between oil and gas operations and adverse health effects. The study observed that congenital defects in calves and other farm and domestic animals were most severe in wastewater spills, leaks and dumping associated with surface level oil and gas operations.[2] The study focused almost exclusively on adverse conditions. Bamberger and Oswald's (2012) study noted that 'complete evidence regarding health impacts of gas drilling cannot be obtained due to incomplete testing and disclosure of chemicals, and nondisclosure agreements' (Bamberger and Oswald, 2012: 51). Based on standards of a controlled experiment, Bamberger and Oswald conceded their study was imperfect because 'one variable could not be changed while holding all others constant' (Bamberger and Oswald, 2012: 55). They also noted that the research 'was not a systematic study that will provide the percentage of farms with problems associated with gas drilling, but the design is such that the study can illustrate what can happen in areas experiencing extensive gas drilling' (Bamberger and Oswald, 2012: 55). Nevertheless, they indicated that it was 'possible to observe temporal correlations between events such as well flaring and air quality, or hydraulic fracturing and water quality leading to toxicity' (Bamberger and Oswald, 2012: 55). Scientifically sound studies of the impacts of oil and gas operations could lead to a better assessment of drilling activities when conducted under both adverse and normal operating conditions. While the availability of some data is better than none, studies done under adverse operating conditions can negatively impact public perceptions against hydraulic fracturing where scientific data of the impact of oil and gas extractive processes remains incomplete. The conditions of data gathering are crucial for sound scientific inquiry into the health and environmental impacts of oil and gas operations.

Comparisons between the tobacco industry and the oil and gas industry abound with respect to the associated health effects. However, tobacco use is a recreational or leisurely pursuit whereas energy development is critical for human civilization. The industry's importance in the overall economy cannot be over-emphasized. The need for balancing soaring demand for energy with environmental risk and degradation is critical for sustainable energy development. Oil and gas operators should not only seek to maximize production output from wells, but also limit the environmental impact of any given project. A part of the turn to sustainable environmental practices is based upon fear of liabilities and fines associated with the failure to abide by environmental regulation, but oil and gas operators, like other corporations are recognizing the role of energy efficiency, risk preparedness and hazardous waste management as economically viable objectives.

Two examples of self-regulation are the reporting of the chemical components of hydraulic fracturing fluids and the testing of available water resources near operated oil and gas wells. The oil and gas operators in Colorado began disclosure and testing prior to any specific government mandates. Based on the success of the initial voluntary programs, the Colorado Oil and Gas Conservation Commission (COGCC) institutionalized the programs and adopted rules to govern them.[3] Future CSR could capture and report compliance with these COGCC rules. The evolution of environmental reporting and monitoring from a voluntary program to a meta-regulated program shows the effectiveness of corporate sustainability efforts. While critics may argue that these efforts are self-serving and do not go far enough, the results do, indeed, enhance corporate transparency and are a step in the right direction.

Initially, the industry organization, Colorado Oil and Gas Association (COGA) established a program to collect data pre- and post-drilling at individual well sites to examine impact on the groundwater quality associated with the drilling and hydraulic fracturing of oil and gas wells. Through the program, baseline groundwater quality samples were collected from two existing groundwater features, located within half a mile of the surface of new well pads or additional wells on existing well pads. These samples were collected prior to the drilling operation and again from each groundwater feature within one to three years following completion of the drilling. The samples were collected by individuals with experience in water quality sampling and sent to an accredited laboratory for analysis. Each landowner who had elected to participate in the program was provided copies of the lab results within three months of the sample collection. Landowners did, however, have the option not to participate. With the landowner's permission, the results would be posted on the COGCC's publically available website. The COGA program was an industry-led initiative. Even though it was voluntary, many oil and gas operators opted to participate to ensure groundwater quality. The oil and gas operators were amenable to the requirements because the groundwater monitoring and sampling program had the potential to restore and reinforce public confidence in the environmental integrity of oil and gas drilling operations. The voluntary program evolved into a government-mandated program. The success of the program to date can be linked to its origins as a form of self-regulation. When corporate actors are able to maneuver through the regulatory regime on their own accord, better results for sustainability are achieved.

When Colorado mandated statewide water sampling and monitoring for oil and gas drilling operations modelled after the COGA program in 2013, adopting the regulatory rules proved relatively smooth (COGCC Rule 318A.e.(4), Rule 608, and Rule 609, 2013). These rules are the first of their kind and arguably the most rigorous rules for groundwater sampling and monitoring in the United States, enabling stakeholders, to be kept abreast of baseline groundwater quality. Apart from the government, other key stakeholders include non-state actors, public officials, community members, NGOs and environmental groups. For example, a team of researchers at Colorado State University initiated the Colorado Water Watch programme to collect groundwater samples from oil and gas sites and report information every hour on a university-operated website. Noble Energy serves as a partner in this university-led program. The oil and gas operator has a vested interest in securing public confidence in its extractive activities. Having a live website that shows results of groundwater monitoring near operating oil and gas wells is one such step. The government regulation sought to aid in early detection of any adverse impacts associated with oil and gas drilling activities along with existing groundwater contaminants, which could be treated. Since contaminants can naturally occur in groundwater, or can be due to agricultural activity, septic system use, household chemical use/disposal, the age and composition of the plumbing pipes or industrial activity, the groundwater sampling prior to drilling and completion operations would provide a baseline analysis of groundwater quality conditions.

Operators choose the sampling locations, but COGCC Rule 609 establishes a hierarchy of preferred water sources.[4] Wells in the Greater Wattenberg Area (GWA) in Northern Colorado and coal bed methane wells have different spacing requirements for the sampling and monitoring rules because of the high level of activity in that area (COGCC Rule 318A and Rule 608, 2013). A modified rule was adopted in the GWA due to the combination of energy development, agriculture and other industrial and residential use unique to the area. Operators in the GWA must sample one source per governmental quarter section both before and after drilling. Operators may select the sampling locations; if there is more than one available water well within the quarter section, or half mile, then similar to Rule 609, the rule sets forth a hierarchy of preferred water sources.

Colorado House Bill 1316 was introduced late in the 2013 legislative session and sought to require the state to undertake the same stringency of groundwater testing in the oil-rich Wattenberg basin as it does across most of the state (Proctor, 2013). Industry leaders criticized HB 1316 saying that it disregarded scientific data presented during the creation of groundwater testing rules and would derail efforts to address local community needs (Lynn, 2013). Environmentalists criticized the exemption in the Northern Colorado oil field, calling it the 'Anadarko-Noble loophole' after two major producers in the region, Anadarko Petroleum Corp. and Noble Energy Inc. Weld County, which lies in the Greater Wattenberg Area, is home to 20,000 of the state's 50,000 active oil and gas wells, according to the state oil commission.[5] The Senate version of the bill, though, was killed.

Post-drilling and completion groundwater sampling facilitates monitoring any change in water quality or the appearance of contaminants over a period of time. The pre- and post-water quality sampling data created as a result of the new rule will be a part of the larger COGCC database, which will be the most comprehensive water quality database in the United States once it is combined with COGCC's existing water sampling date. Rule 609.g. provides that the sampling results "shall not create a presumption of liability, fault or causation against the owner or operator of a Well, Multi-Well Site or Dedicated Injection Well who conducted the sampling, or on whose behalf sampling was conducted by a third party. Rule 318A.e.(4) expressly states that owners or operators shall not be presumed to be liable, at fault, or causally responsible, as a result of under-taking the sampling required by these rules, or based on the sampling results. While such a no-liability provision is standard in corporate agreements, its appearance shows a concern among corporations for liability. That is, the mere presence of a no-liability provision indicates that corporate officials are recognizing the threats posed by environmental lawsuits on many issues, including disposal of hazardous substances, toxic spills and public health. The no-liability provision makes the success of environmental lawsuits more difficult, but not impossible. The threat of liability facing the owner or operator if suspected of being in breach of environmental regulations, the potential costs of defense, critical scrutiny by stakeholders plus the likelihood of reputational damage, all help drive corporate sustainability efforts.

In 2011, Colorado adopted a second measure requiring disclosure of all chemicals used in hydraulic fracturing fluids. Requiring drilling companies to disclose information about the chemicals used in hydraulic fracturing is now becoming well-established. But the particulars of the disclosure requirements can differ from state to state. Colorado's disclosure requirements are the toughest in the United States. What is significant about the Colorado rule is that it requires specific details on the ingredients and concentrations of the hydraulic fracturing fluids – much more detail compared to other states (Jaffe, 2011). Colorado governor John Hickenlooper has said that the disclosure requirements will likely become a model for other states (Jaffe, 2011).

COGCC established a regulatory regime for chemical inventory and disclosure requirements, water protection measures and the hydraulic fracturing process requirements. Tests will be paid for by oil companies, and results will be kept in a database by the COGCC. Colorado is among a number of states that provide for regulatory reporting of chemicals used in the hydraulic fracturing process through posting on the FracFocus.org site – an online database managed by Ground Water Protection Council and the Interstate Oil and Gas Compact Commission. The primary purpose of this site is to provide factual information concerning hydraulic fracturing and groundwater protection.[6] In the 2012 negotiations over the hydraulic fracturing fluids chemicals disclosures, the environmental advocacy group Earthjustice represented the Colorado Environmental Coalition, Earthworks Oil and Gas Accountability Project, National Wildlife Federation, San Juan Citizens Alliance and High Country Citizens Alliance and also worked closely with the Environmental Defense Fund (Earthjustice, 2011). The public participation in the agency rulemaking improved the outcome of the law.

The New Mexico state legislature had also adopted rules for hydraulic fracturing disclosures, but the New Mexico rule limited disclosures if the chemical qualified for trade secret protection (New Mexico Admin. Code 19.15.16.19(B), 2012). In the 2013 state legislative session, state congressional representative Brian Egolf, Jr. introduced a bill similar to the tougher Colorado rule, but the New Mexico House Bill 136 (2013) was not adopted. Idaho allows oil and gas operators to apply for trade secret protection, but limits the exception when state or federal law requires disclosure to a health care professional (Idaho Admin. Code r.20.07.02.056, 2012). Louisiana offers a parallel exception for disclosure to a health care professional, but generally the exact chemical name is not disclosed to the public (La. Admin. Code tit. 43, pt. XIX, Section 118, 2011). At the outset, oil and gas operators did not want to disclose proprietary information and sought protection, but invariably did accept the proposal (Jaffe, 2011).

The environmental implications of the groundwater sampling and monitoring program raise a heightened level of corporate stewardship of the land and its natural resources as well as a sense of greater corporate accountability. The disclosure requirements for hydraulic fracturing fluids also further the goal of corporate accountability and transparency. The hesitation of oil and gas operators about disclosing the hydraulic fracturing requirements, interestingly, was tied more to the protection of trade secrets than a fear of the public discovering the dangerous stew of hydraulic fracturing fluids, most of which are common chemicals found in household cleaning solvents. The concentration of the chemicals is low because it is diluted with water and sand in the fracturing process and varies from 0.5 to 1.0 per cent of chemical concentration.

These examples highlight the value of a meta-regulated hydrocarbon extraction business. The example of the groundwater sampling and monitoring program illustrates the regulatory bridge from self-regulation to meta-regulation. Some Colorado oil and gas operators initially began voluntary testing of groundwater sampling pre- and post-drilling. Seeing the results of the tests increased public confidence in drilling operations, the oil and gas operators accepted mandatory testing requirements. Corporations are willing to expose themselves to layers of additional environmental regulation to advance sustainability as it promotes the 3BL approach. Whether the willingness of corporations to be subjected to additional layers of regulation indicates the belief among firms in the intrinsic value of the 3BL approach, or believe in the probable contribution to public confidence remains to be seen. What is clear is that firms are accepting environmental monitoring as a necessary component of their business model. A meta-regulated governance model bridges the gap between a highly regulated system and one with only limited oversight. The case of self-regulation in Colorado in relation to the groundwater sampling and monitoring program demonstrates the emergence of the corporate conscience. Increasingly companies are seeking to improve the sustainability of their products with an eye on the 3BL model. The viability of future corporate operations hinges of the availability of natural resources in the future and the conservation of such natural resources. For instance, the availability of clean water is critical to future operations, because the community stakeholders rely on safe drinking water. If the community stakeholders suffered harm on account of the loss of access to safe drinking water, they would protest and seek affirmative steps to enjoin the oil and gas operations. Hopefully all oil and gas operators recognize their potential impact on the environment, such as the threat to safe drinking water for community stakeholders, and take steps to ensure the conservation of water resources.

The expansion of a meta-regulatory governance system would be crucial in the oil and gas sector. The next steps for heightened corporate transparency and accountability for hydrocarbon activities include pre- and post-drilling health screenings and testing of animals within a certain proximity to the hydrocarbon activities. The Food and Drug Administration (FDA), in coordination with the Environmental Protection Agency (EPA) and/or coordinating state agencies, can support and eventually mandate pre- and post-drilling testing of domestic livestock, such as cattle, sheep, chickens, goats and other farm animals, used for human consumption. Increasing the availability of scientifically sound medical and environmental studies is crucial for improved sustainability reporting for oil and gas activities. To maintain objectivity, these studies should be conducted by independent research institutions or universities or through government-funded grants. Having oil and gas operators fund these studies may undermine the overall public acceptance and the credibility of the results. Using an independent third party facilitates a more open dialogue on the issue.

Likewise, while tests to assess the impact on groundwater are of primary importance, additional testing could be conducted on wastewater, surface water and storm water in the proximity of oil and gas wells. This expanded testing of water resources could provide additional data on the soundness or detrimental impact of fossil fuel production. Using more layers of accountability would improve the integrity of the collection of the sample; the testing facility should have a requisite level of objectivity in that it should not have any commercial interest in the oil and gas operations. Sweeping restrictions on hydraulic fracturing activities, which may have a level of public support, would adversely affect energy supply. By enhancing self-regulatory efforts of sustainable energy development, the corporate actors will be able to maintain or increase production output to manage rapidly increasing energy demands.

Conclusion

Well-documented evidence suggests that voluntary corporate sustainability strategies can be effective in enhancing both environmental protection and corporate profits. The triple bottom line model for accessing corporate success in sustainability reporting is a corporate best practice for environmental stewardship. The emergence of corporate sustainability reporting (CSR) has resulted from a new wave of globalization where environmental best practices are emerging as a significant contributor to corporations having the ability to perform responsibly, and to be granted, or keep, a 'social license to practice'. As outlined in the chapter, the conceptual framework of CSR has suffered from the lack of a clear regulatory regime. The case study on Colorado's oil and gas industry has provided evidence to suggest that while part of the emergence of CSRs can be attributed to this lack of regulatory oversight, the failure to regulate simultaneously can delegitimize the substantial potential of CSR initiatives at the corporate as well as governmental level. The success of the outcomes highlighted in the Colorado case study provides support for an alternative to mandatory reporting and to that of no reporting; that is, meta-regulation as an emergent form of governance for CSR and as an increasingly valuable corporate tool.

Notes

† Assistant Professor of Law, Barry University Dwayne O. Andreas School of Law. LL.M. University of Denver Sturm College of Law; J.D. University of Florida Levin College of Law; B.A. University of California at Berkeley. This paper has benefited from feedback and questions by the participants of the Sabin Colloquium on Innovative Environmental Law Scholarship at Columbia Law School in 2015, United Nations Institute for Training and Research (UNITAR)-Yale Conference on Environmental

Governance and Democracy at Yale University in 2014 and the Next Generation Environmental Compliance Workshop, sponsored by the Environmental Protection Agency's Office of Enforcement and Compliance Assurance, Environmental Law Institute, George Washington Law School, University of California at Berkeley Boalt Law School, and University of California at Berkeley Goldman School of Public Policy in 2012. It has also been shaped by discussions at the University of Denver's 45th Annual Sutton Colloquium on *Approaching the Limits of Growth in the 21st Century: Sustainable Development vs. Sustainability* and Harvard Law School's Institute for Global Law and Policy 2013 Workshop in Doha, Qatar. Thanks to Federico Cheever, Ved Nanda, Don Smith, Rock Pring, Hari Osofsky, Cary Coglianese, David Marcello, Lee Paddock, Jason Czarnezki, Ann Powers, Nicholas Robinson, Shelby Green, Vanessa Merton, Jill Gross, James Fishman, David Kennedy, Michael Gerrard, Jessica Wentz, Michael Burger, Celia Taylor, Luke Danielson, Cecilia Dalupan, Kristi Disney, Marketa Zubkova, and Lucy Daberkow. A note of gratitude to Akmal, Senan, Hanan, and my parents and siblings.

1   The first major air pollution law in California, denominated the County Air Pollution Control District Act, was enacted in 1947. California Health and Safety Code §§ 24198-24341. Subsequent amendments in 1957 extended regulation over motor vehicle emissions

2   The (Bamberger and Oswald 2012) study explains:

> Exposure to drilling chemicals occurred during a blowout when liquids ran into a pasture and pond where bred cows were grazing; most of the cows later produced stillborn calves with congenital defects. Exposure to wastewater occurred through leakage or improper fencing of impoundments, alleged compromise of a liner in an impoundment to drain fluid, direct application of the wastewater to roads, and dumping of the wastewater on creeks and land. The most common exposure by far was to affected water wells and/or springs; the next most common exposure was to affected ponds or creeks. Finally, exposures also were associated with compressor station malfunction, pipeline leaks, and well flaring. In addition to humans, the animals affected were: cows, horses, goats, llamas, chickens, dogs, cats, and koi.

3   COGCC's power to make and enforce the rules is derived from Section 34_60_105(1), C.R.S. Meanwhile, § 34_60_106(2)(d), C.R.S. gives COGCC the authority to regulate:

> Oil and gas operations so as to prevent and mitigate significant adverse environmental impacts on any air, water, soil, or biological resource resulting from oil and gas operations to the extent necessary to protect public health, safety, and welfare, including protection of the environment and wildlife resources, taking into consideration cost effectiveness and technical feasibility.
>
> COGCC Rule 609 (2013).

4   Locations closest to the well and maintained domestic water wells are preferred and locations in a radial pattern are additionally preferred for sampling. The operator must perform an initial sampling and then two follow-up samples at the exact same locations as the initial sampling. Initial samples are to be taken within 12 months of setting conductor pipe. Two follow-up samples are required upon completion with the first between six and twelve months and a second follow-up between sixty and seventy-two months. Rule 609 provides for certain variances so that "an operator may request a variance if no available water sources are located within one-half mile of the

proposed well or the water sources are improperly maintained or non-operational."
5   By way of disclosure, the author worked in the Denver of Noble Energy during 2013-2014.
6   FracFocus is not intended to argue either for or against the use of hydraulic fracturing as a technology. It is also not intended to provide a scientific analysis of risk associated with hydraulic fracturing.

References

Archibald B, 2008 Let My People Go: Human Capital Investment and Community Capacity Building Via Meta-regulation in A Deliberative Democracy-A Modest Contribution for Criminal Law and Restorative Justice, 16 *Cardozo Journal of International and Comparative Law* 16: 1–11

Bamberger M and Oswald R E, 2012, Impacts of Gas Drilling on Human and Animal Health, *New Solutions*, 22(1) 51–77

Bardach E and Kagan R A, 1982, *Going by the Book: The Problem of Regulatory Unreasonableness* Philadelphia, PA: Temple University Press

Bligh S and Wendelbo C, 2013, Hydraulic Fracturing: Drilling into the Issue *Natural Resources and the Environment*, 27(3). Available at: www.americanbar.org/publications/natural_resources_environment/2012_13/winter_2013/hydraulic_fracturing_drilling_the_issue.html [accessed 14 February 2015]

Braithwaite J, 2000, The New Regulatory State and the Transformation of Criminology, *British Journal of Criminology* 40(2): 222

Braithwaite J, 2002, Rewards and Regulation, *Journal of Law and Society* 29(1), 12–26.

Civins J and Mendoza M, 2008, Corporate Sustainability and Social Responsibility: A Legal Perspective, *Texas Bar Journal*, 71: 368

Coglianese C, 2007, The Case Against Collaborative Environmental Law, *University of Pennsylvania Law Review PENNumbra*, 156: 295–310

Coglianese C and Mendelson E, 2010, Meta Regulation and Self-Regulation in Cave M, Baldwin R and Lodge M (eds) *The Oxford Handbook on Regulation* Oxford: Oxford University Press

Coglianese C and Nash J, 2006, Management-Based Strategies: An Emerging Approach to Environmental Protection, in Coglianese C and Nash J (eds) *Leveraging the Private Sector: Management-Based Strategies for Improving Environmental Performance*, 3–30

COGCC Rule 318A (2013)

COGCC Rule 608 (2013)

COGCC Rule 609 (2013)

COGCC Series 200, 300, and 805 Rules (2011): 3–20

COGCC, Statement of Basis, Specific Statutory Authority, and Purpose, New Rules and Amendments to Current Rules of the Colorado Oil and Gas Conservation Commission, 2 CCR 404–1, Cause No. 1R Docket No. 1211-RM-03, *Statewide Water Sampling and Monitoring (new Rule 609 and amended Rule 318A.e.(4)*. Available at: http://cogcc.state.co.us/RR_HF2012/Groundwater/FinalRules/StatementofBasisPurpose_Rule609_FINAL_012513.pdf [accessed 14 February 2015]

Colorado Oil & Gas Association (COGA), Colorado Oil & Gas Association Voluntary Baseline Groundwater Quality Sampling Program. Available at: www.coga.org/index.php/BaselineWaterSampling#sthash.AOnD5HqC.dpbs [accessed 14 February 2015]

Colorado State University (CSU), Noble Unveil Live Water Monitoring Program near Drilling Sites, *The Tribune*, 24 September 2014. Available at: www.greeleytribune.com/news/13150500-113/colorado-gas-oil-carlson [accessed 14 February 2015]

Deloitte, 2005, *Sustainability Reporting and Integrated Reporting*. Available at: www.iasplus. com/en/resources/resource63 [accessed 14 February 2015]

Dow Jones Sustainability Indices. Available at: www.sustainability-indexes.com/about-us/ dow-jones-sustainability-indexes.jsp [accessed 14 February 2015]

Earthjustice, 2011, *Colorado Adopts New Fracking Disclosure Rule*, 11 December 2011. Available at: http://earthjustice.org/news/press/2011/colorado-adopts-new-fracking-disclosure-rule [accessed 14 February 2015]

Elkington J, 1999, *Cannibals with Forks: The Triple Bottom Line of 21st Century Business*, Oxford: Capstone

Elkington J, 2004 Enter the Bottom Line in Henriques A and Richardson J (eds) *The Triple Bottom Line: Does it All Add Up? Assessing the Sustainability of Business and CSR* London: Earthscan

Endangered Species Act of 1973, 16 U.S.C. §§ 1531–1544 (2000)

Federal Water Pollution Control Act (Clean Water Act) (33 U.S.C. 1251 – 1376; Chapter 758; P.L. 845, June 30, 1948; 62 Stat. 1155)

FracFocus Chemical Disclosure Registry. Available at: www.FracFocus.org [accessed 14 February 2015]

Gill A, 2008, Corporate Governance, As Social Responsibility: A Research Agenda *Berkeley Journal of International Law* 26: 452, 470

green@work, *Corporate Acts: Five Signs that Sustainability's Tipping Point Is Close* (March/ April 2003. Available at: www.greenatworkmag.com/magazine/corp_acts/05julaug.html. [accessed 14 February 2015]

Handl G, 2012 Declaration of the United Nations Conference on the Human Environ-ment (Stockholm Declaration), 1972 and the Rio Declaration on Environment and Development, 1992, United Nations. Available at: http://legal.un.org/avl/pdf/ha/dunche/ dunche_e.pdf [accessed February 17, 2015]

Henriques A and Richardson J, 2004 *The Triple Bottom Line: Does it All Add Up? Assessing the Sustainability of Business and CSR*, London: Earthscan.

Hutter B, 2001, *Regulation and Risk: Occupational Health and Safety on the Railways*, Oxford: Oxford University Press

Idaho Admin Code r.20.07.02.056 (2012)

Indus Canada, 2004, *Corporate Social Responsibility Monitor 2004: Executive Brief*. Available at: www.ic.gc.ca/eic/site/csrrse.nsf/eng/rs00123.html [accessed 14 February 2015]

International Institute for Sustainable Development, *What is Sustainable Development? Environmental, economic and social well-being for today and tomorrow*. Available at: www.iisd.org/sd/#one [accessed 14 February 2015]

Jaffe M, 2011, Hickenlooper: Colorado's frack fluid disclosure rule will be a model for the nation, *Denver Post*, 13 December 2011. Available at: www.denverpost.com/breaking news/ci_19537142 [accessed 14 February 2015]

Morgan B, 2003, *Social Citizenship in the Shadow of Competition: The Bureaucratic Politics of Regulatory Justification* Aldershot, UK: Ashgate.

Louisiana Admin. Code title 43, pt. XIX, Section 118 (2011).

Lynn S, 2015, Water monitoring exemption for oil companies overturned in House, *Northern Colorado Business Report*, 1 May 2013. Available at: www.ncbr.com/article/ 20130501/NEWS/130509992?pagenumber=2 [accessed 14 February 2015]

Native Village of Kivalina and City of Kivalina v. ExxonMobil Corporation et al., CV 08–1138, U.S. District Court, Northern District of California. Available at: http://cdn.ca9.uscourts. gov/datastore/opinions/2012/09/25/09-17490.pdf [accessed 30 September 2009]

New Mexico Admin. Code 19.15.16.19(B) (2012)

New Mexico House Bill 136 (2013)

Norman W and MacDonald C, 2004, Getting to the Bottom of 'Triple Bottom Line' *Business Ethics* Q., 14(2), (April 2004), 243

Ojo M, 2011, Building on the Trust of Management: Overcoming the Paradoxes of Principles Based Regulation, *Banking & Financial Services Policy Reporter*, (July 2011), 1, 4–5

Parker C, 2002, *The Open Corporation: Effective Self-Regulation and Democracy*, Cambridge: Cambridge Unversity Press

Parker C, 2007, Meta-Regulation: Legal Accountability for Corporate Social Responsibility? in McBarnet D, Voiculescu A and Campbell T (eds) *New Corporate Accountability: Corporate Social Responsibility and the Law*, London: Cambridge University Press 207–240

Parker, C., Scott, C., Lacey. N. and Brainwaithe, J. 2004. *Introduction in Regulating Law.* (http://ukcatalogue.oup.com/product/9780199264070.do) accessed 14 February 2015

Pitts J W, 2009, Corporate Social Responsibility: Current Status and Future Evolution, *Rutgers Journal of Law & Public Policy*, 6: 334, 361–63

PricewaterhouseCoopers LLP, 2012, *Sustainability Valuation: An oxymoron?* April 2012. Available at: www.pwc.com/en_US/us/transaction-services/publications/assets/pwc-sustainability-valuation.pdf [accessed 14 February 2015]

Proctor C, 2013, Colorado House approves bill raising oil and gas water testing rules, *Denver Business Journal*, 1 May 2013. Available at: www.bizjournals.com/denver/blog/earth_to_power/2013/05/colorado-house-approves-bill-raising.html?page=all [accessed 14 February 2015]

Rees J V, 1988, *Reforming the Workplace: A Study of Self-Regulation in Occupational Safety* Philadelphia, PA: University of Pennsylvania Press

Richardson J, 2004, Accounting for Sustainability: Measuring Quantities or Enhancing Qualities? in Henriques A and Richardson J (eds) *The Triple Bottom Line: Does it All Add Up? Assessing the Sustainability of Business and CSR* New York: Routledge

Rio Declaration on Environment and Development, 1992. Available at: http://legal.un.org/avl/ha/dunche/dunche.html [accessed 14 February 2015]

Selznick P, 2002, *The Communitarian Persuasion*, Washington, DC: Woodrow Wilson Press Center

Slaughter A, 2004 *A New World Order*, Princeton, NJ: Princeton University Press.

Taylor S, 1984, *Making Bureaucracies Think: The Environmental Impact Statement Strategy of Administrative Reform*. Redwood, CA: Stanford University Press

Tepper Marlin A and Tepper Marlin J, 2003, A brief history of social reporting. Available at: www.mallenbaker.net/csr/page.php?Story_ID=857 [accessed 14 February 2015]

United Nations, 1987, *Report of the World Commission Environment and Development: Our Common Future*, New York: UN Documents

United Nations Environment Programme (UNEP), 1972, *Declaration of the United Nations Conference on the Human Environment.* Available at: www.unep.org/Documents. Multilingual/Default.asp?documentid=97&articleid=1503 [accessed February 17, 2015]

United Nations Environment Programme (UNEP), 1989, *Decision 15/3, United Nations Conference on Environment and Development.* Available at: www.unep.org/Documents. multilingual/Default.asp?DocumentID=71&ArticleID=932&l=en [accessed 17 February 2015]

Wellmer F W and Becker-Platen J D, 2012, Sustainable Development and the Exploitation of Mineral and Energy Resources: A Review, *International Journal of Earth Sciences*

196   *Nadia B. Ahmad*

(Geologische Rundschau) 91: 723, 723–45. Available at: http://link.springer.com/article/
10.1007%2Fs00531-002-0267-x [accessed 14 February 2015]
World Commission on Environment and Development (WCED) *Reports on the World
Commission on Environment and Development: Our Common Future*. Available at:
www.un-documents.net/wced-ocf.htm [accessed 14 February 2015]

9 Timber companies and state building in the Congo Basin

Andrea Iff

Introduction

Imagine a logging concession located in a remote area in a tropical rain forest in a country still recovering from civil conflict. The logging concession hosts 30–40 very small poor villages that lack basic services like water, education and health services. As usual in the Congo Basin, in the concession agreement between the state and the forestry company, the latter agrees in a so called *Cahier des Charges* to build infrastructure (road, health centres and schools) and to pay into a local development fund. While the company fulfils its promises to what might be called a contribution to state building, no public servants are hired to operate the facilities and the agreed upon equal share of the central state is not paid into the development fund. In addition, there is widespread suspicion that the fund, managed by district level public officials together with local actors and the company, does not reach the villages. As the company's smooth operations depend on good relationships with the local communities, such a situation raises questions not only about private and public interests but also about responsibilities.

Interestingly, there are no studies of the impact of company service delivery activities on state building. Despite this lack, there are both proponents and critics of such an approach. In its report of mid-June 2014, the High Level Panel on Fragile States, established by the African Development Bank, states that private sector investment is one of the relevant actors in service delivery and state building in the coming years in Africa (High Level Panel on Fragile States, 2014: 23): '[. . .] a state monopoly on the delivery of public services may not be a viable strategy. Instead we should be willing to support a plurality of institutional forms, with service delivery shared between government agencies, private firms [. . .]).'. Critics however, see international capital as inherently bad and extractive industries even more so, and do not agree business should play an active role in state-building activities. They see private sector actors as too powerful vis-à-vis poor and low-capacity governments as well as weak communities in the Global South. Both narratives have one thing in common: they see the host state as an important, but very 'weak' actor (McCarthy, 2012; Moog *et al.*, 2012), and see most problems that arise as crystallizing around this factor.

The above outlined problems in the provision of public services by non-state actors are not new and not confined to companies. Development actors are also confronted with this issue: how can they support the provision of basic services like water, health and education without weakening the social contract between an incapable or unwilling state with its citizenry (Batley and Mcloughlin, 2010; Riehl, 2001)? However, while development actors have come forward with a framework of how to interact with such states (most prominently OECD Development Assistance Committee's (DAC) International Network on Conflict and Fragility (INCAF) at a bilateral or multilateral level, the engagement of private sector actors often raises additional questions about their role in what is termed 'service delivery' (Batley and Mcloughlin, 2010; Stel *et al.*, 2012) or state building more broadly.

It is questionable whether businesses have to be 'state builders' and whether this is not a new role that is being imposed on them by international NGOs and development agencies (Banerjee, 2008; Haufler, 2010); a role that is not their core business and something they might not be good at. Of course, companies would never see state building as one of their roles (Iff *et al.*, 2012), and would refrain from any involvement that could be termed state building. Still, all large extractive operators are in one way or the other engaged in service provision of infrastructure, health or education. In the following, the state is understood as the 'state administration' or what is sometimes referred to as state apparatus, who is nominally, if not practically, responsible for delivering services to the people.

This chapter aims to examine the ways in which multinational companies can support or undermine a host state (through state building) in fragile and conflict-affected situations.[1] It examines the impact of company activities on the contract between the state and its citizens based on the example of a multinational forestry company in the Congo Basin. Utilizing qualitative data, this impact will be evaluated in three steps: (a) discussion of service delivery activities in fragile and conflict-affected states by reflecting on the state-building literature, followed by insights from other literature on corporate social responsibility (CSR) and corporate governance; (b) analysis of effects of companies' service delivery on state building through processes of substitution, legitimization and distribution and, (c) consequences for the relevance of private sector participation in state building.

This research aim is highly relevant, as fragile and conflict-affected states with high levels of poverty and a lack of sustainable development capacity do need support in public service delivery. Some development cooperation agencies in the Global North see multinational companies as the 'new kings' in development, referring to the potential of the resources they bring (financial, managerial, links with international markets) (see, for example, Commission to the European Parliament, the Council, the European Economic and Social Committee and the Committee of the Regions (2014). Berdal and Mousavizadeh (2010) summarize the characteristics of this new state-building model through multinational companies in three points: (a) a growing preference for trade instead of aid, (b) a movement towards foreign state-backed 'macro-finance' investment and (c) an acknowledgement of the fundamental development benefits of foreign investors coupled with a robust local regulatory framework. However, for reasons outlined below, a profound discussion is needed on the implications of locating multination enterprises (MNEs) as a critical driver of development. Such an approach introduces serious dangers, and before the development community embraces it, it is important to understand the roles the different actors play and their likely impact. This chapter examines the case of a multinational company, analysing their activities and expectations placed on them. The analysis highlights corporate responses to demands from the host government and the community, and the impact of these responses on the contract of the citizenry with their own government. The assessment highlights the consequences for state building and peacebuilding efforts in these countries.

State builder or 'accidental' service provider?

Internationally supported state building

State building is a phenomenon that is tackled mainly in peace and conflict research and increasingly within the development literature. Scholars working on this issue are concerned with the question of how to strengthen or to build a state (meaning an administration with institutions and interfaces for citizens) in developing or fragile contexts. There are different definitions of state building in the literature (Berdal and Zaum, 2013; Chandler, 2010; Paris and Sisk, 2009). The common denominator of these definitions is that state building means the process of how a viable and legitimate state is established, possibly with the support of the international community. Today, most scholars focus on two alternative processes for state building: one is a top-down endeavour of introducing institutions of coercion; while the other involves a relational approach whereby liberal and traditional institutions interact in order to create some kind of legitimate hybrid state order.

In the first process, there is a classical Weberian understanding of the state as a formally constituted legal administrative body (that is also supported by most state-building interventions of the international community) while in the second process there is a more hybrid interpretation of the state, where state functions can be shared with actors not belonging to the formally constituted state administration, such as traditional authorities like chiefs or councils (Boege *et al.*, 2008; Clements *et al.*, 2007; Pollitt and Bouckaert, 2011). In a classical Weberian understanding 'state building is an endogenous process to enhance capacity, institutions and legitimacy of the state' (OECD, 2008: 2). This definition and the accompanying international policy (mainly by the UN agencies and OECD) on state building saw several shifts during recent years. After a critical discussion on the effectiveness and legitimacy of internationally driven state building exercises – particularly in Afghanistan and Iraq (Ottaway, 2002; Paris, 2002), there emerged a view that more local ownership and harmonization in state building efforts are needed (Paris, 2006; Richmond, 2009). While international interventions today still seek to develop the institutions and capacity of a state through supporting the formal state authority, more recently, international bodies have begun to focus more on building the legitimacy of the state through collaborative relationships with its citizens and traditional or local representative institutions.

With this shift, the 'mainstream' literature on state building also started to include those views seeing state building as a hybrid process (Boege *et al.*, 2008; Clements *et al.*, 2007; Meagher, 2012; Richmond, 2009). Scholars supporting this view argue that while there might be a lack of classical Weberian state structures in developing or fragile contexts, this does not mean that there is no 'state'. Rather, that people rely on societal structures they perceive as powerful (Clements *et al.*, 2007: 50): traditional authorities like chiefs, transnational networks of extended family relations, NGOs or other civil society actors but also gang leaders or other criminal networks. Thus, these scholars diagnose a situation where classical Weberian institutions work in parallel with local power-structures leading to the establishment of a hybrid order where both kinds of state structures are relevant (Meagher, 2012). In such an understanding, state building encompasses a lot of different activities by different actors. In this chapter, the focus lies on one particular aspect of state building, namely service delivery. In the following, service delivery as part of state building will be introduced and then, the possible role of companies in service delivery will be discussed.

Service delivery as part of state building

In a paper for DFID, Whaites (2008) distinguishes between different levels of state functions in state building. Apart from so called survival functions like security and the rule of law, he presents what he calls expected functions like service delivery or infrastructure building. In this understanding, the state has an important role in service delivery as a technocratic and de-politicized entity focussing on the provision of equal rights and opportunities for its citizens. Citizens expect the state to provide them with services (health, schooling, water and infrastructure). Furthermore the delivery of these services has the additional purpose of establishing and consolidating the legitimacy[2] of the state by its citizens (OECD, 2007, 2008). In such an analytical frame, service delivery of infrastructure, health and education can thus be seen as core functions of the state (Pollitt and Bouckaert, 2011).

The approach to service delivery as an aspect of state building has changed over the years, analogous to the shift in state building overall as indicated above. Before the 1990s, development agencies provided services themselves instead of the state, but in the early 2000s aid dependency discussions led to the insight that such practices make leaders less accountable to citizens (Duffield, 1997; Riehl, 2001; Soeters and Griffiths, 2003;)Moss *et al.*, 2006). Thus, new models of direct budget support[3] or the provision of multi-donor funds to governments in order for them to provide services have been introduced (Quartey, 2005; Unwin, 2004). However, particularly for fragile and conflict-affected states, it was soon realized that despite direct budget support and capacity building for governments, the quality of state-building was not satisfactory. By way of addressing this failing, together with the ever-growing scepticism of the value of development aid by the voters and parliaments in the Global North, and the accompanying need to show impact of development projects, development actors started to discuss the outsourcing of state-services to specialized private service delivery companies (Batley and Mcloughlin, 2010; Moss *et al.*, 2006; Palmer *et al.*, 2006).

This marked a return to the delivering of services on behalf of the state, but taking different forms, as Bately and Mcloughlin (2010) show in their comparative assessment of service delivery activities in fragile and conflict affected states. They show a variety of types of providers like faith-based organizations, NGOs, communities, individual entrepreneurs operating both in the public and private sector. They argue that supporting the building of legitimate state structures through service provision by non-state actors is a missed opportunity by the international community. They see, however, some indirect functions that non-state actor cannot provide and that should remain with the 'state apparatus': supporting, coordinating and regulating within and between services (setting policy frameworks, developing and enforcing standards, universal take-up of basic services). Not mentioned in their assessment were service delivery activities of large multinational companies particularly those operating in the extractive sector.

From a classical Weberian perspective, companies are taking over functions of host states (expected functions) if they provide health services, schooling opportunities, but also if they build roads or other infrastructure for access to clean water. Big extractive industries as well as agribusiness companies in particular take up the role of providers of goods and services for their workers, but more importantly, for communities surrounding their operations. Even though these activities of 'strategic social investment' are an important part of most large extractive operation sites (timber, oil and minerals) and the expenses for such activities are growing (see, for example, Rio Tinto, 2013) these service delivery activities have rarely been the subject of academic scrutiny. It is difficult to give an overview of these kinds of expected services, as it is difficult to gather detailed data that goes beyond the description of mere singular cases. Certainly, this does not include companies that do service delivery in developing countries as their core business, for example contractors that are providing health care services for the state (see, for example, Liu *et al.*, 2008). What is of interest here is examining MNCs as service deliverer within a state-building frame. Since the new development models (see, for example, Africa Progress Report 2013, or the event by g7+ on private sector investment and job creation in fragile states in April 2013[4]) put the private sector at the centre, it is important to assess the implications of this kind of service delivery by corporate actors. While there are articles that tackle the relevance of building schools and providing water in terms of corporate social responsibility, philanthropy or global governance, the link to what this means for the relationship of the state with its citizens is often totally neglected. In the following, a short review of the literature on both corporate social responsibility and global governance is undertaken in order to show the gaps from these perspectives.

Insights from other disciplinary approaches

In articles on corporate social responsibility (CSR), the provision of public services by multinational companies has come to be termed as the provision of 'social and economic infrastructure' or 'strategic stakeholder engagement' (Eweje, 2007; Idemudia, 2011). In recent years companies and associations of the extractive sector have invested heavily in understanding communities that surround their sites and developed guidance on how to interact with these communities. Companies report on projects involving strategic stakeholder engagement on a global level or regionally, rarely providing exact costs of particular projects, but use project examples as single best case examples. This might change in the future if stakeholder engagement becomes more important for extractive companies. A possible indication in that direction is the shift in the work of the International Council on Mining and Industries (ICMM). This organization brings together 21 mining and metals companies and 33 regional mining associations and global commodity associations. In their 2013 report, they indicate that in 2014, their work will focus more strongly on community relationships, 'increasing both resources for activities in the Social and Economic Development work program and the community focus of projects in the other program areas' of Health and Safety, Environment and Climate Change (ICMM, 2014: 12–13)). So while there is some evidence that 'strategic social investment' or 'community engagement' is gaining in relevance, the question still remains, whether this should be performed as an added element of good business practices (Banerjee, 2008: 74; Newell and Frynas, 2007: 672)), or if it needs to be guided, regulated and driven by broader state-led development priorities. Guidance on this particular issue has started to be produced, not least by the former Special Representative to the Secretary General on Business and Human Rights (Human Rights Council Report, 2011: 15): in his report on principles for responsible contracts, there is guidance on how to provide additional services beyond the scope of a project (principle 5). The provision of such services by business risks a blurring of roles, responsibilities and accountability for their quality and sustainability between government and business. It is furthermore questioned how impacted individuals and communities are informed about the service delivery and how possible adverse human rights impacts are addressed.

A second stream of literature tackling the issue of service delivery of MNCs is the global governance literature from political science. This literature tries to explain 'who governs' in a globalized world and particularly whether MNCs have more power than states in the global economy. It is observed that often, the state is no longer the sole source of authority both in the domestic and international system, and in such a situation, so-called host states are often not capable or willing to provide services for their citizens (Ruggie, 2007). Börtzel and Risse (2010) argue that the missing regulatory function of the host state in a globalized economy can be taken over by external actors and mentions companies as possible regulators. For example, when companies develop codes of ethics or best practice on issues of international significance that are difficult to regulate otherwise (Voluntary Principles on Business and Human Rights, Conflict-free Gold

Standards, bribery and corruption) and then implement them in the host states. However, the impact of these external non-state actors as regulators is strongly dependent on the kind of business, the kind of sector and the home country of the company (Fransen and Kolk, 2007; Moog et al., 2012). Still, more recently, companies are portrayed as solving social problems (Coni-Zimmer and Rieth, 2012; Newell and Frynas, 2007). In this stream of literature, issues of power and legitimacy of the state are raised; contrary to the CSR literature that is rarely tackling the question of the state or the impact of service delivery activities on the state-society relationship. In this stream of literature one state function that companies have taken over has been widely discussed: security (see, e.g. Kinsey, 2006; Meagher, 2012; Schreier and Caparini, 2010). Following the distinction made between survival and expected functions, security is a survival function (which is already widely researched) and will not be examined here.

To summarize, the literature on state-building recognizes the existence of non-state actors in service delivery, but the question of the legitimacy of service delivery by MNCs in weak and fragile states has seen limited discussion. In the field of CSR, issues around stakeholder engagement are more pronounced, however, there is no focus on service delivery of expected functions, and impacts are not understood as impacts on state capacity. Finally, the global governance literature has focused on the delivery of security by companies. However, this is security as a core business by private military companies and not security as part of stakeholder engagement, possibly understood as human security. This chapter aims to fill the gap and start to understand and include private sector actors and their activities of service delivery in an overall framework of state building.

Methodology

The approach taken here is from a state-building perspective; however, it is not a classical Weberian perspective where we diagnose a 'governance gap' with a state not delivering services, but rather a hybrid order perspective where we observe who the powerful actors are that are delivering services and what the implications of this are (another example taking such an approach is Boege et al., 2008). This enables us to see private sector actors as one possible and powerful actor in fragile situations, without promoting any normative position. The aim is to describe how service delivery activities are implemented by one company as part of its CSR, allowing for a discussion of the effects of service delivery on the state, and on the local community[5].

In order to understand the possible impact of the company's service delivery activities on state building, first an examination of the company's activities will be undertaken and secondly, the impact on state building will be described through three possible effects that their service delivery might have: substitution, legitimization and distribution effects (Anderson, 1999). The first effect refers to the possibility that the provision of services might replace existing systems or structures of service delivery by the state, traditional authorities or other social structures; the substitution effect. This can lead to a situation where the state relinquishes responsibility for civilian welfare. The second effect might be to give additional legitimacy to a possibly corrupt state and might help to maintain a national and local government, that is, for example, complicit in human rights violations. The third (distribution) effect, points to the danger that the more powerful segments of the society may hijack particular services such as health and schooling, and the use of infrastructure provided by companies.

The methodological approach involves a case study of a timber company in the Congo Basin, who shall remain anonymous. The research draws on empirical data that was collected in August 2013 during field research in the Congo Basin, where 29 interviews and five focus group discussions have been conducted on the overall social impact of the company's activities. In order to secure reliable and valid data, the interview partners have been selected taking a triangulated approach, involving government representatives at the national and local level, civil society bodies and the company personnel[6]. The following individuals or groups were interviewed:

1) Govt Nat Levl 1–5: five representatives from national government bodies;
2) Govt Regnl Levl 1–5: five from the regional level, relevant to the forestry sector;
3) Civl Soc Nat Levl 1–10: ten representatives of national level civil society organisations working in or on the forestry sector:
   a   Focus Gp Civl Soc Nat Levl: one focus group discussion with national level civil society representatives;
   b   Focus Gp Civl Soc Regnl Levl: one focus group discussion with 5 representatives of civil society organizations at the regional level;
   c   Village Gp 1–2: two village group discussions 'under the tree' with representatives of villages in the concession area.
4) Comp Staff 1–9: nine interviews with company staff including: head Africa division HQ, CSR responsible HQ, national management, national finance director, 3 community relations officers, a union representative, a representative of the eco-guards. Additionally, informal discussions were undertaken with mid-level management (Comp Infml).

Internat Orgs 1–4: three additional interviews with representatives of international organizations working in the forestry sector;

1) Bilateral Dons 1–2: two interviews with bilateral donors financing forestry projects in the region;
2) Forest Comp X: in order to familiarize with general practices in this sector, one interview with a representative of another forestry company;
3) Security 1–3: three interviews to understand the security situation, with village level representatives of the police and gendarmerie, as well as eco guards.

While the civil society and most of the company representatives were very open and collaborative, the government interviews were often ceremonial and required in order to get the official consent of doing research in the area. Moreover, a distinction between civil society representatives that are close to the government (what has been termed by others as government organized NGOs, Governmental Non-Governmental Organizations (GONGOs) (Brown and Korten, 1989)) and those that are more independent became obvious during the interviews. While most of the NGOs at the national level were rather close to the government, those active at the regional level were very familiar with the local context and less political in their statements.

The analysis also utilizes gray literature (documents in print and electronic formats not published commercially (GreyNet, 1999)) including environmental impact assessments of the operation site, market research reports, working papers, government documents on the forestry sector in the Congo Basin generally, and national and international regulatory documents relevant to the region. The chapter offers a first attempt at conceptualizing the issue of service delivery within the state-building literature, and provides tentative suggestions about where possible policy strategies could go.

Case study: a timber company in the Congo Basin

The case study starts with a description of the quality of service provided by the 'official' state administration, based on interview data and literature research. Then, the legal framework and obligations of the company towards the communities are discussed.

Quality of state-provided service provision

The quality of governance in the lower Congo Basin is diverse (see country reports of Worldwide Governance Indicators[7]). However, what unites most of the few countries in the south of the basin is the large contribution (between 8 and 17 per cent in the last five years) of natural resource extraction to the overall GDP (Natural Resource Governance Institute, country data[8]). These undiversified economies provide employment opportunities only for a few well educated people and the remainder work in the informal economy (Alemagi and Nukpezah, 2012; De Merode and Cowlishaw, 2006; International Labour Office, 2009). Poverty is widespread and it is often women, young people and ethnic minorities, such as indigenous people, who are most affected. Several of the governments in the lower Congo Basin are characterized by a lack of transparency, accountability and high levels of corruption – at all ranks (Corruption Perception Indices 2011–2013 lie between 150 of 177[9]) (Clark, 2002; Hodges *et al.*, 2013; Tati, 2005). Like most of the foreign business operating in the basin, the international logging industry is seen as 'profitable to public officials' (as a member of a local NGO said) but not the common population. While most of the forest legislation in the basin specifies that a definite amount of taxes paid to the national treasury are reserved for regional development and should flow back to the regions, these amounts often do not reach the concerned populations (Brack, 2012; Clark and Poulsen, 2012; Poulsen and Clark, 2010). While there exists many appropriate laws and regulations on the timber sector particularly, and governments have signed a number of international regulations and conventions, the implementation of these is often missing (Bayol *et al.*, 2012; Dellicour and Sacaze, 2012)[10]. Most importantly for this analysis, the state administrations in several parts of these countries are only partially able to perform their duties and to provide basic services like water, electricity, infrastructure, education and health in all of their regions (Alemagi and Nukpezah, 2012).

Companies like this timber company, headquartered in the global North, often depart from a classical Weberian understanding of the state where the state is responsible for basic services like health, water and infrastructure (informal discussions with company representatives). As indicated above, in a hybrid order understanding of the state, local communities rely on a web of diverse and culturally distinct norms and practices to organize their societies parallel to the 'official' state structures. Often, if the state is not able or willing to provide basic services, the company becomes the service provider. This, however, leads to a situation characterized by legal pluralism, where the coexistence of official state law and traditional rights leaves companies and communities uncertain over a variety of issues (e.g. land access and land ownership rights).[11] These uncertainties lead to situations where conflictive issues are regulated ad hoc, often favouring the stronger party, usually the companies, in the negotiations. The following section describes how company responsibility has been defined vis-à-vis local communities in existing legal documents.

Company obligations towards the communities

The timber company's core business activities include the selective felling of tropical trees and their processing in an in-house sawmill, as well as some export of logs. This company bought a concession in the Congo Basin (over one million hectares) in 2005, and in 2007 presented their Forest Management Plan[12], including a *cahier des charges*, describing their plan for meeting the social obligations of the company towards the communities (documents from the company, interviews Comp Staff 1, Comp Staff 2). The term *cahier des charges* (literally 'specifications') is an old term that has been introduced by the Ancien Régime in France. In the forestry sector, it designates a document that is negotiated between the forestry company and the Ministry of Forestry and defines the social obligations of the company towards the local community. It enumerates the quality, quantity and schedule of infrastructure construction (schools, health centres, roads and water pipes). These documents are regulatory standard in most of the Congo Basin: the management plan divides the concession into zones (*séries*) according to a set of specific objectives: conservation, community development and harvesting. The harvesting zones are further divided into forest management Units that specify the operating schedules taking into account constant annual production (volume/species) and regrowth and regeneration. The forest management plan *cahier des charges* also includes a section on wildlife management and socio-economic impact, where baseline studies on particular issues are undertaken and mitigation strategies are discussed.[13]

The company employs approximately 1,000 people, but estimates that 8,000 people depend on its activities (Comp Staff 2). In the *cahier des charges*, an overall amount of €450,000 is budgeted for the logging period of 30 years (Comp Staff 1, Comp Staff 2). This covers the building of roads, schools and health care centres, as well as facilities in the vicinity of the operation site. In the immediate surroundings of the operations, the company built houses for employees and their families and provides several services: they support a butcher (in order for the local people to get affordable proteins and not to rely on bush meat), built food stores, a water pipe, as well as roads. Close to the company but not in the village, there is also a school originally built for indigenous children (now open to Bantu's too), as well as a water pipe close to the school (Comp Staff 1, Comp Staff 2, Comp Staff 5). Apart from these services for the village close to the operation, the company supports approximately 30 smaller villages within their concession. The *cahier des charges* defines in which villages the company will build schools or health centres, and where the company will build roads.

Voluntarily, the company agreed to pay €60,000 into a Local Development Fund, which should be financially complemented with the same amount through tax transfers by the central government (Comp Staff 4, Comp Staff 5). The aim of the fund is to support the alternative livelihoods of the communities living in the forest, as it is assumed that through the felling of the trees they lose part of their livelihood (gathering of caterpillars, selling of firewood, charcoal, hunting, etc.). The fund is administered by a board composed of local administration, the company, and civil society representatives (a committee of five people) (Comp Staff 2, Comp Staff 3, Govt Regnl Levl 2, Govt Regnl Levl 3, Internat orgs 2). Projects are implemented after they have been proposed by the communities to the management board of the fund. Currently, there have not been enough projects presented to the board and the money in the fund cannot be spent (Comp Staff 2, Comp Staff 5). Additionally, the company engages voluntarily in different capacity-building programmes. For example, they have raised awareness of, and explained, the new law on indigenous people during visits of their social team to villages in the concession, and supports a local radio station, which, however, does not reach the whole logging concession (Comp Staff 4): Finally, in collaboration with the state administration and the Wildlife Conservation Society (WCS), the company pays eco-guards (Poulsen, 2009; Poulsen and Clarck, 2010) to protect the wildlife in the concession area. These are paramilitary patrols with the task of catching 'poachers' and protecting wildlife (Comp Staff 9, Internat orgs 4, Internat orgs 3). While this is by no means a legal requirement in the Congo Basin, there are several such projects throughout the region (WCS 2013).

Analysis: company service delivery activities and effects on state building

The above initiatives can all be understood as service delivery activities that might be provided by the state in other circumstances. While the company does engage in other discretionary CSR activities, these are not relevant to the research focus.

The activities were categorized into three different forms of service delivery (a) the building of roads, schools and health centres (*cahier des charges*), (b) the support of local development projects and (c) the protection of wildlife through eco-guards. The impacts of these activities were then analysed in terms of state building effects (legitimacy, substitution and distribution):

Building of roads, schools and health centres

The places where schools, roads and health centres are built are determined during the writing of the *cahier des charges*. This document was finalized between the central state and the company, with the communities back in 2007 being only partially involved in the process (Govt Regnl Levl 1, Village Gp 1, Village Gp 2). Some NGOs see it as a problem that the ministry has very close relations to the company: 'The presence of the ministry on the site of this company but also other companies is huge. Why is this?' (Focus Gp Civl Soc Nat Levl). In the interviews, it did not become clear how the local and regional communities were able to participate in these decisions, for example whether they could indicate that instead of a school, they would prefer something else in order to improve their livelihood (Civl Soc Regnl Levl 2, Focus Gp Civl Soc Regnl Levl 1, Village Gp 2). The communities say they do not know the contents of the concession contracts or the *cahier des charges* of the company, even though company staff responsible for community engagement was carrying out information campaigns to inform communities about these issues (Comp Staff 5, Village Gp 1, Village Gp 2). As one village elder said, 'There is no one that knows really what stands in the *cahier des charges*. And if a worker asks, he gets a request to explain himself and then has to leave work'. It seems to be only a selected group of village elders or NGO representatives that do understand the commitments provided in the *cahier des charges* or the additional agreements on the development fund and eco-guards. It seems this information is not necessarily passed on to the other members of the community. This can create conflicts. According to one company employee, 'The people sometimes also ask for things that have not been foreseen in the negotiations between the ministry and the company. (. . .) They are then able to block the logging for several days.' (Comp Staff 7).

There were, and still are, traditional ways of providing education and health to communities. However, the impact of health centres and school buildings as potentially substituting for these activities is insignificant, as most of these facilities remain empty, because there are no teachers or nurses that would work in these remote areas (Comp Staff 5, Village Gp 2). Thus, if the buildings are not used for something else (village hall), these often remain 'white elephants'[14] (Comp Staff 5, Village Gp 1, Civl Soc Regnl Levl 3, Focus Gp Civl Soc Regnl Levl 2). The roads are seldom determined based on their usefulness for local communities (e.g. trade routes) but follow the path of timber extraction, taking sustainability issues into account (Village Gp 1, Village Gp 2, Civl Soc Regnl Levl 2, Civl Soc Regnl Levl 1). Thus, there is no substitution effect that can be observed based on service delivery activities in this realm.

It is difficult to say if there is a legitimization effect through the building of roads, schools and hospitals. It is argued that in constructing and providing these services the company may undermine the role of the government by creating a substitute for government responsibilities, which, in turn, may result in the weakening of government legitimacy. In most of the interviews with civil society organisations and villagers, the common view is that 'the company is in league with the central government' (Village Gp 1, Village Gp, Civl Soc Regnl Levl 1). Arguably, the legitimacy of the government is being undermined as most of the services and support provided for the people in the concession are provided by the company only, and not by the (central) state structure. The effect on state building is a de-legitimization of the state – a state that communities see as an instrument of rent seeking by corrupt officials on every level. Service delivery has also a negative effect on the company. By building public facilities, the company inadvertently creates expectations that it will also delivery appropriate services (Comp Staff 1, Comp Staff 2, Comp Staff 5). For example, if infrastructure is not delivered on time or if facilities are not maintained and staff recruited, this can create a further source of conflict between the communities and the company. As on NGO representative said: 'There is very good legislation on different policy issues, but the implementation remains a problem' (Focus Gp Civl Soc Regnl Levl 1).

The building of schools, health centres and roads shows there is a strong distribution effect. Most of the schools are built for the dominant ethnic group, the Bantus, while the indigenous peoples of the area are not profiting from these (Village Gp 1). In the interviews, we learnt of the case of a school the company built originally for indigenous children., but turned into a Bantu school after some time (Comp Staff 2, Village Gp 1). The people surrounding the school do not understand why only indigenous children should be able to go to school there and felt discriminated against; 'what about mixed kids?', they asked (Village Gp 1). Thus, some of the services are mainly or even exclusively claimed by the more powerful segments of the society. Also the issue of corruption became evident again: some of the village people that were responsible for building the school, together with the company, were accused of having taken some of the money that was intended for a the village. One villager observed: 'We don't know how much the material for the school cost, but to construct something like this, that can never cost 20 million *franc congolaise*.'

Supporting livelihood through local development fund

A second service delivery activity expected of the timber company, companies is the support of livelihoods through the local development fund. In contrast to the *cahier des charges*, this instrument tries to take into account the needs of the local communities by empowering them to come up with development projects. The *cahier des charges* was in this case a process that was strongly steered by regional and central government, without the consent or even participation of the people (mostly indigenous) living within the concession. Contrary to the *cahier des* *charges*, the establishment of a local development fund is not a legal requirement (Comp Staff 2, Comp Staff 5). The rationale of the fund is to support communities that have traditionally been dependent on timber forest products, to develop alternative forms of livelihood, such as developing agricultural activities. Most of the people in the remote villages do not understand the mechanism of the fund. 'They have changed the procedure after we did a project to plant manioc, but it did not work out. Now they changed it again, so it is a bit of a mess.' There is no substitution effect that can be observed, as there has not been support of livelihood programs by either the state or other social structures before the company's operation started. However, what can be observed are pronounced legitimization and distribution effects connected to the management of the local development fund (Civl Soc Regnl Levl 1, Govt Regnl Levl 3, Govt Regnl Levl 4). These effects are no different to those of NGO-led development projects (see, for example Acemoglu and Robinson, 2006; Dasgupta and Beard, 2007; Garred, 2006; Platteau, 2004). Thus, the fund is administered by a delegated committee comprising: five representatives (two from the district government, one from the company, and two from representatives of regional level civil society) (Comp Staff 5, Govt Regnl Levl 4, Govt Regnl Levl 5), Though it is unclear how those representing civil society have been selected (Village Gp 1). However, all these mechanisms are based on existing power structures that are supporting those segments of society more affluent or have higher status than more vulnerable groups (indigenous people, youth or women). Thus with this fund, the company and the state are legitimizing existing power structures within the local communities, which often lead to additional conflict. Several interviewees complained that the money never reaches the communities, even though it has been promised for them (Village Gp 1, Village Gp 2). Hence the company finds itself confronted with recurrent demands for expenditure, and failure to deliver may turn into obstruction or violence against the company, even though they have already paid their share into the fund. Concerned to somehow manage this situation, the company buys material that villagers often need (e.g. for building) instead of giving cash (Comp Staff 2, Comp Staff 5). Without financial oversight and no support for local people to help them prepare proposals and manage projects, the local development fund risks creating more conflict than doing good. The usurping of funds by higher status individuals and sub-groups (elite capture) is a major weakness of the community development fund programmes and can cause local tensions (Dasgupta and Beard, 2007; Iversen *et al.*, 2006; Platteau, 2004). As a member of the company's social engagement team said 'some people in the villages have the impression that these projects are for them [the village elders, A.I.] and not for the whole village' (Comp Staff 5). Ethnic hierarchies within the society between indigenous and Bantu's are prevalent, and exist within each ethnic group. There is also a constant threat of misappropriation of funds by individuals of these groups. For example, one representative of an indigenous community said: 'There was one of us, an indigenous, his name is ***, he was the contact person with the company [responsible for managing the development project on behalf of the community, A.I.], but now he is gone [and took the money of the project with him, A.I.].' (Village Gp 2). This is a lost opportunity because the local communities perceive the fund as an important source of support and a legitimate way to share benefits, in contrast to other existing instruments (i.e. taxes) that are not trusted.

Protecting wildlife through eco-guards

Eco-guards are mostly young local men employed to control illegal poaching and hunting activities in the concession area (Comp Staff 5, Internat Orgs 2, Comp Staff 9). They are formally subject to the ministry responsible for forest management, receive training through the armed forces, wear similar uniforms and carry weapons (Comp Staff 5, Internat Orgs 2). Their wages are mainly paid by the World Conservation Society, an international NGO, and the timber company (Comp Staff 5, Civl Soc Nat Levl 3). While the local community agrees on the importance of protecting endangered species, the conduct of eco-guards towards the local community, as well as the governance of their activities, is often problematic. One interviewee observing these activities said: 'eco-guards sometimes share the confiscated meat with the representatives of the local administration or sell it through middle men in the market' (Civl Soc Reg Levl 3, Village Gp 2). Protection of wildlife is one area where substitution effects can be observed. Many indigenous people see the eco guards as intruders that do not have a traditional connection with the forest (Village Gp 1, Village Gp 2, Civl Soc Nat Levl 5). They feel their knowhow of managing wildlife is not taken into account. Most of the indigenous people believe it is [their] traditional legacy to protect the forest 'and that they know very well how to do that' (Village Gp 2). Clearly, the policy of employing eco-guards undermines the traditional role of indigenous people; delegitimizing their role as guardian of the wildlife. More-over, indigenous people see eco-guards as unreasonably targeting them and their reliance on bush meat. One old indigenous woman got very agitated arguing that 'eco-guards were harassing me because of a porcupine' (Village Gp 1). The eco-guards had taken it away from her and she was certain they ate the meat themselves. Legally, the eco-guards have to bring seized bush meat to the local government representative (Comp Staff 5). The local communities perceive that wildlife protection is being mainly used against them, and for the benefit of the eco-guards and the local government. Thus, forest protection is undermined by the prevalence (or suspicion) of corruption and this creates conflict between the eco-guards and the local community.

The timber company's reaction to this issue varies with the hierarchical level within the company. While top management is responsive to these kinds of questions (Comp Staff 1, Comp Staff 2, Comp Staff 3), middle management questions the company's responsibility for such issues. As one employee said 'in my view, our responsibility ends at the gates of our company'. Some company employees are clear that they are 'not development agencies' and that they do not have the knowhow and financial resources like international NGOs (Comp Staff 4, Comp Staff 6). They were also highlighting that it is not their task to provide these services in the first place, and that they are doing their best. During the interviews, it became apparent that the local communities see the company as their benevolent ruler and that they are expecting a lot from this entity. As one villager said 'the company is all we have, there is no other livelihood in this area. They are taking our trees so they should also look after us' (Village Gp 1). However, the company sees the state administration as the main responsible body for most of the service delivery activities and whilst unhappy about the situation, the company rarely complains, because it is dependent on maintaining good relations with the government (Comp Staff 3). As one company representative said, 'if [we] say something [that the local government does not like], the next day I'd have a new local law on the table and I would not be able to export for the next six weeks'.

This leads to a situation where local communities do not expect the state administration to deliver services, and local state administrations are happy to delegate some of the responsibility to companies. However, this profoundly undermines state involvement in, and capacity to providing services in the long run. This situation also discourages companies from being sensitive to local traditional authorities and in supporting their legitimacy in state building or state like functions.

Conclusions and further research

What are the effects of MNCs delivering public services in fragile environments? How do they influence the relationship between the local citizens and the often powerful central state? Through the example of a MNC timber company in the Congo Basin that delivers public services in the realms of schools, health centres, roads, local development and wildlife protection, the chapter set out to answer these questions. Introducing the concept of state building in fragile environments, it analysed the effects on substitution of public services by the company, with a possible negative effect on the legitimacy of the government who should be the main service provider. It furthermore discussed the distribution effects of the services provided by the company, showing how the more powerful segments of the community benefitted more than others, for example the indigenous people or women and children. Several conclusions based on the analysis are noteworthy.

The public role of MNCs in fragile environments

It is a fact that MNCs are service deliverers in health, roads, livelihood support and security, in addition to their core business. In a hybrid order understanding of state building this is neither bad nor good. In these hybrid arrangements companies might sometimes be perceived as more legitimate public service providers than the state. As indicated in the analysis, companies are then seen as part of a system of social transfers to the local communities. As this study shows, while the state may be formally responsible for organising local development, in practice the MNC can find itself sucked into performing this function., Indeed, the MNC is likely to see this service provision as part of their CSR strategy, engaging in act from philanthropy to direct involvement is social development. They do not want to be framed as a public service provider. Such an interpretation does not fit their self-perception and frames their activities as too political.

Service delivery needs a different self-perception by companies: Companies are often seen as a central actor in the social order, faced with all-encompassing expectations from the local community. For Western MNCs this is difficult because they do not see their task as including service delivery for the local community, or livelihood projects, or wildlife protection; these are all tasks of the state administration. If the leverage of MNCs in fragile contexts really is to be utilized as several policies of the international community suggest, like the report of the African Development Bank High Level Panel on Fragile States , or the recent EU Communication on Private sector and development (Commission to the European Parliament, the Council, the European Economic and Social Committee and the Committee of the Regions, 2014), then a shift in the self-perception of companies needs to take place. Such a shift would not only have implications for the framing of company purpose, but also for the host government and the civil society. Service delivery needs partners: Service delivery by companies is often discussed with the partners at the national level. Only very rarely are the needs and interests of the local community that might benefit from these services taken into account. This leads to conflicts with the company, even though the company provides the services agreed upon with the national-level administration. For most of the local population, the company is just another resource they can rely on, as they have never experienced a state that 'cares' for them; they have always relied on other social structures for service delivery.

Service delivery needs a particular focus on vulnerable groups within the local communities: Contrary to what is stressed in the literature, it is not only the unwillingness or lack of capacity of host states that leads to problems. The picture is much more complex. Public service delivery by companies is problematic where it is not done in conjunction with the host state, and where responsibilities towards the local population are not clearly defined, carefully implemented, and effectively communicated. Companies need the support of development agencies on how best to collaborate with government agencies on these issues outside of their core business.

Conceptually, the chapter was able to show that framing service delivery activities from a state-building perspective has the advantage that companies do not perceive these activities as enhanced one-off philanthropy but as part of a broader state-building project that needs to include an active state administration, the local communities, as well as the traditional community leaders. As companies will be the most powerful actor in the triangle, it is important they look into questions regarding coordination and regulation within and between services (policy frameworks, developing and enforcing standards, as well as universal take-up of services) and empower and enable the state administration to slowly take over this role. As service delivery activities of companies do affect the legitimacy of state building, foreign donor support will be necessary together with close collaboration with the host state and local civil society organizations. This has been envisaged already by the company in our case. They created a position for a development specialist that would support the development projects financed by the Local Development Fund in collaboration with an international donor, the local administration, the local civil society and another forestry company (Comp Staff 5, Internat Orgs 4). However, despite the fact that the position was advertised for more than a year, no one applied for it.

Further research in this area should go into how companies understand their relationship in the triangle with local community and the government. More and more companies are hiring staff who have been working in the development field before, and it will be important to analyse if and how this changes the self-perception of the overall company activities. More research should look into the relations of MNCs with the state, not only their home state, but mainly the host states, and should tackle issues that are not restrained to questions of corruption, but rather on the kind of state partners that companies have (central, regional and local).

A pragmatic approach to state building would see a multinational company as one of several actors that build sustainable and long-term services, operating in fragile and conflict affected states. This, however, is yet to translate into significant and sustained changes in the practices of actors on the ground. Consequently, businesses, international organizations and NGOs miss opportunities to enhance the strategic impact of engagements in fragile states.

Notes

1 The terms 'home' and 'host' states have been introduced by a scholar of international relations, John Ruggie, and are now commonly used in the 'business and human rights' literature (Ruggie, 2007).

2 However, already in the so-called Madisonian understanding of the state, which puts more emphasis on private service delivery (e.g. in schooling with the charter schools), this view is contested (Held, 2013: 59).

3 The OECD DAC defines direct budget support as an aid modality in which foreign funds are transferred to a recipient treasury, managed and spent according to national budgetary regulations and priorities (OECD, 2006: 17).

4 www.etouches.com/ehome/fragilestates/114332/

5 The field research was partly financed by the company itself, partly by the Swiss Commission for Technology and Innovation.

6 To do research on companies in complex environments is very difficult; it has been agreed with the company in advance, that the material collected can be utilized for scientific analysis. As confidentiality is crucial when working with and on companies, no names and affiliations of interview partners are publicized in this chapter.

7 www.info.worldbank.org/governance/wgi/index.aspx#countryReports

8 www.resourcegovernance.org/

9 www.transparency.org/research/cpi/overview

10 The lower Congo Basin countries were the first to introduce and sign the new EU Regulation on the traceability and legality of timber: EU Forest Law Enforcement Governance and Trade (FLEGT). Furthermore, their forest codes.

11 While this issue has been discussed more in Latin America (de Jong *et al.*, 2006; Kaimovitz *et al.*, 1998; Peluso, 1995; Schulze *et al.*, 2008) and South East Asia (Sirait *et al.*, 1994), it remains under-researched in Africa.

12 Forest management plans detail the amount of wood, the kind of wood and the cycle in which logging is done in a particular concession. It entails mainly the technical details of the logging process and issues of species protection and regrowth cycles.

13 The local communities often rely on specific trees for their livelihoods, as they sell caterpillars, bark, oil or fruits from them (this has been termed non-timber-forest-products and has been widely discussed in the literature (see, for example Arnold and Pérez, 2001; De Beer *et al.*, 1989; Ndoye *et al.*, 1998). Companies are therefore obliged to take this into account in their harvesting plans and are bound to support alternative livelihoods of the communities (Cerutti *et al.*, 2011).

14 A white elephant is a metaphor from the ancient kingdom of Thailand, where the king used to give white elephants to people he wanted to ruin. Because of its spiritual value, a white elephant was very costly, and the owner was not allowed to kill or give it away. Thus, a white elephant is a possession with a lot of cost but no other value to the owner.

References

Acemoglu, D., and Robinson, J.A., 2006. *Persistence of power, elites and institutions*. National Bureau of Economic Research.

Alemagi, D., and Nukpezah, D., 2012. Assessing the performance of large-scale logging companies in countries of the Congo Basin. *Environment and Natural Resources Research* 2, 38.

Anderson, M.B., 1999. *Do no harm: how aid can support peace-or war*. Boulder, CO: Lynne Rienner Pub.

Arnold, Je., and Pérez, M.R., 2001. Can non-timber forest products match tropical forest conservation and development objectives? *Ecological economics* 39, 437–47.

Banerjee, S.B., 2008. Corporate social responsibility: the good, the bad and the ugly. *Critical Sociology* 34, 51–79.

Batley, R., and Mcloughlin, C., 2010. Engagement with non-state service providers in fragile states: reconciling state-building and service delivery. *Development Policy Review* 28, 131–54.

Bayol, N., Demarquez, B., de Wasseige, C., Eba'a Atyi, R., Fisher, J.-F., Nasi, R., Pasquier, A., Rossi, X., Steil, M., and Vivien, C., 2012. Forest management and the timber sector in Central Africa. *The Forests of the Congo Basin–State of the Forest 2010*, 43–61.

Berdal, M., and Mousavizadeh, N., 2010. Investing for peace: the private sector and the challenges of peacebuilding. *Survival* 52, 37–58.

Berdal, M., and Zaum, D., 2013. *Political Economy of Statebuilding: Power After Peace*. Oxford: Routledge.

Boege, V., Brown, A., Clements, K., and Nolan, A., 2008. *On hybrid political orders and emerging states: state formation in the context of 'fragility'*, Berlin: Berghof Research Center for Constructive Conflict Management.

Börtzel, T.A., and Risse, T., 2010. Governance without a state: can it work? *Regulation & Governance* 4, 113–34.

Brack, D., 2012. Excluding illegal timber and improving forest governance: the European Union's forest law enforcement, governance and trade initiative. In P. Lujala and S. A. Rustad, *High-value natural resources and peacebuilding*, London: Earthscan.

Brown, L., and Korten, D., 1989. *The role of voluntary organizations in development* (IDR Working Paper No. No. 8), Boston University School of Management Boston, MA: Institute for Development Research.

Cerutti, P.O., Assembe-Mvondo, S., German, L., and Putzel, L., 2011. Is China unique? Exploring the behaviour of Chinese and European firms in the Cameroonian logging sector. *International Forestry Review* 13, 23–34.

Chandler, D.C., 2010. *International statebuilding: the rise of post-liberal governance*. Oxford: Routledge.

Clark, C.J., and Poulsen, J.R., 2012. *Tropical forest conservation and industry partnership: an experience from the Congo Basin*. Hoboken, NJ: John Wiley & Sons.

Clark, J.F., 2002. The neo-colonial context of the democratic experiment of Congo-Brazzaville. *African Affairs* 101, 171–92.

Clements, K.P., Boege, V., Brown, A., Foley, W., and Nolan, A., 2007. State building reconsidered: the role of hybridity in the formation of political order. *Political Science* 59, 45–56.

Commission to the European Parliament, the Council, the European Economic and Social Committee and the Committee of the Regions, 2014. *A stronger role of the private sector in achieving inclusive and sustainable growth in developing countries*, COM (2014) 263.

Coni-Zimmer, M.M., and Rieth, L., 2012. CSR aus Perspektive der Governance-Forschung, in: Corporate Social Responsibility. *Springer*, 709–29.

Dasgupta, A., and Beard, V.A., 2007. Community driven development, collective action and elite capture in Indonesia. *Development and Change* 38, 229–49.

De Beer, J.H., McDermott, M.J., and others, 1989. *The economic value of non-timber forest products in Southeast Asia: with emphasis on Indonesia, Malaysia and Thailand*. The economic value of non-timber forest products in Southeast Asia: with emphasis on Indonesia, Malaysia and Thailand, Netherlands Committee for IUCN, Amsterdam, The Netherlands.

De Jong, W., Ruiz, S., and Becker, M., 2006. Conflicts and communal forest management in northern Bolivia. *Forest Policy and Economics* 8, 447–57.

Dellicour, D., and Sacaze, J.P., 2012. Promoting good governance through development aid: the European Commission's approach. *Crime, law and social change* 58, 55–62.

De Merode, E., and Cowlishaw, G., 2006. Species protection, the changing informal economy, and the politics of access to the bushmeat trade in the Democratic Republic of Congo. *Conservation Biology* 20, 1262–1271.

Duffield, M., 1997. NGO relief in war zones: towards an analysis of the new aid paradigm. *Third World Quarterly* 18, 527–42.

Eweje, G., 2007. Multinational oil companies' CSR initiatives in Nigeria: the scepticism of stakeholders in host communities. *Managerial Law* 49, 218–35.

Fransen, L.W., and Kolk, A., 2007. Global rule-setting for business: A critical analysis of multi-stakeholder standards. *Organization* 14, 667–84.

Garred, M., 2006. *A shared future; local capacities for peace in community development*. Monrovia, CA: World Vision International.

GreyNet, 1999. GL'99 Conference Program. *Fourth International Conference on Grey Literature: new frontiers in grey literature*. Washington D.C.: Grey Literature Network Service.

Haufler, V., 2010. *Governing corporations in zones of conflict: issues, actors and institutions*. Who governs the globe 102–30. Cambridge: Cambridge University Press.

Held, D., 2013. *Political theory and the modern state*. Hoboken, NJ: John Wiley & Sons.

High Level Panel on Fragile States, 2014. Ending conflict & building peace in Africa: a call to action. *African Development Bank*.

Hodges, A., Notten, G., O'Brien, C., and Tiberti, L., 2013. Are cash transfers a realistic policy tool for poverty reduction in Sub-Saharan Africa? Evidence from Congo-Brazzaville and Côte d'Ivoire. *Global Social Policy* 13, 168–92.

Human Rights Council Report, 2011. *Report of the Special Representative of the Secretary General on the issue of human rights and transnational corporations and other business enterprises*, John Ruggie (Agenda item 3 No. A/HRC/17/31/Add.3). Geneva, Switzerland: Human Rights Council.

ICMM, 2014. Enhancing mining's contribution to the Zambian economy and society (Spotlight series No. 18), *Mining: Partnership for Development Spotlight series*. Chamber of Mines of Zambia & ICMM.

Idemudia, U., 2011. Corporate social responsibility and developing countries moving the critical CSR research agenda in Africa forward. *Progress in Development Studies* 11, 1–18.

Iff, A., Alluri, R., and Hellmüller, S., 2012. The positive contributions of businesses in transformations from war to peace. *Swisspeace* Working Paper 2.

International Labour Office, 2009. *The informal economy in Africa: promoting transition to formality: challenges and strategies*. Geneva, Switzerland: ILO.

Iversen, V., Chhetry, B., Francis, P., Gurung, M., Kafle, G., Pain, A., and Seeley, J., 2006. High value forests, hidden economies and elite capture: evidence from forest user groups in Nepal's Terai. *Ecological economics* 58, 93–107.

Kaimovitz, D., Vallejos, C., Pacheco, P.B., and Lopez, R., 1998. Municipal governments and forest management in lowland Bolivia. *The Journal of Environment and Development* 7, 45–59.

Kinsey, C., 2006. *Corporate soldiers and international security: the rise of private military companies*. Oxford: Routledge.

Liu, X., Hotchkiss, D.R., and Bose, S., 2008. The effectiveness of contracting-out primary health care services in developing countries: a review of the evidence. *Health Policy Plan* 23, 1–13.

McCarthy, J.F., 2012. Certifying in contested spaces: private regulation in Indonesian forestry and palm oil. *Third World Quarterly* 33, 1871–88.

Meagher, K., 2012. The strength of weak states? Non-state security forces and hybrid governance in Africa. *Development and Change* 43, 1073–1101.

Moog, S., Böhm, S., and Spicer, A., 2012. *The limits of multi-stakeholder governance forums: the crisis of the Forest Stewardship Council (FSC)*. American Sociological Association (meeting in Denver, August 17–20, 2012).

Moss, T., Pettersson, G., and Van de Walle, N., 2006. *An aid–institutions paradox? A review essay on aid dependency and state building in sub-Saharan Africa*. Washington, WA: Center for Global Development.

Ndoye, O., Ruiz Perez, M., and Eyebe, A., 1998. *The markets for non-timber forest products in the humid forest zone of Cameroon*. London: Overseas Development Institute.

Newell, P., and Frynas, J.G., 2007. Beyond CSR? Business, poverty and social justice: an introduction. *Third World Quarterly* 28, 669–81.

OECD, 2007. *Principles for good international engagement in fragile states and situations*. Paris.

OECD, 2008. Factsheet: *evaluating conflict prevention and peacebuilding activities*. www.oecd.org/dac/evaluation/dcdndep/39289596.pdf [accessed 6 September 2014].

OECD, D., 2006. 2006 Survey on monitoring the Paris Declaration. Overview of the results. *OECD Journal on Development* 8.

Ottaway, M., 2002. Rebuilding state institutions in collapsed states. *Development and Change* 33, 1001–1023.

Palmer, N., Strong, L., Wali, A., and Sondorp, E., 2006. Contracting out health services in fragile states. *BMJ* 332, 718–21.

Paris, R., 2002. International peacebuilding and the 'mission civilisatrice'. *Review of International Studies* 28, 637–56.

Paris, R., 2006. Bringing the Leviathan back in: classical versus contemporary studies of the liberal peace. *International Studies Review* 8, 425–40.

Paris, R., and Sisk, T.D., 2009. *The dilemmas of statebuilding: confronting the contradictions of postwar peace operations.* Oxford: Routledge.

Peluso, N.L., 1995. Whose woods are these? Counter-mapping forest territories in Kalimantan, Indonesia. *Antipode* 27, 383–406.

Platteau, J.-P., 2004. Monitoring elite capture in community-driven development. *Development and Change* 35, 223–46.

Pollitt, C., and Bouckaert, G., 2011. Public Management Reform: A comparative analysis-new public management, governance, and the Neo-Weberian state. Oxford: Oxford University Press.

Poulsen, J., 2009. Building private-sector partnerships for conservation (PSPCs): lessons learned from the collaboration between WCS, CIB, and the Republic of Congo in forestry concessions. (No. Report to USAID and WCS).

Poulsen, J., Clarck, C., 2010. Congo Basin timber certification and biodiversity conservation, in: Shield, D. (ed.), *Biodiversity Conservation in Certified Forest.* Wageningen, The Nertherlands: Tropenbos International.

Quartey, P., 2005. Innovative ways of making aid effective in Ghana: tied aid versus direct budgetary support. *Journal of International Development* 17, 1077–1092.

Richmond, O.P., 2009. Becoming liberal, unbecoming liberalism: liberal-local hybridity via the everyday as a response to the paradoxes of liberal peacebuilding. *Journal of Intervention and Statebuilding* 3, 324–44.

Riehl, V., 2001. *Who is ruling in South Sudan? The role of NGOs in rebuilding the socio-political order.* Stockholm, Sweden: Nordic Africa Institute.

Rio Tinto, 2013. Sustainable development: supporting our licence to operate. London. www.riotinto.com/sustainabledevelopment2013/_pdf/rio_tinto_2013_sustainable_devel opment.pdf (accessed 27 March 2015).

Ruggie, J.G., 2007. Business and human rights: the evolving international agenda. *American Journal of International Law.* 101, 819.

Schreier, F., Caparini, M., 2010. Privatising security: law, practice and governance of private military and security companies, Geneva, DCAF Occasional Paper.

Schulze, M., Grogan, J., Vidal, E., 2008. Technical challenges to sustainable forest management in concessions on public lands in the Brazilian Amazon. *Journal of Sustainable Forestry* 26, 61–76.

Sirait, M., Prasodjo, S., Podger, N., Flavelle, A., Fox, J., 1994. Mapping customary land in East Kalimantan, Indonesia: a tool for forest management. *Ambio* 411–17.

Soeters, R., Griffiths, F., 2003. Improving government health services through contract management: a case from Cambodia. *Health policy and planning* 18, 74–83.

Stel, N., de Boer, D., Hilhorst, D., 2012. *Multi-stakeholder processes, service delivery and state institutions (synthesis report).* The Hague: Peace, Security and Development Network.

Tati, G., 2005. Public–private partnership (PPP) and water-supply provision in urban Africa: The experience of Congo-Brazzaville. *Development in practice* 15, 316–324.

Unwin, T., 2004. Beyond budgetary support: pro-poor development agendas for Africa. *Third World Quarterly* 25, 1501–23.

Whaites, A., 2008. States in development: understanding state-building (Working Paper), Governance and Social Development Group Policy and Research Division. London: DFID.

Wildlife Conservation Society (WCS). 2013, *Annual report 2013*. New York.

10 Conclusions

A spectrum of responsibility for sustainable development

This book explores the notion of a nexus as a site where patterns of interaction among stakeholders generate a developmental agenda, institutional commitments and a regulated environment that together with industry approaches to social responsibility generate a spectrum of reciprocal responsibilities. Building on theory and the perspectives presented by the contributing chapters, we propose responsibility be understood as a nexus of interactions, giving rise to reciprocal and collective rather than as an individual organizational or institutional undertaking. We further suggest the nexus to be dynamic, in both spatial and temporal terms, shifting back and forth along a spectrum of possibilities depending on prevailing ideological attitudes to economic and social development.

Many of the chapters support the dimension of nexus as a developmental environment. Many of the contributions are grounded in the industrial organization economics paradigm: firms exist to maximise profit while government's role is to correct market imperfections and protect the public welfare, through some combination of direct and indirect regulation. We see this in Mocle's chapter (Chapter 2) on the need for regulation to better secure human rights, and Ahmad's chapter (Chapter 8) on ways of encouraging firms to comply with environmental regulations. Similarly Manning's thrust is for government to be more active in regulating the food industry in order to protect the socio-economically vulnerable, while the underlying idea in Fontefrancesco's chapter (Chapter 3) is that government is failing to provide the support mechanisms that enable small and medium-sized businesses (SMEs) to pursuit their economic goals. Radavoi (Chapter 4) is concerned that multinational firms have governments at a disadvantage because the former can, and does, use international law to compel government to honour contracts for exploiting natural resources, even when affected communities object to such investment. Iff's (Chapter 9) account of the challenges facing a multinational timber company operating in the Congo highlights the firm's worry that its legitimate right to maximize profit is being undermined by the host government wanting to see more local social and economic investment from the firm.

Nexus as institutionalized commitments is also evident in several chapters. Fontefrancesco's account reveals a tradition among SME owners in north-west Italy of a deeply held belief that government is responsible for the welfare of SMEs in times of hardship, and are critical of their trade association for failing to present their collective interests. Such expectation is perhaps consistent within what Weible *et al.* (2009) would describe as a European corporatist political regime. Iff's account also highlights the significance of institutionalised commitments, in the form of the ongoing power of traditional tribal hierarchies operating outside of the formal governmental machinery. Failure to recognize these hidden currents undermine any external intervention with a development agenda, for example the UN relying for cooperation only on the formal government of the target country.

Several chapters reveal a variety of patterns of interaction among stakeholders. In some contexts there are clear legal rules guiding the direction of interactions as well as how to resolve any disputes among stakeholders. We see this in Radavoi's review of three legal cases. He shows international law protects the rights of (multinational) firms in any dispute with governments that encourage firms to invest in the extraction of their natural resources, and then later have a change of heart because of community objection. Moreover, affected local communities appear to have no legitimate voice in objecting (or accepting) such projects. In these cases, the policy-making terrain does not recognize local interests. In contrast, Manning worries there are too few rules governing the existence and sale of poor quality food to the socio-economically disadvantaged of society. There are many stakeholders and food production and sale is a very competitive market. There are regulations about food safety, but in the United Kingdom monitoring is light and the food industry is left to regulate itself to a large degree. Here the pattern of interaction is global and networked, and stratified according to interlinked supply chains. Such complexity makes tracking the source of food ingredients difficult and costly. Stakeholders at the end of the supply chain, such as supermarkets, attempt to deal with such complexity and attendant costs, by pushing responsibility for authenticity of ingredients back down the supply chain.

While some chapters hint, others are clear, about the ways that public and private stakeholders interact, or should interact, in the shaping of social and economic development. Partnerships are presented as the way forward to achieving successful sustainable outcomes. Windsor (Chapter 7) is clear about what is required in order to make public–private partnerships (PPPs) work. Drawing on three case studies (the Chad–Cameroon Petroleum Development and Pipeline Project; the Merck Mectizan® Donation Program (MDP); and Transparency International's (TI) work on anti-corruption), he puts forward lessons that seem instructive for PPPs to be effective: the motivations of business, government, international agencies, and civil society organisations; the need for patience as such cooperative effort takes time and they evolve; and the need to evaluate PPP value creation on the particular merits and demerits of each case. Iff brings a different perspective, arguing that in some developing economies, partnerships between business and the formally anointed government to deliver social development and environmental stewardship alongside economic development are prone to fail if they ignore the significant leverage of traditional and tribal hierarchies in any socio-economic development commitments. Iff worries that multinational companies become drawn into the role of state builder where the existing regime lacks strong public institutions or a commitment to public service, and is predatory toward its citizenry. While Windsor is concerned with drawing out universal lessons, Iff highlights the need for international agencies (UN, World Bank) to rethink their assumptions about how to intervene in state-building initiatives in a developing economy. Ahmad's focus is on improving disclosure by oil and gas extraction businesses of their impacts on the environment, while not forgetting that there is a strong economic imperative at stake for the local economy. Her partnership model involves government regulating and firms self-regulating. In these three chapters we see different models of PPP, depending on partner goals and the peculiarities of their individual context.

In the introduction of this book we introduced the concept of nexus as a spectrum of influence of responsibilities that is determined to some degree by the nature of the industry and the jurisdiction. This spectrum was shown as Figure 10.1 and we invited you to consider how each of the chapters addresses the nexus of private and public interests and where it lies within the spectrum. Now we conclude with our perspective on the application of this spectrum to the chapters.

In her chapter, dealing with the activities of timber companies in the Congo basin, Iff describes a situation where governments are 'characterized by a lack of transparency, accountability and high levels of corruption' and how a timber company has voluntarily engaged in capacity building in the local community. This is consistent with corporate responsibility as a form of government in that the firm has found itself initiating its own institutional processes to improve not only the lives of its employees (approximately 1,000 in total) but also the general condition of the local community numbering over 8,000 people. Self-governing corporate responsibility is represented by Karassin and Bar-Haim's 'explaining corporate social performance through multilevel analysis'. In their chapter they studied firms in the industrial sector of Israel to investigate what influences self-governing corporate responsibility of these firms. Ultimately their research suggests that the greatest influence on a firm's corporate social performance is found at the individual level of the firm, and consistent with the typology of self-governing corporate responsibility operating as an alternative to government regulation but not as a replacement. Both Fontefrancesco and Radavoi have touched on cases where the government's involvement in influencing corporate responsibility has either been lacking or misleading; weaknesses highlighted by corporate responsibility facilitated by government within the typology. In Chapter3, Fontefrancesco examines the impact of a lack of government assistance for small and medium enterprises (SMEs) during the recent economic crisis and found that this influenced SMEs to feel more isolated and abandoned, causing them to feel a reduced sense of responsibility (social and economic) toward the wider community.

On the other hand, in Chapter 4, Radavoi addresses how governments who provide political support in the form of industry-supporting rhetoric can influence firms into believing that their current levels of corporate responsibility are

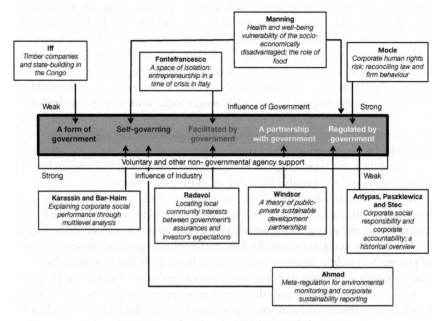

Figure 10.1 Chapters applied to the spectrum of responsibility for sustainable development

Source: Adapted from Gond et al. (2011)

adequate when in fact they are not, as consequently shown through either local community protests or legal challenges. As the typology suggests, while political incentives can promote corporate responsibility on the part of industry, if such facilitation by government leads to firms' responsible actions being misaligned with the needs of associated communities, then the results can be costly for the companies involved. Partnership with government can be seen in Windsor's Chapter 7, in which he presents three cases in order to advance the theory that sustainable development can be best served through collaborative actions in the form of public–private partnerships. His work identifies governments, private sector firms and non-governmental agencies as contributing complementary resources that promote sustainable development and provides greater societal benefits than can be derived by any one party operating independently. Chapter 1 by Stec *et al.*, and Chapter 2 by Mocle provide arguments supporting government-regulated corporate responsibility where it is desirable for government to be a strong influencer of how industry behaves when it comes to corporate responsibility. Their observations indicate insufficient responsibility on the part of industry and therefore they argue, increased regulation is required in order to protect the public interest. Finally, Manning's Chapter 5 and Ahmad's Chapter 8 could be seen as representing self-governing corporate responsibility and government regulated corporate responsibility, but with different recommendations about the relative role of industry and government. Manning examined the UK food industry and found that self-governing corporate responsibility was lacking when one considered the health issues associated with lower income sections of society that consume less expensive food that is also less healthy. The inability of the food industry to adequately address these issues leads her to call for more government regulation that requires firms to take greater corporate responsibility for the health of consumers. Ahmad, in contrast, looks at the Colarado oil and gas case study, and puts forward an argument for combining government regulation and self-governing corporate responsibility, to create a meta-regulation framework to encourage greater corporate responsibility.

Certainly the authors may be able to provide even greater insight into where their chapters fall on our spectrum of responsibility, perhaps arguing that the nexus as they see it is in a different place to that put forward in our observations. Nevertheless, this book does present a diverse range of relationships between corporation, state, and other forms of economic organisation (e.g. NGOs, charities, social enterprise), in addressing some of humanity's most pressing issues. This book contributes to a more nuanced understanding of the interdependence of corporate interest and responsibility and the public policy interest landscape, in terms of practice, theory development, empirical research and analysis. In doing so, they provide some insight to questions concerning the extent to which it is sensible to seek a merging of public and private interests, whether or not we can define private–public interest boundaries, and whether managerial and political ambition necessarily undermine public service and corporate stewardship. However, one thing remains certain. Seeking the appropriate balance of public and private responsibility in pursuing a healthier planet, socially, environmentally and economically, can only be enhanced by dialogue such as offered by this book.

Index

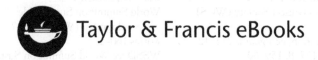

For Product Safety Concerns and Information please contact our
EU representative GPSR@taylorandfrancis.com Taylor & Francis
Verlag GmbH, Kaufingerstraße 24, 80331 München, Germany